My Life

OSKAR KOKOSCHKA

My Life

Translated by David Britt

MACMILLAN PUBLISHING CO., INC.

New York

Macmillan Publishing Co., Inc.

866 Third Avenue, New York, N.Y. 10022

Library of Congress Catalog Card Number: 74-2645

My Life was originally published in German under the title *Oskar Kokoschka: Mein Leben.*

First American Edition 1974

Printed in the United States of America

Contents

Childhood and Schooling

I am supposed to write my own biography. Does writing a biography mean juggling with dates? Idealizing?

That would mean writing a story that is not true. Some spoiled readers might, in all innocence, expect a life story to be an essay on contemporary taste and philosophy. But, clearly, I can write only about what concerns me. Like one of the ancient Greeks, I have found one principle alone to be valid, that man is the measure of all things. And since I am a man who experiences the world through his eyes, not his ears, I will speak of what I have seen.

How did it begin? How did I become a human being? For one does not become human just by being born. One must become human again at every instant. I think it was Herder who said that.

My earliest childhood impressions were purely visual, and to me that seems typical. We stare blankly at the world, until we learn to understand the wonder of creation in terms of light and shadow. And even then, unless we learn insight along with sight, we can long remain in the dark.

I can piece together only episodes of my infancy; for instance I remember lying in a cot, one of those old cots hung with a net of green string. I stuck my nose against the net when, for the first time, I heard my mother coming. I must have heard her voice, although I couldn't understand what she was saying, however hard I pushed my face against the net. I felt trapped, unable to get out of myself. The more I groped around, the more net there was: I screamed and then opened my eyes.

Today, eighty-five years later, I know that it was then I began to learn about the world – the world from which there is no escape, not even by landing on the moon.

Learning about the world is a matter of experiencing space. The decisive discovery of my childhood was that eyes can reach much farther than hands, that we first come in touch with the world through our eyes. I can very well understand that the representation of the human figure is taboo in the visual arts today, as it often has been in the past: whenever you are frightened by the endlessness of space, you shut your eyes.

The child's feeling for its mother is fundamental and intense. At first the child doesn't see its mother at all, it only feels her. It lives by and from its mother. Even when it has left her womb it lives by her warmth, her contact, her tenderness, as it does by her milk.

When man in the machine age finds himself a mere piece of refuse in civilization's rubbish bin, his purpose in life reduced to the turning out of commodities, it is understandable that the young revolt against the Establishment and, in their alienation, confuse love with sex. But sex cannot replace love.

I loved my mother. I owe my being to her. People in desperate need have always consoled themselves with the hope of a utopian world created by gods, or demigods at the very least, but not by themselves. The ideal world, however, comes only after death, since the Immortals are not so pressed for time as we are: they know nothing of five-year plans.

My mother often lifted me from my cot and carried me to the window, to show me what it was like outside. Once I lay in the arms of an aunt – a very beautiful one, I was told later – who wore a huge feathered hat. Her husband was captain of the guard at the Imperial palace of Schönbrunn, near Vienna. It was the first time I had ever laid my cheek on the breast of a woman who was not my mother. She too held me tenderly – and she wore this extraordinary apparatus on her head. On the balcony outside the window there were stucco caryatids with big breasts. I could not tell one woman from another.

Though I was unable to reach the wall from my cot, I remember the pattern of wallpaper on it – a scattering of gaily coloured flowers. To my wide-open eyes, the wall was a three-dimensional space. For as long back as I can recall, I have lived in space, not in time. Space is infinity; hence, eternity resides in that wall I saw, and not in time. This has never been a mystery to me; I have never changed or felt the need to outgrow this experience, even as I grew bigger and older, even as I grew old. I have the feeling of passing from room to room, of going through the world by moving through rooms, whether in this country or that, in this city or another, here or next door. I am always on my travels simply because I am alive – a wanderer.

My childhood memories are not co-ordinated chronologically, as you might expect in a biography, but visually. Must I, in writing the story of my life, go about it with the absolute precision of an accountant, and satisfy my reader with a logical presentation of events, as historians do? I can only call back the moments that are held fast in my memory.

One thing that happened at home long remained a mystery to me, because it did not fit in with the world as I knew it. One day – I had long since learned to walk and talk – I noticed my mother looking at me in a peculiar way and crying; then she took me by the hand. I clearly remember going with her in the carriage to the cemetery, to the grave of my little brother Gustav. I was too young to understand the loss, or to be affected by my mother's tears. Much later, my mother showed me childish drawings done by the dead boy. Only then did I really miss the playmate with whom I myself had often drawn pictures.

I liked school very much at first and looked forward to it every day. It must have been a newly equipped school; I can still remember the pleasing scent of the fresh wood of the benches and tables. The ink, too, in stoneware inkwells let into the tops of the desks, had a special smell. There were many things in the classroom which attracted my curiosity: the big blackboard with its sponge and chalk, the teacher's desk, the coloured map on the wall. And there were all those children I did not know. But my strongest impression was of the teacher who taught the first-year class. She wore a low-necked black dress. I could not take my eyes off her; she was a constant source of wonder. My mother never wore black, and in any case she was quite another sort. The teacher stood before me, decisive, different, strong.

I often deliberately provoked the teacher to haul me from my bench and lay me across her knee for a spanking. I would stare at the golden bracelet, in the shape of a snake with red eyes, which encircled her white arm. The spanking hardly mattered; it didn't hurt, just gentle slaps on the behind. But I had learnt in the scripture lessons that Adam and Eve, being tempted by the snake, fell, and were driven out of Paradise.

That teacher made a lasting impression on me. Now I know that I had fallen into original sin, as one catches mumps or measles. Here was the antithesis of mother-love. It was a significant experience, a very early one, of something that had broken in from the world outside and upset me, an experience that did not end with the sight of the snake on the bare arm, but struck deep into my heart. I could not comprehend it. I was probably in love with that school-teacher.

My parents had moved to a second-floor flat in an apartment house on the outskirts of Vienna. It had a gallery-like veranda, facing south, with carved posts; I liked to pretend that the carvings were dragons' heads emerging from the deep. On fine days one could see across the rolling countryside, over the green of the trees and bushes, as far as the mountains. I used to play on this balcony with my younger sister Bertha; she was small, but lively and full of tricks. As her elder brother, I was expected to look after her. But one day she leant out a little too far over the balustrade and lost her balance. Luckily I was able to hold her by the legs until, hearing cries, our mother came. I was almost at the end of my strength. And down below dragons might lie in wait! At least there was certainly a poisonous plant whose name was deadly nightshade.

The garden behind the house was usually locked, and we children could not get in; it was reserved for the landlord. Between the house and the garden was the courtyard, in the middle of which was a well that had been boarded over. The water was not drinkable; drinking-water used to be brought in great barrels or horse-drawn carts from which each household had to fetch it in buckets and cans. I remember that as a reward for fetching water I used to get a copper coin worth four kreuzers. The well was used on washing days, but was always covered again afterwards for safety's sake. We and the other children liked to play about on top of it. I liked most of all to lie there on sunny days, blissfully drinking in the smell of the old, rotten wood, and watching mites scurrying round in the joints and cracks, disappearing into the hole through which the rope passed down into the abyss, and popping up again. They may have been ants; I no longer remember.

Once when I was fetching water I saw a thick tube emerge from the belly of one of the great carthorses – they were Pinzgauers, a particularly heavy Alpine breed – and let out water. I confused this in my mind with the hose of the municipal water wagon that used to clean the dusty streets in summer, and in my curiosity I went too close; the horse struck out with its hind leg. One of my knees is not right to this day.

When I grew a little older, I found a particular friend in a maiden lady who lived near by and had a wooden leg, which intrigued me. She would call me in and tell me fairytales or stories of Margrave Rüdiger of Bechelaren (Pöchlarn, where I was born), and other heroes. I was particularly fond of the story of the water nymph, Melusine. I was embarrassed because she would sometimes caress me with tears in her eyes. I wonder why she was sad.

Suddenly, one evening, a fearful noise in the yard. People came running. What had happened? They said the lady had drowned in the well. And indeed the next morning she wasn't there. I couldn't really understand what dying meant. All that registered in my mind was that she had disappeared, as I thought, in the way that one does when going from one house to the next, from one room to another. You can't see through the wall, of course, but the person still must be there.

I can never disappear, I thought. Of course she isn't here, but she must be somewhere, perhaps under a spell, like someone in one of her stories.

Two days later I saw from the window a hearse drawn up outside the main door: black horses draped in black, with white plumes on their heads, harnessed to a silver carriage in which lay a white box. People told me she was being taken away in it; but I could not understand. Someone who can cast spells doesn't just get carted off like a piece of baggage. After all, Melusine went down into the water too, and yet she lived on. I gazed after that strange carriage for a long time.

This departure woke the memory of that past occasion when I saw such a vehicle for the first time. Dimly I began to realize that the external world also has limits. This experience of the irretrievability of loss was for me like a transition from the light of day to the fate-ridden terror of night. I became aware that it was possible for part of my world to disappear into the unknown, and I grew pensive and melancholy. I began to walk in my sleep. I was what country folk call moonstruck. My parents had to bar the window in the room where I slept, after they had caught me several times standing on the window-sill, ready to set forth for the moon.

Around that time my father started giving me books. My first book has influenced my entire life: it was the *Orbis pictus* of the seventeenth-century bishop of the Moravian Brethren, Jan Amos Comenius. In this book he set out in pictures, for the young, everything that he knew to exist. You could read the explanation of each picture in four languages. I kept to the pictures at first, for this was the real world that lay in wait for me. One-legged people were not to be found there. I forgot about fairytales and about my Melusine, hoping that her wooden leg had turned into a fishtail in the water. Comenius was a humanist, and from the *Orbis pictus* I learned not only what the world is, but how it should be in order to become fit for human beings to live in.

My father also gave me an illustrated edition of the Greek myths. Again, I found the pictures more impressive than the text which took too long to spell out.

For Christmas I received a paint-box with paints that tasted of honey. I often licked the brush while colouring the black and white pictures in the book of myths. In life everything has a colour, and so I started to paint with colours, using those I liked best: red, green, yellow and blue. When I had finished my homework after school, painting was my favourite activity.

I was never very close to my father; yet he influenced me, and in a very different way from my mother. He did not concern himself with people but with such things as gold, jewellery, and precious stones. He was a skilled goldsmith, with a tradition of that craft in his family. As far as he could tell, his ancestors were Bohemians, from Prague; one strain came from Augsburg. They had, or so the tale ran for generations back, been armourers and swordsmiths, and had wrought all manner of ornament on weapons and utensils, chalices and other jewelled articles. They were *Petschire*, workers in precious metals, who went in search of employment from one country, or one art-loving court, to another.

My father was born in Prague, of a patrician family that possessed a fine house in the Brentegasse with its own shop and workroom. He had assisted his father on the restoration of the Gothic chapel of St Wenceslas in the Hradčany Castle. Artists and musicians of note, including Dvořák and Smetana, used to come to the house. My father always laughed when he retold the story of his encounter with the Emperor Ferdinand I. The Emperor, who was living in exile in Prague at the time, had ordered a snuff box from my grandfather. While the Emperor was talking to my grandmother, who is said to have been a good-looking woman, my father, then a small child, slipped away into the anteroom and tried on the Emperor's top hat. He got stuck in it, and had to be rescued, amid howls, by His Imperial Majesty.

Nearly a century later, I looked for my father's house in Prague, and found it. It had all been given up – house, shop, workroom – while my father was still a young man. He had even been forced to abandon his craft. The family moved to Vienna during the financial collapse which followed the war in Bosnia, the former Turkish province handed over to Austria to administer as one of the Great Powers. Today I realize that the social upheavals of that period were caused less by the war than by the rapid industrialization of the country. The machine had supplanted the craftsman. Precious things were no longer made by hand, and factory-made goods were changing people's taste. That was the end of the skill my father had learned, for no one can fight such a course of affairs. He turned in on himself and seldom remained at home, as if he found no more joy in it. He became a partner in a relative's jewellery business, and travelled constantly to London or Paris. He always brought me back toys from his journeys. Of them, I was most attached to a magic lantern which had coloured pictures that moved because of the heat given out by a little lamp. Will people now say that I owe the dynamism of my paintings to that magic lantern?

My mother was often alone in the house with my younger sister Bertha, my even younger brother Bohuslav and myself. Visits from relatives became less and less frequent as our financial circumstances got worse. We moved to smaller and smaller flats in poorer and poorer neighbourhoods. My mother had no one to confide in but me. To take her own mind off her worries she liked to tell stories of her past life, of where she came from, and how I was born. She wouldn't name the hour of my birth, however, not even much later when I had become well known in Vienna and people wanted to cast my horoscope.

It had been in the last days of February 1886 – my father was on his travels – that my mother decided to have her baby at the house of her brother, who owned a sawmill at Pöchlarn on the Danube. There I was born on 1 March. The very next night, she told me, a fire broke out which spread to almost the whole town. My uncle's sawmill and house were burned down. She was taken to safety, with me, on an improvised bed of hay on a tall haywain. When I heard this story, the siege and destruction of Troy became so real to me that I could also understand why as a child, in an unwatched moment, I had grasped a red-hot coal that had fallen from the stove. I couldn't let it go, although I got badly burnt in the process and still bear the scar on the palm of my right hand. I love fire above all things. The burning town on the night after my birth must somehow have imprinted itself on my consciousness; I have no other way to explain this strange passion of mine.

My mother came from a family of ten children, not all of whom survived, however. Her parents lived high in the mountains of Styria, far removed from any other human habitation. Her father was an Imperial forester. With such a large family, money was short, and clothes were handed down. The descent from the mountain to the village school each day was long and hazardous. At dusk they began to get frightened of ghosts and the wild man of the woods. One piece of dry bread had to last them all day; they came home at night exhausted and ravenous.

On many evenings my mother talked to me about the hard, laborious life of my grandmother, who must surely have been a brave woman. On one occasion, apparently, the house was besieged for a whole day and night by a band of gipsies. Her husband was out after poachers in the forest. She took his shotgun and, from the window, behind half-closed shutters, held the marauders at bay for twenty-four hours.

My grandmother had the gift of second sight, and could predict the future. This probably came from the loneliness of her existence up there in the mountains, where there were no neighbours. Of all the legends about her, that of her premonition of death I find the most unforgettable. One fine May

morning she took her wedding dress out of the chest and had herself dressed
in it. For a day and a night, although in perfect health, she waited for death.
She ate and drank nothing, and foretold the exact hour at which she would
die.

My mother had inherited the gift. For example, once, many years later
when we were living in a suburb of Vienna, she left my younger brother
Bohuslav alone at home – he wanted to work in the garden – while she went
into Vienna to visit her sister. In the middle of a casual chat my mother
suddenly broke off and cried out, 'I must have a cab quickly, I must go home!
The boy's in the garden, bleeding!' Her sister tried to talk her out of it.
'Sheer imagination, don't make such a fuss.' But my mother insisted, made
the driver go as fast as he could, and in the nick of time arrived to find my
brother lying covered with blood in the garden. Though barely fourteen
years old, he had tried to chop down a tree, and cut himself badly in the leg
with an axe. He would surely have bled to death if she had not come back
in time.

No doubt most people will say there is no such thing as second sight. The
world really looks just as it does in photographs. Beyond that, there is
nothing. After all, don't those who know better, the truly wise, teach us that
man is simply a product of his material environment? But I wonder, where
does reality reside? Where are the frontiers of the real, when a great mathe-
matician in his theory of relativity can call in question even the traditional
concepts of time and mass?

I believe, on the contrary, that a world in which we can feel at home exists
only by virtue of our experiencing it as we do. The worm sees it differently;
for him it is not made of the same stuff as it is for us. Only the human mind,
thanks to its forming power, makes us capable of grasping the immense
possibilities of creation.

Might life, therefore, be a dream, and might the world, as it appears to
us, exist only for the time being?

After the financial crash, Austria became impoverished. As in all industrialized States that have to compete for markets, production had to be artificially
stimulated. The objective was to bring as many people as possible within the
industrial economy; there was no future for the traditional craftsman. The
danger that the masses streaming from the country to the cities would go
unprovided for was remedied by the new factories which absorbed the
flow of human raw material. The State-controlled educational system
became a problem. The Welfare State did not yet exist, and not everyone

with an education could become a civil servant with pension rights. The authorities restricted access to secondary and higher education by making the entrance examinations more difficult.

That I did nevertheless manage to continue my education after elementary school I owe, as in so much else in the decisive phases of my life, to my mother. My father lived in a world of his own, and had no faith left in the possibility of making one's own way. However, he went along with my mother's wish to send me to the Realschule, the 'modern' high school. I would personally have preferred the Gymnasium, the classical high school, because at the Realschule they taught mainly physics, chemistry and mathematics, for which I felt no aptitude. But a Gymnasium education lasting nine years would have been too expensive, and the Realschule took only seven. And so fate decreed that I was to go to the Realschule, where I did well enough in the entrance examination to be awarded free tuition.

In those seven years I often sweated blood. Only foreign languages came at all easily, perhaps because of a very good teacher who got through to me. Dr Leon Kellner came from a family of rabbis in Czernowitz (now Chernovtsy), a university and garrison town in the Bukovina, on the Russian frontier. He was president of the Austrian Shakespeare Society, and it is to him that I owe my particular love of England. Having grateful memories of him as a teacher, I inquired long afterwards about his fate. Fortunately he had not lived to see the Anschluss; after the war a little street was named for him in Vienna.

I vividly remember one day in class when I did something I was ashamed of. He had brought in an English magazine, perhaps the *Illustrated London News*, to be passed round to the students; and in an article about some excavations, the statue of a half-naked Aphrodite was pictured. Thus began my love of the art of antiquity as a sensual experience. If I had understood as a child that the Greeks worshipped goddesses, I would certainly have become a devout pagan and not a lukewarm Christian. The Greeks had kept their eyes open! I could never understand how I did it, but I stole the page. When Dr Kellner discovered that a page was missing, he went from one boy to the next along the bench, questioning each in turn. As he approached my place, I held the torn-out page compressed in my fist. I'd rather die than give it back, I thought. I was wholly infatuated and unhappy at once, for I was also very much afraid! Just before he reached me, he gave up and said, looking straight at me: 'One of you will have a guilty conscience, because he has mutilated a work from my library.' That is the only time in my life I have stolen anything. His penetrating eye must have told him who the thief was.

Perhaps he understood me, for he knew a lot about human nature. I loved him.

The school was in Währing, in Vienna 18. My long walk there, every morning and afternoon, took me past a bookshop with a display of Reclam pocket editions laid out in the window. I soon knew the titles by heart. Over the years, with the pocket-money my mother set aside for me out of my scholarship, and which was intended for buying a bread roll or something in the break between lessons, I bought almost all those cheap little books; and so I got to know the great literature of the world in translation. Reclam did a great service to young people with its cheap editions. Later, too, when I was a student at Kunstgewerbeschule, in the midday break when the others went off to eat, I used to sit on a park bench and read. This reading did more for me than all my seven years' schooling – except for the knowledge of Shakespeare that I gained from Dr Kellner.

For mathematics, the higher mathematics, I had no gift at all. The master who taught us mathematics, physics and chemistry was strict beyond all reason, and made my life a misery. Yet it was chemistry that interested me most of all, at first. I had even wanted to go on studying chemistry, because I was possessed by a Faustian desire to penetrate the world of cells and molecules, the primary material of organic and inorganic matter. But for the chemical formulae of the elements and compounds I was going to have to invent a new, simpler and more comprehensible notation; that was what I had decided, because I have no memory for abstract concepts that cannot be visualized. I kept going, after a fashion, but in the end that stony-hearted science master nearly stopped me from passing the school certificate examination. He wanted to fail me because I had rebelled against the orthodox method of teaching. I had decided, if I failed the examination, and thus lost my scholarship, to commit suicide. Armed with the hunting-knife that had belonged to my grandfather, the forester, on the eve of the final examination I wandered around all day in the cold, until I finally crept home exhausted and hungry.

The vote of my drawing master, Professor Schober, saved the day at the masters' conference. I had first attracted his attention long before, in the course of his weekly lessons, when I put together a still-life and painted it, instead of endlessly copying the one plaster head of a faun that we had in the school. I was a born artist, he said; and his intervention at the conference tipped the balance, I had passed though I think a quarter of the boys failed that year. It was the toughest year ever.

When I think back to my schooling I have the feeling that it was a reflection of the whole history of Austria. Many peoples were joined together in the old Austrian Empire, each retaining its individuality, its particular aptitude, and all contributing to weld the whole 'cultural commonwealth', as I would call it, into an organic unity. There has never been anything like it in history. By contrast, the British Commonwealth was a basically economic institution. In my class there were boys from the Alpine countries, Hungarians, Slavs, Jews, Triestines, Sudeten Germans. A real gathering of peoples. And every second master came from a different country and had brought with him some unmistakable national element, a colouring in his voice, his manner, his way of thought. In this sense, school was a preparation for my later life, in which I became a wanderer. In fact, in my modest high school in Vienna, I got to know my world just as well as a schoolboy in England at the same period learned about the far-off continents where his parents were ruling colonies. Actually, it is a pity that the Great Powers which signed the peace terms after the First World War, having no idea of geography, broke up this unit, and could find nothing better to put in its place. But it's no use lamenting the past.

Every Sunday, my younger brother and I crossed the Schmelz – the big parade-ground near the Hofburg, often deep in snow in the winter – to go to church; a magnificent organist and choir accompanied the Mass with classical music. The great music of the Baroque! And the great Baroque paintings in Viennese churches! A few years before, when I was still a choirboy, my voice had broken in the middle of a solo in a Mozart mass, and, with a majestic dome fresco by Maulbertsch before my eyes, I had passed out cold.

The kind offices of Professor Schober, my sympathetic drawing master at the Realschule, had managed to get me a scholarship to the Kunstgewerbeschule, the Vienna School of Arts and Crafts. It came from the bequest of the Fröhlich sisters, who were friends of Franz Grillparzer, acknowledged to be Austria's greatest and last dramatist; he had once translated Calderón's *La vida es sueño*. Again the idea that life is a dream!

I was to become a teacher of drawing. One could go either to the Akademie der Bildenden Künste, the Academy of Fine Arts, or to the Kunstgewerbeschule. At the Akademie they trained artists. It never entered my head to go there and pass myself off as an artist in a velvet jacket and beret. I opted for the Kunstgewerbeschule.

STUDIES

All over Europe at that time the new ideas of Jugendstil, Art Nouveau and the Arts and Crafts movement were taking hold, with their emphasis on rescuing and ennobling the vanishing tradition of craftsmanship. The principal impetus came from England, the land of slums and factory chimneys. The utilitarian objects of everyday life were to take on new forms, and life itself was to have a new face. In that shabby transitional period society longed for reforms; man felt in danger of becoming a slave of the machine. Progress had shown its ugly side.

At the turn of the century the Kunstgewerbeschule in Vienna was one of the most progressive educational institutions in Europe. The growing international movement, Art Nouveau – known in its German incarnation as Jugendstil – had had a decisive influence on its curriculum. The school possessed a well-stocked library where one could keep up with what was happening in France, Holland, Belgium, Germany and England in the applied arts and in the pursuit of a pattern of domestic life – a *Wohnkultur* – suited to the needs of modern society.

Vienna was already becoming rather provincial at that time, and the ideas propagated by the Kunstgewerbeschule were hotly contested. They were basically the ideas of John Ruskin and his spiritual heir William Morris (who died in 1896), further developed in Scotland by the group known as the Glasgow School, and in particular by George Rennie Mackintosh and his wife Margaret Macdonald Mackintosh.

There were close links between the Kunstgewerbeschule and the Wiener Werkstätte, a workshop co-operative which also played a leading part in this stylistic change. Most of the professors at the school were also members of the Werkstätte, including Alfred Roller, Josef Hoffmann, Koloman Moser and Carl Otto Czeschka, to whom I shall return presently. In 1898 Olbrich had built the imposing building of the Wiener Secession, with its dome of gilded openwork scrolls which the Viennese irreverently called the 'cabbage'. Perhaps the artificial revival of craftsmanship that the Jugendstil preached provides a new angle on the human comedy.

The Secession, an association of artists who had withdrawn from the official art association, the Kunstverein, had Gustav Klimt as its president. The motto on the cornice of the new Secession building was the somewhat provocative phrase 'To the age its art, to art its freedom.'

I took the drawing course under Professor Anton von Kenner, but I was equally interested in craft subjects – in type forms, book composition, bookbinding, woodcuts and lithography, as well as the use of leather, parchment and other materials such as handmade paper; in everything, in fact, that was to be learned there.

For prospective teachers a special life class and lessons in anatomy were offered. At the beginning of the course, as in a real Academy of Fine Arts, we drew from a model in addition to composing still-lifes. Our model was an old man, naked except for the inevitable loincloth. He had to pose completely still on the podium for a week on end, leaning on a stick. The life room was large, but so was the number of students, all with easels and sheets of paper stretched on great frames, which cut off one's view. The model had to be drawn lifesize and very accurately, with charcoal. As a newcomer, I had my place far at the back, and from where I was working the old man looked very small. So on my gigantic piece of paper I put him down as small as I saw him.

Professor von Kenner said 'What are you doing? Why aren't you drawing the model lifesize, like all the others?' Professor Czeschka having come into the room, I showed him what I saw and took him as a witness. 'Even you, sir, can't see the man any bigger from where I sit.' He laughed and said, 'So you want to go into solitary confinement?' and gave me a tiny studio all to myself, a solitary cell.

There I got the children of a circus family, who used to live by modelling in the winter when there was no other work, to play and leap around, so far as the space allowed. Every day I made great sheaves of lightning studies. Capturing the various movements and twists of the body in action really stimulated me, unlike the tedious academic instruction.

This appealed to Czeschka. He was an exceptional teacher, and later he helped me in every way he could. Soon I was entrusted with running the evening course for the whole body of students; drawing from models in motion was something entirely new. So now I was both a student and a teaching assistant at the same time, and my idea for teaching drawing was afterwards adopted in several countries.

During this time a whole series of important exhibitions of modern foreign artists must have taken place at the Secession; I did not see them. I hardly ever went to see even the extraordinary collections of old masters in the Kunsthistorisches Museum on the Maria-Theresia-Platz. I felt it would be presumptuous to stand before the works of the great masters unprepared, a mere beginner.

In the Naturhistorisches Museum, on the other side of the magnificent square with its statue of the Empress Maria Theresa, I felt more at ease, free of the shyness, even the awe, which I still feel today when I encounter the works of the great masters of the past. In the ethnographical department I found something on a more human scale, something I could grasp. Masks, implements, weapons, textiles and tapestries – these products of a vanishing world – testified to the uniqueness of the human life of ordinary men like myself. However wide I opened my eyes, I was still not ready to judge the works of a Titian or a Rembrandt. I would have felt myself ridiculous if I had claimed to understand them. But seeing a Polynesian mask with its incised tattooing, I understood at once, because I could feel my own facial nerves reacting to cold and hunger in the same way. For all my sympathy with primitive art, it would not have occurred to me to imitate it. I was not a savage. I would have had to live like them for my imitation to be genuine. And I had just as much feeling for fossils, stuffed animals, meteorites, or any documents of a time which is lost for ever.

In my last year at the school, Professor Czeschka brought me into close contact with the Wiener Werkstätte. I received minor commissions, and painted a considerable number of postcards which were printed as chromo-lithographs. I also painted fans, a fashion that was coming back at the time, using swan-skin stretched over ivory frames. Much of what I drew and painted then has vanished.

My first self-contained series of graphic works, *Die träumenden Knaben* ('The Dreaming Youths'), was published in 1908 by the Wiener Werkstätte. I had been commissioned to draw a children's picture-book to be printed as a series of colour lithographs, but I followed my brief only as far as the first page. The remaining sheets appeared with verses of my own, as a picture-poem. I chose the title because the book was a kind of record, in words and pictures, of my own state of mind at the time. I was in love with the heroine, the girl Li 'from the lost bird-forests of the North', in real life a young Swedish girl called Lilith who attended the Kunstgewerbeschule, and wore a red peasant-weave skirt such as people were not used to seeing in Vienna. Red is my favourite colour, and the book was my first love letter. But she had already gone out of my life by the time it appeared.

In the summer of 1908, the Wiener Werkstätte, in co-operation with the Kunstgewerbeschule and the Klimt group which had broken away from the Secession, mounted the first Kunstschau, an international art exhibition in a temporary building on a vacant lot on the Schubertring, near the Schwarzen-bergplatz. The artists invited were chosen from among those who were still not fully understood or appreciated in their own countries. Gustav Klimt, then the leading spokesman of modern painting in Vienna, was chairman of the selection committee. Thanks to Professor Czeschka, I had been invited to participate, and was given a small room to myself, rather apart from the big exhibition galleries. In a short time I had painted a tapestry cartoon, in tempera on four large canvases, which I called *The Bearers of Dreams*.

When you strive to create what people are not yet prepared to understand, you are bound to suffer the consequences. Their incomprehension turns to laughter, and they feel superior because your effort to solicit their attention has failed. I feared this would be my fate. So, when Klimt came to my room, flanked by Hodler in top hat, frock-coat and sash, with the other gentlemen of the jury following behind, I refused to let them in. 'I won't open the door,' I said, 'until you promise to show my work to the public, whatever the jury thinks.' They were furious; but Klimt, though a little taken aback, did not stay to bandy words with me. Goodnaturedly, he motioned the group on, and said only: 'Let the fellow get himself torn apart by the press, if that's what he wants.'

In addition to the tapestry cartoon I also exhibited a painted clay bust, on a pedestal, which I called *The Warrior*. In fact this was a self-portrait with open mouth, the expression an impassioned cry. As far as the Viennese public was concerned, my room became 'the Chamber of Horrors', and my work a laughing-stock. Every day I found bits of chocolate and other debris in the mouth of my bust, probably put there by girls as a further expression of scorn they felt for the *Oberwildling*, the Chief Savage, as I had been dubbed by the critic Ludwig Hevesi.

In spite of all the gibes, I had the consolation, though only a beginner, of selling several drawings to artists of note, among them Emil Orlik and Koloman Moser. These were my first 'public' sales. My much-debated sculpture was bought by the architect Adolf Loos, whom I now met for the first time, and who kept it until his death. The tapestry cartoons were purchased by Fritz Waerndorfer, the commercial director of the Wiener Werkstätte and a collector of Beardsley, who wrote in a letter to Czeschka on 5 June 1908: 'The scandal of the Kunstschau is Kokoschka. I do like the paintings in the exhibition however, and we have bought them from him for two hundred crowns cash, with the guarantee that if we get some money we will turn them into tapestries.' Unfortunately these *Bearers of Dreams* seem to have disappeared; at any rate they have not yet come to light.

My development at that time is linked to my discovery of the work of the Belgian sculptor George Minne, who was represented in the second Kunstschau exhibition in 1909, in which I also showed a number of new drawings and portraits, including one of my friend Ernst Reinhold (of whom more anon). I now encountered the paintings of Van Gogh, Gauguin, the Fauves: the whole world of modern art, of which I had been ignorant. But what impressed me most were the sculptures of Minne. In their chaste forms and their inwardness, I seemed to find a rejection of the two-dimensionality of

Jugendstil. Something was stirring beneath the surface of these figures of youths, something akin to the tension which, in Gothic art, dominates space and indeed creates it.

Jugendstil represented a warning to society to change its ways. But in the pursuit of surface embellishment, its exponents had forgotten space, three-dimensionality. The idea of a *Gesamtkunstwerk*, a fusion of all the arts, which preoccupied the artists and designers of the movement, had also governed the work of medieval builders. But in the Gothic age master builders, stone-masons, sculptors, carvers, painters and glaziers worked in accordance with a higher plan. Not content to mirror the tangible, transient world, they sought an image of Eternity, of Space without limits.

But in the age of the Industrial Revolution, wherever one looked, the struggle for existence remained superficial: factories with their smouldering chimneys, the arid waste of industrial production, the slums swelling with the pressure of the population streaming in from the countryside. The objective retreated as fast as it was pursued. The loss was in direct proportion to the gain. Progress thundered down its single track, unstoppable.

The social situation, similarly, looked progressively dingier. The old observation was confirmed, that there is never so much talk of reforms as when people have no idea where to start. With a touch of sadness, one acknowledges, today, the superficiality of that whole movement – of its sun and fresh-air cult, its clothing reform, its promotion of hiking (the *Wandervogel* movement) and of the House Beautiful (*Wohnkultur*).

Perhaps this has something to do with the fact that the technological revolution came too quickly, and that society was wrenched out of its conservative style of life before it had found a new one. Painters and poets saw themselves bound to their times, captives in a cage from which there was no escape. They took refuge in far-away countries, Gauguin in Tahiti, Rimbaud in the land of frankincense, gold dust, ivory and slaves. To this day, that part of society which concerns itself with cultural matters still feels similarly alienated, because it does not participate in the creative act. Modern artists have offered, in lieu of original creativity, their own interpretation of African art, or that of the Inca, the Maya, or the Pacific islanders. Anyone who felt like going into it more deeply would be unable to ignore the inference that there exists a logical connection between technological revolution and the pursuit of exoticism.

It all began with the *fin de siècle* movement, when people were intoxicated by the cry 'Après nous le déluge'. Like any bout of drunkenness, this one was inevitably followed by a grim sobriety. Practicality (*Neue Sachlichkeit*) and

non-objective art led at last to the sterile elimination of the human image –
and not only art but existence itself threatens to become objectless. Nor is it
paradoxical that society seems to be turning to promiscuity, and art to porno-
graphy: this reflects no true return to human value, nor even a tentative
rapprochement with figurative art. Ruskin and Morris dreamed a beautiful
dream. Nowadays a brush and paints (non-toxic, let us hope) are placed in
the hands of a chimpanzee in order to determine empirically, from the psyche
of a primate, the essential nature of art. I should be much more likely to draw
a few conclusions about the psyche of *Homo sapiens*. In keeping with a vul-
garly materialistic theory, they are already at work in America on a computer
that can paint and write poetry. However, I digress. It is not my trade to
unmask society, but to seek in the portrait of an individual his inner life, that
measure of all things, and never to rob humanity of its value.

Over a cup of coffee my friends and I, all about twenty years old, used to
discuss the things closest to our hearts. My friends were mostly Jewish bank
clerks. One was an unpublished poet who earned his living reporting burgla-
ries, burst water-mains and adulteries for the local paper. He had a wooden
arm which we used to knock against the table when we wanted to call the
waiter. Another was a drama student who had broken with his prosperous
family in order to live a free life. Another, a Finn, was learning to be a singer.
In the coffee-houses we read the newspapers and heard, or sensed, political
conflict disturbing the air where once one had been able to drink a cup of
coffee in peace and quiet.

Ideas akin to those of the French Revolution were waking again. Murderous attacks on crowned heads and ministers were becoming a matter of
course. The elected representatives of various interests – of employers or
workers – all pulled their separate ways. Students demonstrated outside the
university, workers outside the parliament. The mounted police swung into
action. In parliament politicians threw inkwells at one another, or came to
blows over their nationalistic or socio-political differences. Though the world
we knew was moving towards its end, we stood firm against what for most
was the compelling slogan of the day: 'Into the streets!'

At the turn of the century one was still able to travel without a passport
from the Mediterranean far across the Alps, to the north, east and west.
People of forty nationalities had learned to live together; they had inter-
married and done business with one another. One could even believe that
this ancient Habsburg Monarchy, in its thousand years of rule, had learned
the art of teaching the nations to co-exist in peace. Was it possible, then, that

such a model of social adjustment had lost its meaning as a result of the march of progress? Charles V, under whom the Habsburg Empire had reached from Mexico to India, had subscribed to the rights of man and forbidden the slave trade, long before the Church itself had come to such enlightened ideas. Now this same Empire seemed suddenly to have become so small that people were everywhere treading on one another's toes. In each province forbidding difficulties arose which appeared soluble only by breaking up the whole family of nations. Whereas in the old Danubian monarchy the various nationalities had more or less lived on the things they produced, industrialization was changing the pattern of life. Supply and demand required that, to match the increased productivity of the machine age, new markets should be opened up and wars should be waged to that end. The State, to speed industrialization, felt compelled to organize all of society in ways that ruthlessly suppressed the individual. Nationalist politicians demanded the natural resources of their countries for exploitation, at the expense of the community as a whole. The intellectual *élite* of various nationalities started smashing windows, and the internationalist workers built barricades of paving-stones. No one remembered the truth once expressed by a Roman statesman in a parable: that the limbs separated from the body cannot exist on their own.

Coming as I did from a simple home in the suburbs, I had remained largely untouched by the intellectual and political contagions of the day. To begin with, it was all beyond me, but I had also deliberately opted out. My instinct led me to pursue my own affairs. I had no eyes or ears to spare for the events of the world. But also I could not and would not be merely a statistical unit in a world in which work had ceased to be a human activity and had become only a matter of mechanical efficiency. And so I stayed a political innocent, but I also stayed free.

The Kaffeehaus Central was the meeting-place of the respected leaders of the Social Democratic workers' movement. People rather self-consciously pointed out representatives of the Communist International, who held aloof from the Social Democrats. They were mainly Russians; Trotsky, a regular customer, played chess every evening. Here, as elsewhere, the plans being laid for a future social order were as various as the pale faces in the smoky darkness. Vociferously, the politicians defended their own ideas: Pan-Germans wanted to join the German Reich, the various irredentist groups wanted a united Italy or a Greater Serbia. A group of Pan-Slavs hoped for union with the empire of the Tsars. Each believed in his own future State. But my friends and I had no problems except personal ones. I, above all, had no money.

Sometimes I used to bring drawings. One or the other of my friends might have an acquaintance among the regular customers of the coffee-house to whom he would offer them. Then we could all go and eat at a Jewish place that stayed open late, where the Viennese *bohème* used to gather.

For a young painter the situation then was very different from what it is now that the art market is inflated. In Vienna there was no art market to paint for. A few antique dealers, yes, but no art dealers, such as those who today buy up youthful talent like a racehorse and expect it to run like hell until its breath gives out. Nor had the idea yet emerged of being bound by a contract to produce works of art.

I cannot say why I wanted to paint. The only answer is in the pictures themselves, not in any examination of the circumstances. When my new friend and patron Adolf Loos took pictures off my hands, he did so not with the intention of collecting them, or in order to sell them for me, but rather to prevent my painting over them for lack of a new canvas. Society in general – the world my friends and I referred to as 'The Adults' – possessed varying conceptions of art. The middle class, in whose eyes I was still a standing offence, viewed art as something to decorate a wall. For the nobility it was an adjunct of their ancestor cult, to be used like the Court Photographer. The workers had more pressing priorities than that of employing creative artists: higher wages, shorter working hours, the task of strengthening their own organization, and one day, if possible, becoming a State within a State.

The ideas of Progress and Enlightenment were still casting a romantic glow over the social gatherings of those days, but they did not seem to offer the hope of personal happiness. I myself had no illusions that ideas, plucked from the air, would provide an answer to the proper direction of mankind.

Along with the scent of incense that I had loved in my last years at school, and the magic of classical church music and Baroque art, the intellectual atmosphere of Catholicism long held me under its spell, although I resisted dogmatic religion. Calderón with his 'Life is a Dream', Cervantes with his immortal *hidalgo* who tilts at windmills and bows down before a half-witted maidservant; Shakespeare with his characters who are never allegories but people of flesh and blood; the wise and sceptical Montaigne, restoring all things to their human proportion in an age that was becoming inhuman; even Voltaire with his ironic 'best of all possible worlds'; none of these had been driven by mere repression, as was Jean-Jacques Rousseau, to place their trust in utopias, a future earthly paradise beyond the horizon. They all experienced the mystery of the divine incarnate in the Son of Man: God become man, denied, despised, tortured, delivered to the hangman by false judges and the hypocritical Pilate, and nailed to the Cross. The Passion is the eternal story of man. Even the miracle of the Resurrection can be understood in human terms, if it is grasped as a truth of the inner life: one does not become human once and for all just by being born. One must be resurrected as a human being every day.

In my perplexity these wise minds helped to set me on the right path; they pointed to a goal, however many different answers they supplied to the question 'What is man?' The saints, the priests, the laymen, even the heretics, the apostates who deride the spiritual struggle and yet in their own hearts plead desperately for grace; the mystics, De Fiori, Suso, Tauler, Eckhart; St Theresa, who ceased to believe that God was in heaven and found him in her own heart – they all went their own Way of the Cross, the way of inner experience. Nourished by the spiritual food of *charisma*, love as spiritual grace, they form a fellowship whose insights differ fundamentally from the materialist conception of history. Even the word *charisma* has now been twisted to mean its opposite.

Emigrés who have lost their homelands may sympathize with the nostalgia felt by those who have given up the spiritual life on the Catholic model and yet still long for the bitter cup which the alliance of throne and altar has placed before so many, and which some martyrs have been forced to drain to the last drop.

Waking from a shadowy, formless existence, I had found support in these thinkers; or, to put it less grandly, I had learned to stand on my own feet. They had shone a light on the human consciousness, and my fears of isolation were now no more than the swiftly fading spectres of a dream. Beyond, more dangerous and intriguing depths remained to be explored. The erotic advance of the female principle almost at once put my hard-won equilibrium in jeopardy. Strangely enough, for me men always had only one face, which showed their character, experiences, passions, even when the face was a mask. No man could lead me, as a woman could, into a guessing-game. I had just begun to read Bachofen on matriarchy with the same enthusiasm as others were reading Karl Marx, and I had met one of Bachofen's pupils, the Englishman Briffault, in Vienna, in the salon of my friend Dr Eugenie Schwarzwald. I still have the copies of his books which he gave me, although I have kept hardly anything else from those days. To him I owe my understanding of the Greek ideas of Eros and Thanatos – the counterparts of progress and enlightenment – out of which our dreams are spun. I pondered day and night on the secret that lies beyond love and death.

I was not the only one treading dangerous waters. The whole world seemed to be in the grip of an existential malaise, no longer believing in the possibility of individual action or the control of one's own future. I looked on the concept of human progress as no more than a fertile soil for the growth of heroes and martyrs. To see humanity in the light of progress is to impose on it an abstract concept which leads to endless utopian fallacies. To me, one thing was certain: the instinct for self-preservation which begins with the first movement in the womb and ends with death. I could confront reality and come to terms, as many others do, with the fact that life is a mortally dangerous thing. Thus, I was spared the panic which strikes those who refuse to open their eyes, and I suffered none of the erosion of self-confidence which periods of uncertainty tend to inflict on the mind. Fear makes for inactivity, but behind that shadow of Thanatos, which had dogged me from my childhood onwards, there lurked the ever more enticing abyss of Eros. Here, in this new existence to which I began to seek the key, is perhaps the secret of my first stage play, *Mörder, Hoffnung der Frauen* ('Murderer, the Women's Hope').

I was now adult in every sense, and different from before, but my curiosity remained unassuaged. An inner voice tormented me, like a hermit in the wilderness, with imaginings about the female sex. In Greek mythology there is a lot about Eros, but nothing analogous to the unhappy story of Brunhilde and Siegfried, or Tristan and Isolde. And how is one to explain, I wondered, this almost instantaneous transformation when one becomes possessed by another and bestows upon this being such beauty, wit, and spiritual qualities as nothing in the world could equal? The power of attraction is strong enough to render passion itself speechless, and you will take any risk, shrug off any folly, for the sake of a smile or of words you imagine were never heard before from mortal lips. You can feel icy cold and boiling hot at the same moment. When you timidly try to put an arm around the one with whom you are mortally in love, your heart begins to beat as if you were committing a sacrilege; only God, if he exists, could know how much you suffer. One may try, at a certain age, to remain unshaken by this vision of the magical countenance of Hypnos, or Eros. I know it took a world war, with all its carnage, to enable me to overcome this fatal confrontation. But more of that later.

The pen drawings I had done in my last year at the Kunstgewerbeschule were entirely new: they documented my own inner transformation. Adolf Loos later showed them to the Berlin editor Herwarth Walden, who printed them in the first few issues of his magazine *Der Sturm*, along with my play *Mörder, Hoffnung der Frauen*.

The first performance of this play, in Vienna in the summer of 1909, came about in the following way. On a grass plot alongside the temporary exhibition building which housed the Kunstschau, the Wiener Werkstätte had set up an open-air stage for the performance of modern ballet and music. I pressed the members of the committee to allow me to use it for staging a play of my own. Although they laughed at me, they agreed that I could put up a poster and announce the performance: 'You can do what you like, as long as it doesn't cost the Kunstschau anything.' That was enough for me.

Immediately I designed and got printed a poster expressing the content of the play. The man is blood-red, the colour of life. But he is lying dead in the lap of a woman who is white, the colour of death. If in art the label 'Expressionism' has a meaning, then this poster was one of its earliest manifestations. And, as I had intended, it sent the Viennese into paroxysms of rage. Thanks to the notoriety of my pictures, the tickets were sold out a week before the performance, and the proceeds went at once to pay the costs of the printer.

I wanted the actors to offer the public a gesture of defiance on my behalf. I was angry at the insults I read every day in the Press where I saw myself treated as a criminal. So I had my head shaved in order to look the part, and in my drawings for the play, and in a second poster, I showed myself in this guise to the public.

Since not much has changed in the theatre since 1909 to waken audiences from their lethargy, the storm that broke out at the open-air theatre at the Kunstschau constitutes an event of a kind that doesn't happen often. My wildest hopes and fears were exceeded. By chance, in an adjoining barracks, a regiment from the Balkan province of Bosnia was quartered. The soldiers who lined the garden wall became more and more excited during the performance, and were clearly only waiting for a disturbance as an excuse to intervene. Additionally there was the eerie effect of the firebrands that the Amazons in the play snatched from the warriors' hands at the storming of the citadel, and which at first menaced the makeshift wooden set with their flames and then smouldered red in the darkness. The wild atmosphere was intensified musically by drumbeats and shrill piping, and visually by the harsh, shifting colours of the lighting. My performers, most of them drama students, hurled themselves into their parts, as if acting for dear life. They were not acrobats, but even so they could run, jump, stand and fall better than any of the Burgtheater actors, who often took a quarter of an hour to lie down and die. As there was no money, I dressed them in makeshift costumes of rags and scraps of cloth and painted their faces and bodies, where exposed. In this, I had been helped by my visits to the ethnographical museum. There

I had learned how primitive peoples, presumably as a reaction to their fear of death, had decorated the skulls of the dead with facial features, with the play of expressions, the lines of laughter and anger, restoring to them the appearance of life. In a similar way I decorated the actors' arms and legs with nerve lines, muscles and tendons, just as they can be seen in my old drawings. The actors entered into the spirit of the play body and soul, without a trace of false pride or false emotion. In the end some emerged bloodied and bruised.

The heroine was played by a lovely, wild Croatian girl with a mane of red hair, Ilona Ritscher, whom I sketched in 1912 to use in a poster for a Wedekind festival. Other members of the cast were Karl Etlinger*, later a famous actor in Germany, and Rudolf Forster, who made a big name for himself in Berlin in the 1920s. Above all there was the male lead, my enthusiastic helper and friend, Ernst Reinhold, whose portrait I had already painted.

The savage review in the *Neue Freie Presse* on the next day, 5 July 1909, names a few more actors who have remained in obscurity.

A flimsy barrier separated the stage from the rows of seats, which were full to bursting-point. The garden was too small to hold the throng of society, intellectuals, and the merely curious, all of whom had come to see what outrage this bull in the china shop was about to commit. The audience maintained a chorus of catcalls throughout the play, but my actors were not deterred. Eventually, as the foot-stamping, scuffling and chair-brandishing increased in pitch, the soldiers stormed in and a free-for-all followed between them and the audience. In the tumult the police had to be sent for. Fortunately for me, Adolf Loos and his friend, the satirical writer Karl Kraus, knew the chief of police, Dr Schober, and arranged for him to come with a squad of men and restore order. Only the personal intervention of this senior official saved me from being arrested for a breach of the peace. Instead, I got off with a warning, thanks to Kraus and Loos whose friendship and support earned my lasting gratitude.

But I have not yet said anything about the play. Actually, I had simply improvised it at a night-time rehearsal in the garden with my friends. I gave the principals and other players an outline of the action and wrote down each of their parts in short key phrases on slips of paper, after first acting out the essentials of the play for them, complete with all the variations of pitch, rhythm and expression. Now, more than sixty years later, *Mörder, Hoffnung der Frauen* has been rediscovered. Theses are written about it at European and American universities. My plays are now regarded as forerunners of Expressionism, like those little fish that act as pilots to whales; people have begun

*Asterisk here and hereafter directs reader to Location of Works Mentioned in the Text, p. 232.

to read into them influences from Freud or Claudel, or to interpret them in terms of solar and lunar myth. I don't go in for such interpretations. Whatever the learned journals say, my play had nothing to do either with a rejection of society or with projects for its reform – and these two characteristics are proper to the literary movement that is called Expressionism. But it is no wonder that Viennese society of the time, like the Berliners later, could not understand my plays. I created them simply because I could not afford to go to the theatre. They are not didactic; they don't belong to the tradition of theatre as a moral institution. They simply express my attitude to my world. The only succeeding playwright in a similar vein, whose work I admired, was August Stramm, whom I met later at Herwarth Walden's house in Berlin. Unhappily, he was killed in the autumn of 1915. My play is not for reading. It must be spoken, acted and lived, as an antidote to the torpor that, for the most part, one experiences in the theatre today.

By midnight, when I set off for home with Ernst Reinhold, I was not very steady on my feet. On the way, something happened that I still find incomprehensible, although I have often talked about it to friends and acquaintances. Let me make clear that I was not drunk. My new patron Loos had indeed stood me a glass of whisky at the Kunstschau bar, my first whisky, as it happened. It was strong enough to relieve my tiredness, but not to make me lose control. Understandably, after such an initial and highly charged confrontation between the public and what I can now admit was the youthful exposition of my own views, I was in a state of great excitement. Pull yourself together, I thought. If the crowd doesn't understand me, at least my friends will. Keep calm, don't be afraid of being left alone. But I had to drop Reinhold's arm and press my hands to my temples to soften the shrill ringing agonizingly audible in my inner ear, like the ocean's roar in a seashell. Then, suddenly, I lost control. Probably the light of the full moon contributed to my state of mind. I had started walking faster to catch up with Reinhold, who was now a few steps ahead of me, when something strange occurred at the edge of my visual field, as if my own shadow were moving away and lagging farther and farther behind. My legs appeared to be freeing themselves from the network of shadows which framed the moonlit cobblestones. I caught hold of my legs in order to weight them down to the ground. I had an eerie sensation of floating in mid-air. I still vividly remember hanging sideways three feet above the pavement. I was slanted downwards to the left, my legs in the air, the back of my head perilously close to the ground, my arms flailing, trying to get hold of something. I was completely beside myself. Having lost my shadow, I felt as if I had lost my very being. But this happens to no one, living or dead, I thought: I will not give up so easily. I cupped my hands in front of my mouth to call out after my rapidly disappearing companion – then let them fall without a sound. I would permit myself no feelings of inferiority, no cries for help before strangers.

I have never forgotten the look of total incomprehension on the face of my friend. He had no idea of my condition, tossed about like a moth in a whirlwind. In the desolate moment when I had a right to his support, not even so close a friend could understand me. I had no choice but to suppress my cry.

Suddenly I felt a jerk, as if I had been caught up in a net of moon-cast shadows, thrown by a fisherman down below. My feet touched the ground, and my shadow returned; I could hardly believe it. Reinhold had evidently noticed nothing. But he had stopped and called out to me: 'Where are you?' 'I was nearly gone,' I stammered. 'Don't be funny, you must have had one too many.' And without sympathy he looked me up and down and said coldly: 'You're lying.' 'Yes, of course, now that I think about it, there wasn't anything wrong,' I answered, and let him go on alone.

I did not forgive him for years.

When in the First World War I suffered a head wound, which for a long time caused me difficulty in keeping my balance, the effect was very like what I have just described. During the lengthy and unpleasant treatment I underwent, I was able to make a leisurely study of the phenomenon, but now as a purely clinical one, not a hallucination.

I had painted Reinhold's portrait shortly before this incident; afterwards I entitled it *The Trance Player*, because I had many thoughts about him that I could not put into words.*

The party was over. The *furor* in the Viennese press following the performance of my play went far beyond the criticism which in 1908 had greeted my paintings in the 'Chamber of Horrors'. I was called a 'degenerate artist', 'bourgeois-baiter' (*Bürgerschreck*), 'corrupter of youth', and 'common criminal': all the expressions that came into common use in Hitler's day.

Soon after the performance the director of the Kunstgewerbeschule, the celebrated stage designer Alfred Roller – a well-meaning gentleman who was not much good at standing up to the authorities – showed me a telegram from the Minister of Education: the Minister could no longer answer to the press for the presence in the school of a disruptive element such as Kokoschka. My time there was up, anyway; but I would now also have to abandon any idea of continuing to work at the school.

My Early Paintings

Since the Second World War the human image in art has been steadily losing ground. In literature humanity held on to its special status somewhat longer, although only in the detailed description of man's animal functions, in a sordid language laying maximum emphasis on their least appetizing side. Lately a number of writers, like the painters before them, have set out, with all the confidence of their youth, to expel the human being altogether. Instead of man, the material environment becomes the hero of their novels.

I was astonished to read in a paper some time ago that the then director of the National Portrait Gallery in London has attempted to redefine the portrait on the grounds that photography, film and voice recording express more of the personality than the traditional painted or sculptured portrait. That you can deduce useful information from details – whether a gentleman's trousers are well pressed, or whether the shoes of life's victims are down at heel – only argues for not piling up quantities of trash in museums. Goya painted a woman's body once naked and once in a diaphanous costume. This is interesting as a fact, but tells us nothing about the art of portraiture. However, when Queen María Luisa de Borbón-Parma had herself painted by Goya several times in the garb of a *pétroleuse* of the French Revolution, the result is a revelation of her character and of Goya's genius.

A violent stimulus produces a trauma in an organism. So too a work of art – if it really is a work of art – can create a genuine experience, a visual shock, in the consciousness of a receptive observer. Since I am not a pessimist, I venture to suppose that one or other of my readers will give more credence to me than to the director of the National Portrait Gallery. I see creative art as a source, a spring, like Nature itself. I defend it as the constantly active, living material of thought. Had the politicians and generals not spared a few of the testimonies of art, what, today, would we make of history with its long record of millions slaughtered for the sake of abstract ideas?

When I paint a portrait, I am not concerned with the externals of a person – the signs of his clerical or secular eminence, or his social origins. It is the business of history to transmit documents on such matters to posterity. What used to shock people in my portraits was that I tried to intuit from the face, from its play of expressions, and from gestures, the truth about a particular person, and to recreate in my own pictorial language the distillation of a living being that would survive in memory. I usually start my paintings without having done any preliminary drawing: and I find that neither routine nor technique is of any help. I depend very much on being able to capture a mental impression, the impression that remains behind when the image itself has passed. In a face I look for the flash of the eye, the tiny shift of expression which betrays an inner movement. In a landscape I seek for the trickle of water that suddenly breaks the silence, or a grazing animal that makes me conscious of the distance or height of a range of mountains, or a lonely wayfarer whose shadow lengthens as evening falls. It would be too high-flown to call these things decisive experiences: they are simply what make me a *seeing* observer of nature. So too I could never have accepted as a sitter everyone who wanted to be painted: the sitter must have something worth noticing about him. I can't paint bemedalled gentlemen, or dressmaker's dummies festooned with pearls. A bare canvas has always filled me with a *horror vacui* until, initially in a half-indecipherable form, I am able to bring out from its prepared surface the vision of my inner eye.

I try to keep my sitters moving and talking, to make them forget they are being painted. This has nothing to do with extracting intimate secrets or confessions, but rather with establishing, in motion, an essential image of the kind that remains in memory or recurs in dreams. I could not do this if my sitter had to keep still, as he might for a photographer, or to hold a stiff pose until we were both sick of it. A person is not a still-life – not even a dead person.

I once drew the likeness of a dead girl in her coffin, at the request of her parents. I had known her briefly at the private school where I taught drawing. She was carried off by the murderous influenza epidemic at the end of the First World War. The scent of lilies and hyacinths in the room where the body was laid out could not entirely mask a faint smell of corruption, and I dropped my charcoal in fright when I suddenly saw moisture dripping from the dead girl's nose.

Simple records of fact bear no fruit; like the winter sun, they do not warm the heart. For example, the portrait of Reinhold, a picture especially important to me, contains one detail that has been hitherto overlooked. In my haste, I painted only four fingers on the hand he lays across his chest. Did I forget to paint the fifth? In any case, I don't miss it. To me it was more important to cast light on my sitter's psyche than to enumerate details like five fingers, two ears, one nose.

I also did an early portrait of Reinhold's father – Father Hirsch, I entitled it; his son's name was a stage name. Relations between the two were bad and, naturally, the portrait did nothing to improve them. I saw the father as an obstinate old man who, when roused to anger, as he very easily was, would bare his great false teeth, I liked to see him angry. Oddly enough, Father Hirsch was fond of me and proud to have his portrait painted. He hung the painting in his flat and even paid me for it.

I owe the faculty of capturing an expression in a few lightning strokes to the movement studies of my college days. But it often takes all my long experience in dealing with people to prise open a character sealed fast in convention. In addition, people often reveal their pretensions rather than their selves. This is almost always the case with young people, the larvae who have not yet discovered their shape as butterflies. When, in London during the Second World War, I painted the Russian ambassador, Ivan Maisky, he read *The Times* throughout the sittings. I could not get him to talk: perhaps he regarded a portrait as some new form of brainwashing. Finally, after hours of sitting, I suggested he reverse the paper behind which he was hiding, for I had finished reading the part turned to me. At length he became a little more talkative, and told me about his student days in Vienna and Munich. I donated the fee for this picture to the Stalingrad Hospital Fund, with the stipulation that it be used to help the German as well as the Russian wounded, but I don't know whether my wish was carried out. The fee was a thousand pounds, the only time in my fourteen years in London that a person unknown to me paid so much for a single work.*

I had shown my portrait of Reinhold as early as the 1909 Kunstschau, the exhibition at which I discovered there was such a thing as modern painting. Soon I also did portraits of Adolph Loos and his wife Bessie, and of Karl Kraus. The portrait of Kraus, editor of the much-feared periodical *Die Fackel*, was not, as the critics alleged, an unmasking of him but of Viennese society, on which his writings and speeches acted like vitriol in the country of the Phaeacians.

It was Adolf Loos, however, who first aroused interest in my paintings in certain circles of Viennese society. From time to time he persuaded one of his acquaintances, perhaps a customer for whom he was building a villa or designing an apartment, or even a complete stranger, to commission a portrait from me. Most of my sitters were Jews. They felt less secure than the rest of the Viennese Establishment, and were consequently more open to the new and more sensitive to the tensions and pressures that accompanied the decay of the old order in Austria. Their own historical experience had taught them to be more perceptive in their political and artistic judgments.

In my opinion Loos was outstanding both as a creative personality and as a critic. My meeting with him during the Kunstchau of 1909 was decisive not only for my career but also for my life. It may seem immodest, but I must say of Loos what Dante said of Vergil: he led me through the heaven and hell of life as a faithful companion and guide. He was the most important architect of the modern movement. Le Corbusier, Gropius, Mies van der Rohe, all paid due tribute to him as their forerunner and as a source of inspiration. But he never received a public commission; they were for the most part assigned to Government architects, without a jury to decide on the merits of designs submitted in open competition.

So Adolf Loos had time to help me. 'You must paint!' He had a wide circle of supporters and acquaintances, whom he was able to interest in my work. To paint his portrait – to come into such close contact with so great a man and artist – was a major experience for me. He had learned the trade of a stonemason, but had decided against taking over his father's business on the latter's death. Despite his diploma in architecture, he took pleasure in calling himself a mason to set himself apart from those architects who work only with blueprints. In America, though he led a harsh existence as a penniless casual labourer living in Welfare Committee hostels, he also kept his eyes open for what the architecture of the New World had to teach him. Loos was worlds apart from the individualist Frank Lloyd Wright. He remained highly disciplined after his return to Vienna, where as a radical innovator he declared total war on Jugendstil, concerning himself with man's creation of his total environment. In his designs, in his writings and in his lectures, which were always given to packed audiences, he covered every aspect of modern life right down to the way we walk, sit, stand, lie down and cook. He spoke out against a retrograde society which in some respects still persisted in eighteen-century habits of life. He disliked the pseudo-Renaissance architec- ture of the Victorian period, with its false stucco façades, as well as the japonoiserie of Art Nouveau ornament. He opposed even Otto Wagner and his school, although Wagner, as head of the Secession, had by then gained international recognition. Adolf Loos was the first, and for a long time the only, architect to concern himself with the education of society – a task which State organizations, in Britain and elsewhere, are even now only starting to attempt. He said: 'In the age of overpopulation, the most pressing problem for mankind is housing.'

His few completed buildings show how modern production methods could be used to evolve an organic architecture to meet the requirements of contemporary life. As a mason, he had a lively feeling for the beauty of his materials; he denounced Jugendstil as mere embellishment, inadequate in itself and, to make matters worse, often applied to inferior constructional materials. His gospel was the appropriate handling of the material itself, together with the use of architectural elements in a formal language whose essence must remain, as in antiquity, the expression of function in space. Vitruvius was his bible; he showed me with pride an early Italian edition that he possessed.

Loos was the prime architect of modern times, but people did not let him build. One of his writings is called 'Ins Leere gesprochen' – 'Spoken into the Void'. I painted him in his own flat; today there is not even a commemorative plaque on the house where he lived for forty years.*

At approximately the same time, I also painted Karl Kraus, the scourge of the Viennese conscience, like Abraham a Sancta Clara of the Thirty Years War. This first portrait has to my great sorrow not been traced. It is said, however, to have been offered for sale, together with the portrait of Bessie Loos, by a Russian officer in the devastated city of Berlin, shortly after the Second World War. Perhaps a kindly Fate has preserved it in East Berlin or elsewhere.

Art Nouveau basically ignored the portrait; plant forms and geometric ornament were preferred. Strangely enough, there was a good reason – an unconscious one, certainly – for avoiding the human image, as there has always been in transitional periods. My surmise is that Darwin's theory of evolution reduced too shockingly the distance between us and the related species of primates. The sense of familiarity and intimacy within mankind gave way to a feeling of alienation, as if we had never really known ourselves before. I myself was more affected by this than I would admit, which is why, to confront the problem, I started painting portraits. I wanted to have a really good look at people, to watch their behaviour, to get to know the nature of the society in which I had to live. Whatever has been said about my being a humanist, I do not really *love* humanity; I see it as a phenomenon, like a flash of lightning from a clear sky, a serpent in the grass. The human soul's propensity for goat-like leaps, its tragedy, its sublimity, and also its triviality and absurdity, attracted me, as a visitor to the zoo is attracted by the idea of observing the life of his own forbears – or as a scientist examines stones, plants and fossils to assemble his data. I could have foretold the future life of any of my sitters at that time, observing, like a sociologist, how environmental conditions modify innate character just as soil and climate affect the growth of a potted plant.

But there was no common language in which I could talk to people about the things I saw in them. Even to myself, I could express my insights only in paint. The form of official portraiture was quite different, being either directed towards smoothness and beauty of finish or intended to express the social status of the subject. Nor would 'art for art's sake' have summed up my objectives. Of course the whole Press, and the judgment of society, were against me – to my great good fortune. It was good for me too that I escaped the influence of the Impressionist fashion, eternally pregnant as it was with a scientific potential that the ensuing, disillusioned age rejected as barren. That Loos treated my pictures as works of art was barely comprehensible to me; it seemed like flattery. Nevertheless, it strengthened my feeling that I must not pursue routines or theories, but must find through my painting a basis for self-knowledge. At that time, I think, all young people felt essentially the same way about Expressionism. What is said about it today is entirely misleading – the whole core of the idea is lost. There is no such thing as German, French or Anglo-American Expressionism: there are only young people trying to find their bearings in the world.

I still met my friends, about four or five intimates, in the coffee-house in the evenings; in the daytime each of us went about his private business. Outside, the world was waiting for us; in the coffee-house we did not wait for the world. Then, in 1907 the first bar opened in Vienna: the Loos-Bar in the Kärntner Strasse, mainly frequented by Americans and other foreigners. There the bartender tolerated us until the foreigners came in from their hotels after dinner. Our money would buy us just one drink, but it was worth it. When you came through the outer door, with its angled glass sign in harsh shades of red, white and blue, like something in a Western film, the subdued indirect lighting on the coffered marble ceiling and under the glass table-top gave you a feeling of well-being. You sipped your drink like a blasé man of the world. The ice in the glass seemed positively warmed by the golden evening light that filtered through the onyx-paned fanlight over the narrow entrance. The discreet quiet of the bar afforded a change from the unrest that had begun to affect the coffee-houses.

Once we went to the Loos-Bar to celebrate the recovery of one of our friends, the young Finn from a Swedish family who was training to be a singer. We used to become as melancholy as he, when, in the Stadtpark at night, he followed his Schubert Lieder by singing songs from his own country. He was a reserved character, with a boyish prettiness, strawberry-blond hair, and delicate features like those of Gainsborough's *Blue Boy*; but he had ice-cold blue eyes. I painted his portrait too, later on. He had strange relationships with men, particularly the robust Bosnian soldiers, who carved him up one night in the park and left him unconscious. The park-keeper found him in the morning, half-dead from loss of blood, and called the police. The ambulance took him to hospital, where they patched him up again. We were not allowed to mention this too often in his presence; for all his mildness he was subject to sudden rages. We were happy to have him back among us.

When the Americans came along and wanted their usual table, one of them, who was already rather tight, started passing remarks about how long these young men took over one glass. To keep the Finn out of it, I accepted the American's proposal that whichever of us could drink the other under the table should have all his drinks, and those of his friends, paid for. I was young and had stamina: it was the American who finished on the floor. If it had ended otherwise, the bill would have been sent to Loos, and I should never have been able to face him.

Once more – and not for the last time – I crawled home at three in the morning to find my mother still up, waiting patiently with a glass of warm milk for me so that I shouldn't wake my father. Exhausted by his long working day, he had long since gone to bed. In my youth I often suffered pangs of conscience, but always soon forgot my good intentions.

Adolf Loos and Karl Kraus were close friends, linked by a profound intellectual affinity. Neither ever made concessions to the public. The story of Karl Kraus's life is contained in the pages of the magazine *Die Fackel*, which he founded in 1899, and which continued to appear for thirty-seven years in spite of war and revolution. When Kraus died, independence of thought in Austria died with him. Like Loos, he saw his existence as a mission to be carried out until the last day of his life: the mission of bringing light into the 'verbal morass' of the Press. As his poetry shows, he was, again like Loos, a man of great sensitivity. His poem 'Wiedersehn mit Schmetterlingen', for example, is a vision breathed into words.

> *Hier, fern von Trug und Tadel,*
> *leiht Rittersporn den Adel,*
> *mein Muth ist Löwenzahn!*

Die Zeit mir zu begleiten,
erzählt der Bach von Zeiten,
die hat die Zeit vertan.

Und dass ich wieder singe,
erscheinen Schmetterlinge,
o grenzenloses Glück!
Auf einem Sonnenstrahle
die stolzen Admirale
sie kehren mir zurück! . . .

His highly developed feeling for language is the one common denominator between his poetry and the satirical genius with which he mirrored the comedy, tragedy and ignominy of the world. He needed – as did Loos – the personal reaction of an audience. They were both masters of the art of reading aloud, and their lectures and readings were always crowded.

Kraus slept during the day and worked at night. He had his dinner at the coffee-house, and always followed it with innumerable cups of black coffeee. It was a great mark of distinction to be invited to his table, while he went over every letter, every comma and full-stop, in an article for the next issue of *Die Fackel*. In the war years, even the blank spaces were expressive. On several occasions, the censors insisted on cuts, against his obstinate resistance, to avoid having to prosecute him. The Imperial Royal Censorship Board feared his popularity in Vienna more than it feared the rumours of military defeats.

I painted Kraus's portrait at his home. His eyes flashed feverishly in the lamplight. He gave an impression of youthfulness, shut away behind his huge spectacles as if behind a black curtain, gesticulating animately with nervous, fine-boned hands. His voice had a cutting edge. Loos, whose hearing was failing, caught every word. Kraus's personality was utterly compelling. He would pounce like a wild cat on a red-covered copy of *Die Fackel* and rip a sentence out of it like a chunk of flesh, in order to convince Loos of the absolute accuracy of an expression. Both had forgotten I was there. In their company I came to understand that some men earn the right to criticize society, and to reform it. Kraus had a right to douse the German and Austrian press with vitriol, because he had the keenest possible ear for the corruption of language. Every false note, every unclear, mishandled expression, every cliché perpetrated by the carpetbaggers of the Press, gave him physical pain; it was a crime against the language that was dear to him above all things. For Kraus the spiritual environment of a people was its language; for Loos it was the way in which a man builds his home.

After the publication of each new issue of *Die Fackel*, everyone at the two friends' coffee-house table was subjected to a stern *viva voce* examination on its contents. I used to plead that I had not yet read the issue in question. I had, of course, but surreptitiously. Kraus was merciless. If I admitted to having read it, and then misinterpreted some line, devoted primarily to the definitive expression of some fine shade of meaning, and only secondarily to some polemic, I would have convicted myself of the grossest ingratitude to the last custodian of the German language. But I was only a painter; and, just as in the East they regard halfwits as sacrosanct, I was granted the privilege of sharing a table with the others, as a mute.

Seventeen years later, in 1925, I painted Karl Kraus's portrait again, at our house in the Liebhartstal. He apologized most charmingly to my mother for disturbing her by his presence, and she made him some specially strong coffee because he had come such a long way to see us. At the last sitting – Kraus had been coming out with Loos, in a horse-drawn cab, every day for about a week – the chair collapsed because he was arguing rather vehemently with Loos. I made a note of this on the back of the painting in these words: '*Pro domo et mundo*. The chair on which Karl Kraus sat for this picture fell apart after the last sitting on 7 February 1925, and the carpenter had to be sent for. Your desk was a plank borrowed from the shipwrecked world of those who are born with their heads barricaded. OK.' That pleased him.

The lyric poet Peter Altenberg – whose real name was Richard Engländer – was a lifelong friend of both Kraus and Loos. Altenberg looked like a seal, or rather a newborn seal-pup that has just been put into the sea; such was his habitual expression of astonishment. He could be full of sparkling gaiety at one moment, and surly and miserable the next. To make us laugh, Kraus sometimes used to goad him into one of the childlike outbursts of anger which were so easily provoked. Especially when as a joke they got Altenberg's rich patron Herr von Lieben to delay payment of the weekly pension which Altenberg regarded as his by right of custom. But Karl Kraus was his truest benefactor all his life. Altenberg was a bohemian, and always lived from hand to mouth in the same shady little hotel in the city centre, frequented by prostitutes whose poet laureate he became. Thanks to them there was always a bottle of slivovitz under his bed, and his room was papered with their postcards and pictures. He was a dreamer who, in his checked shirt and brightly coloured homespun jacket, looked like a clown. But in painting him I went deeper. Later, when I saw the famous aquarium in

Naples, where tourists used to pay ten lire for a glass rod with which to tease an octopus asleep in his tank, I was reminded of Altenberg and his outbursts under provocation. The sea-beast would flail its tentacles faster and faster so that it came to resemble a wheel, rotating round a plump pinkish-white body from which the great eye flashed yellow, blood-red, ice-blue, black with fury.

Loos brought my painting things to the coffee-house, the best place to get hold of the poet, while Karl Kraus was having dinner. Loos had fixed everything, even getting Altenberg to sit still. The surroundings did not disturb him at all; and in Loos's view, whatever my objections, I simply had to paint Peter Altenberg. I loved to hear him telling stories, and to catch his often dazzling witticisms in the circle of his intimate friends and benefactors. Even on a bleak Viennese winter evening, his podgy, animated hands could conjure up the houris of Arabia, the geishas of Japan, and the concubines of the Thousand and One Nights. But this time, when the teasing began, I could bear the look of desperation on his face no longer. 'How can you torment Peter like this and still claim to be his friends? He's done nothing to you! You have fun, but he really takes it to heart. It hurts him and it hurts me too!' I must explain that Altenberg had a reputation for being a miser, no doubt because he was constantly short of money. When I jumped up in anger, Altenberg held me back, and amid the universal astonishment that followed my little speech he called spontaneously for the waiter and ordered me a pair of frankfurters with mustard, and in addition a whole packet of cigarettes! It was unheard of for Altenberg to overcome his parsimony in this way, and the evening ended in general affectionate hilarity. My portrait of Peter shows him not as a clown but as an angry octopus in human shape.

In this same period, I painted my first landscape. Altenberg's patron Herr von Lieben had a beautiful estate on the Plattensee, a lake on the Austro-Hungarian border. He invited Loos and me to spend a week there, principally in order to get Loos, who was in poor health again, away from Vienna for a few days. The picture, a view over the endless expanses of the *puszta*, is called *The Hungarian Landscape*. Loos took it back with him to Vienna. He was really depressed at this time, because another of his great plans had come to nothing. Full of hope, he had travelled to Nice with a suitcase full of completed plans for what he wanted to call the 'Grand Hotel Babylon'. A speculator on the Riviera had taken an interest in it. It was the prototype of the stepped terraces that are often built nowadays: light from all directions, balconies everywhere, a pyramid as big as those of the Pharaohs.

Loos had put me in touch with another of my sitters, the former reader to poor Empress Elisabeth, Franz Joseph's estranged wife, who was stabbed to death by an Italian anarchist on Lake Geneva. Her rather sentimental monument stands near our house, and I often pass it. Dr Constantin Christomanos was a Greek, a hunchback, a highly educated man with an extraordinary capacity for empathy. During the sittings he told me a lot about the Empress, to whom he had given lessons in ancient Greek every morning; to his great pride she reached the stage where she could read Homer. His portrait was unfortunately one of those I overpainted because Loos did not get it away from me in time.

Another habitué of Kraus's table was Ludwig Ritter von Janikowsky, whose feeling for language Kraus prized particularly highly. Janikowsky came from an aristocratic Polish family, and had long held a senior post in the Austro-Hungarian Foreign Ministry. In my time he lived in the Steinhof clinic, near Vienna, suffering from an incurable affliction which the Viennese elegantly called 'The French disease'. Loos wanted me to paint his portrait before the disease attacked his brain, which it was soon expected to do, and indeed not long afterwards he died. I liked Herr von Janikowsky very much, but a certain reserve was necessary on my part, for he insisted on my learning to smoke a pipe. To this end he kept offering me his own pipe, which he was always chewing. Now, I did not want to learn in the first place, and to take his pipe in my mouth took a major effort of will. But he insisted, and in the end, out of the kindness of my heart, I gave in; he never noticed how much it revolted me.

Dr Emma Veronika Sanders, a very gifted Dutchwoman with a considerable reputation as a scholar, was a frequent visitor at my friend Dr Eugenie Schwarzwald's house in Vienna at that time. She always seemed strangely distracted when she was sitting for me. Although on the surface calm and composed, her thoughts were obviously far away, and her great, sad eyes, gazing into nothingness, made me think of a madwoman. It was this feeling that I expressed in my picture, as if I had had a premonition that she would be in an asylum a few years later. It's odd that throughout my life I've known so many suicides and people who were mentally ill: clearly this hasn't been the best of all possible worlds.

I had by now become more self-confident, and my whole bearing was less retiring. Part of this came from dressing well. Loos always saw to this. To be really modern one must not go around looking like an artist. His great model was the English gentleman. Neither of us had any money, but he knew the best tailors in Vienna whose shops he had redesigned. The court tailor, and chairman of the association of gentlemen's tailors, was Kommerzialrat Ernst

Ebenstein, who used to dress old Emperor Franz Joseph. Ebenstein was himself a distinguished old gentleman, and he was *the* Viennese tailor. He was elected president of one of the specialized committees of the British wool industry in Scotland, and had to go to Aberdeen every year to give his judgment of the choice of patterns for woollen fabrics. This meant a lot for a foreigner. It was he who dressed me in suits made to measure just as they were for his exalted clients. In return I painted his portrait, in which I captured the essence of conservatism better than any court photographer could have done.

While he was taking my measurements, I learned from him, the tailor, my first real lessons in anatomy, which has to be taken into account in tailoring if the body is to move freely, with true elegance, in the clothes. It was a far cry from the anatomy class at the Kunstgewerbeschule where I remember being sick when the Professor demonstrated on a corpse; the air had entered the knee-joint with a hissing sound, and I had caught sight of the severed head, lying open-eyed in a pail under the marble slab.

For a time I did portraits of children. The tailor Goldman, who a few years later was to kit me out for the war, commissioned me to paint his child, then only a few weeks old. It was the Goldmans' first child, they were happy, and to show this I included both parents' hands in the picture, holding up the little creature in its white dress, its expression stoical because it did not know why it was loved so much. The parents noticed something strange about the father's hand in the painting: the middle finger seemed thicker than it should. At first they assumed this to be a sadistic distortion on my part, taking it out on the parent for the howling of the infant. But later, after much thought, the father remembered falling off his bicycle as a child and breaking a finger. It was proof of how exactly I had observed; for Loos, this trifle confirmed my clairvoyance.

I also painted the children of the Viennese bookseller Stein. For children anything can be a decisive experience. Unlike adults, they have no need of a shock to bring them out of themselves, out of the confines of the ego. In childhood this process of leaving the self behind is the secret of all growth, development and being. Children are still half spiritual creatures, not habituated to life as grown-ups are. This is true of all children, but especially of those under school age, and this is why they can always communicate with one another, even when they have no language in common. Adults fail to grasp this secret. We imagine we've made ourselves clear to children when all we've done is to talk down to them. We are no more than vulgar interlopers in their kingdom of dreams – a realm in which, however childishly we behave, we share very little. Yet sometimes in the midst of all our self-deception, we are taken unawares by a moment of sharp regret at ever having become outsiders: it is the moment when a child suddenly looks at us as if we were not there.

The Stein children came before me flushed with playing, clothes rumpled, the girl in a pink and white striped garden frock of the kind that parents always seemed to think appropriate for the occasion, the boy in the inevitable Sunday sailor suit – dressed, in fact, as bourgeois children were in those days. To keep them diverted while I was painting, I asked whether they liked to play, and whether they wanted any new toys. There was a sudden silence. I myself could no longer believe what I had said. Even their clothes now looked like a disguise. But it was done and could not be remedied. They ran away, and just to have something to do, I started clearing up the dirt they had tracked in from the garden. Looking at their footmarks, I felt a need to tread carefully lest I step on the snake that had been the downfall of Adam and Eve. Dear God, how can we go about so pleased with ourselves, when we know at heart how much we still long for the Eden we have lost!

I also painted the young son of a psychoanalyst who collected works of art in order to put some money aside for the future, and who wrote about art as well. The picture shows the boy wide-eyed, with his left hand raised.

It was Holy Week when I saw the boy for the first time. He was playing with a green caterpillar which was rearing up on his little finger, turning its tiny dark head this way and that, as if it had no eyes and was nevertheless seeking the light. The boy barely acknowledged my presence. I had a faintly ironic awareness of how the boy and the caterpillar were alike in their helplessness because the world was not as it should be. How his eyes would suddenly darken with delight if the caterpillar were to turn into a butterfly!

The father asked me what I thought the boy would be when he grew up. I answered without hesitation: 'A cardinal.' In a family of assimilated Jews this would have been something of an event. I thought of the draught of hemlock drunk by Socrates: once a man has drained the bitter cup of life, no disappointment can affect him. The helpless worm in the grass can be crushed underfoot by no one. Then, the pantomime over, he spreads his wings and escapes from the confinement we think of as freedom but which, as Socrates knew, is only self-deception. I wonder what happened to that particular family later, when the Anschluss came.

There is no need for us to despair about everything, not even about painting, for it isn't necessarily restricted to so-called facts, such as gentlemen with or without moustaches, or ladies wearing low necklines or nothing at all.

Pictures are not mere signposts on an endless road: they give us pause. God himself, on his heavenly throne, must sometimes say to himself: 'Infallible I may be, but that was still an unforgivably stupid thing to do', as he considers that he permitted the Fall of Man with all its consequences. Man the dwarf blames God for what he has done to him, but history rolls on its way even though the dwarf has now taken the business of creation into his own hands.

The master of the house invited me to share the family's Easter lamb. It was fresh from the market, and he took me into the kitchen to see it. Usually I don't give a damn about food; but how could I put something into my mouth that, even after being slaughtered, looked at me with such reproach in its eyes? I was left alone in the kitchen for a while. The corpse lay on the table. It was Good Friday, and my mind turned to the Son of Man, whose fate was not very different. Every Sunday in the Holy Mass the faithful eat his body, and God be thanked that Christ can no longer feel it, even in sympathy. The lamb's eyes seemed to cloud over and become lifeless as I watched. But the thought that this dead thing was now to be roasted and consumed! When the master of the house lifted it by its stiff legs to give me a better view of it, blood dripped out of its mouth. I had had enough.

Suddenly I had an idea. Instead of accepting his invitation to eat the lamb on Sunday, I wanted to take the freshly skinned carcass into the next room, which was hardly ever used except as a boxroom, and to paint it at once. My host accepted the suggestion; for one thing, the lamb had been expensive, in the Easter rush, and this was a way of making extra use of it. The portrait of his son was finished, and the only reason I had come on this particular morning was to stand the painting in the boxroom to dry. If I started the still-life right away, there would be enough time before Sunday. All the accessories I could want were in the son's playroom: an old tortoise and an aquarium containing an axolotl, a pinkish-red amphibian which lives in deep caves in Carinthia and shuns the light. There was a white mouse, as well, which the little boy had trained to nibble cheese from his hand without running away. In painting you can do a lot with technique, but there was still something more needed, some little thing to add a highlight to the objects my host and I had assembled. Not even the tomato providing a spot of colour right at the front was quite enough; nor was the reflection of light from outside, falling on the old smoke-blackened wall and on a battered antique oil-jar – the abandoned relic of an Italian holiday. It was all grey, sad, soulless, like the realm of the forgotten, the shades of the dead in Hades; it was too much like a cemetery. Ferreting around, we discovered on the window-ledge of the maid's room a dazzling white hyacinth in full bloom. It seemed waxen,

artificial, and glowed like the Light Eternal, even in the dark. I could have
hoped for nothing better, although its scent reminded me of the room where
I had once painted a dead girl. The hyacinth, pouring forth its fragrance in
the frosty, early spring air, when everything still seems lifeless, points a finger
towards heaven, and assuages the eternal fear that all – except experience – is
in vain. I hoped my painting would convey a subliminal impression of the
individuality of the little boy, whose parents could do no more than wonder
at his strange otherness.

Baron Victor von Dirsztay had me paint a portrait of his nephew, Jacques
de Menasse. A delicately chiselled little face, a late generation of a robust
family. At the same time I painted Dirsztay himself, who was a complicated
character. He had a great gift for music, and was always playing Richard
Strauss's *Till Eulenspiegel*, which was then new and much decried in Vienna.
Somewhat later he wrote a book called *Das Lob des hohen Verstandes* ('In
Praise of the Lofty Intellect'), and an autobiographical work called *Der
Unentrinnbare oder der Doppelgänger* ('The Inescapable, or the Double'),
perhaps to impress his family by getting something into print. I had to
correct his manuscripts and illustrate his books, in return for presents, such
as a pair of cufflinks. He suffered from a skin disease which probably affected
his whole body, and hence was always scratching himself. It made him
furious when I told him about his habit; kind words could never assuage his
inner fury but only made things worse. Even Freud, whom he went to for
years, could not heal him, because the cause of his illness was the contempt
he felt for his family. They were *nouveaux riches* from Hungary who had not
the faintest conception of the romantic impulses that lurked in the heart of
this prodigal son. He suffered from *Weltschmerz*. I became aware of this one
day when Dirsztay stood upstairs in the family mansion in the fashionable
diplomatic quarter of Vienna, and pointed scornfully at the bundle of dirty
linen that lay unregarded on the magnificent staircase. Downstairs several
corpulent members of the family could be seen through the open door of the
drawing-room, noisily drinking and playing cards in their underwear. That
was how he saw his family: an underworld. I could understand the profound
disgust he felt at such a shameless display of vulgarity.

He used to spend hours outside Caruso's dressing-room at the Vienna State
Opera, just to catch a glimpse of the singer he idolized. Once, he refused to
wash his face for days on end because the great man had boxed his ears.
Caruso had been in his dressing-room, busy with a girl from the chorus,
when he heard a noise and threw open the door to discover Dirsztay, whom
he took for a voyeur. Well might Caruso give free rein to his fiery tempera-

ment; what he did not see was that my friend was really Rigoletto, the clown. We are all trapped in our own skins, clowns trying to shield ourselves from the absurdity of transience by imagining ourselves to be more or less worthy images of God. And in the end fate always throws a custard pie in our faces. Victor von Dirszstay eventually killed himself. I saw Caruso again in Naples, as a shrunken mummy in a glass coffin.

On one occasion I was summoned to attend a court case. A flower-pot had fallen from a balcony on to the head of a gentleman passing in the street; it had not hurt him, but it had crushed his top hat. I was an eye-witness, and aroused general hilarity by giving my occupation as 'painter, poet and habitué of the Yiddish theatre'. Kraus, Loos and I went often to the Jiddisches Theater in the Leopoldstadt area, not far from the Prater, a district where many families of Jewish immigrants from Galicia lived. The most famous Yiddish theatre companies from the Austrian sector of Poland, and from Hungary, used to make guest appearances. There was considerable rivalry between them. It is impossible to forget those performances, full of originality and fantasy; down-to-earth comedy rubbed shoulders with high-flown emotion. I was able to follow the action, more or less, partly because it was often based on classical plays, partly because my young coffee-house friends in that polyglot city had not forgotten all their Yiddish, but mostly because the Middle High German I had learned at school gave me a head-start with Yiddish, which is largely derived from it. The house was always sold out. The Shakespeare evenings, travesties with added music and songs, provided a special attraction. I can still see the broad-beamed, high-bosomed Ophelia singing her farewell aria in melting, heartfelt tones, while the Prince of Denmark took ship for England, pulling a wooden toy boat across the stage behind him on a string. The music and dances, the solo numbers and duets, had so much sheer theatrical verve, and the Jewish humour was so wild, that one did not know whether to laugh or cry. Every number was greeted with frenetic applause. A Chassidic ecstasy, a forgetfulness of self, such as I have since encountered only once, among the dancing dervishes of Cairo. This kind of Jewishness has been pretty well wiped out. But it was the Jews from Russia, Poland and Hungary who invented the American musical. Some of them became important in theatre and film, and capitalized on their own ghetto experiences in Broadway revues.

I remained faithful to this Yiddish theatre in Leopoldstadt in the 1920s, when the golden age of the Habimah Theatre began on the Continent. In Germany I used to see and admire the actress Rovina, who played the lead in *Der Golem*; I can compare her only with Duse. Rovina lives in Israel now, and sends kind regards to me and to my brother, who was also in love with her, whenever our paths fail to cross in the course of our travels.

Adolf Loos was a man full of contradictions. For all his fury at the incomprehension of his contemporaries, he had still delivered his lectures – 'spoken into the void'. In despair at the coming collapse of his native Austria, which he could foresee, he travelled several times to Paris to go to the Moulin Rouge. It was in Paris, many years later, that I saw him for the last time. Already a sick man, he had been brought to Paris by his faithful cabinetmaker, who for years had made the chairs for the flats Loos designed (Loos tolerated no mass-produced articles), and his long-time cleaning woman. Obviously no one else was prepared to do it. I found Loos in an unmade bed, though it was already about midday. His mind was failing. He had wanted to come to Paris after spending many years in Austria in desperate search for a way out. I was very upset and, after we had talked desultorily for a while, I wanted to leave. But with his irresistible force, irresistible in spite of his illness, he held me back, got up out of the bed in his tattered pyjamas, lifted the dirty counterpane and pulled out, to my revulsion, a huge lobster dripping with tomato sauce. *Homard a l'américaine* was his favourite dish. He pulled off one claw, scooped out the flesh with the gesture of a seasoned gourmet, and crammed it into my mouth. With a flash of his old wit he told me: 'The Austrians lost the war because instead of seafood they ate nothing but dumplings, strudels and chocolate cakes.'

When called up as a reserve officer in the First World War, Loos had nearly been court martialled because he presented himself in a uniform specially designed for him by his devoted tailor Goldman, with an open collar instead of the regulation stiff one and puttees instead of jackboots. In his view the Germans lost the war, in spite of all their strategic plans, because of their boots: the army had got trench-feet. Loos had ideas of his own.

One day he had turned up at my mother's flat and said: 'Your son needs to get out of Vienna; I'm taking him to Switzerland.' At the time Bessie Loos was in a sanatorium at Leysin, above Lake Geneva. Sunlight had been discovered as a therapy for tuberculous patients, and sanatoria had been built near the Swiss glaciers – a measure good for employment and for the rural economy generally. Bessie Loos had been one of the Barrison Sisters, the first cakewalk dancing act to reach Vienna; they appeared at the Cabaret Tabarin, and were much admired by Altenberg, Kraus and Loos. Adolf Loos at once took charge of the pretty English girl; she was already ill and would certainly soon have died if she had not left the stage. He married her in

1905 and took her to Leysin, which he knew because he had built a villa near there for a Viennese doctor.

So Loos negotiated with my mother, answering all her objections to my first trip abroad. Naturally she had to agree in the end. She wrapped a gold coin in my handkerchief, in case of need; she had been keeping it for years in the linen cupboard. Loos was taking a number of valuable old oriental carpets with him to sell in Switzerland, and because the trains out of Vienna in mid-winter were badly heated, we wrapped ourselves up in them. With the proceeds from their sale Loos paid Bessie's sanatorium bill, and got me an attic room in the same clinic with half-board. Loos could be very charming; he knew how to talk people into good deeds, so long as he was asking nothing for himself. He had not forgotten to pack my box of paints, and he proposed that the patients should have me do their portraits to while away the time. (My first picture, however, was a landscape). When everything was set up to his satisfaction, he had to leave, and he entrusted Bessie to my care.

I was devoted to her from the first. She had the delicate complexion of those Lancashire girls who work all day at their looms and never see the sun. Even when she was spitting blood into the hated blue glass bottle that all the inmates of a tuberculosis clinic carry around with them like a holy relic, she had a joyous, childlike laugh. I was supposed to keep an eye on her; but how can you hold back a pleasure-loving young thing like Bessie? When the doctors had gone to bed, she used to climb out the window and go off dancing with the other patients – those anyway who still had enough life left in them. She was the embodiment of a kind of Englishness that no longer exists.

From my attic window I watched Loos's departing sledge. He looked up at me, the horses trotted on, my patron turned round once more and waved; then the sledge disappeared in a little cloud of steaming breath from the galloping horses, white and grey in the seemingly endless expanses of the mountain landscape. Here was empty space as I had never before been aware of it, living as I had for many years cooped up in city flats from which the sky could be seen only as a crack between the smoking chimneys of the houses along the street. At the station in Vienna, I had studied the travel posters, large photographs of Swiss winter landscapes. But when I stood at the open window of my room at Leysin, and the world of the Dents du Midi unfolded before me in all its vastness, the memory of the posters paled. They had nothing in common with the Nature which transformed itself before my eyes into an ever wider and deeper interplanetary space, as the rising sun flooded with light the glacier-hung massif, a giant crystal amid the encircling mists. My awe and amazement grew, as down below, over ice and snow, along the pinewood and past the signposts and the telephone wires, Loos disappeared into the distance. The pain of parting grew in my heart alongside my awe at the sunrise. From that moment it became clear to me that a landscape cannot simply be depicted objectively, captured by Kodak, painted like a still-life. Landscape too is something living, something experienced; and I tried to give shape to this new insight in a painting.

A good two years later, in the summer of 1912, my *View of the Dents du Midi* was bought at the Sonderbund exhibition in Cologne for the large sum of 1800 gold marks by Herr Hagelstange, the director of the Wallraf-Richartz-Museum in Cologne. This, my first sale to a public institution, was Loos's doing. The painting hung in the museum until the late 1930s, when, along with a number of other works, it was declared to be 'degenerate art' and sold abroad. After the Second World War, when I visited Cologne and made inquiries about the picture, I heard to my despair that it had 'fallen prey' to the destroyers. To my delight, it later turned up in a private collection in Tyrol. I never saw Bessie Loos again after that stay in Switzerland. The portrait of her I painted at Leysin at the same time as the Dents du Midi was considered lost until recently, when Dr Werner Haftmann, Director of the Nationalgalerie in Berlin, found it wrapped in newspaper in a store-room in New York.*

I occupied my attic in the sanatorium at Leysin for quite a while. It was a long, severe winter. Loos visited from Vienna only rarely. Some of the patients sat for me, talked into it by Bessie Loos. They were like shrivelled plants, for whom even the Alpine sunshine could not do much. They set little store by my painting; to them it was a minor distraction in a succession of identical days spent awaiting a cure – or the end. I painted the Conte Verona, who had a caved-in face coming to a point at the chin; I also painted the Duchesse de Rohan-Montesquieu and her husband. My portrait of this delicate, aristocratic lady is illustrated in the derisive catalogue of the Nazi exhibition of 'degenerate art' (*Entartete Kunst*) held in Munich in 1937. I was moved by her beauty. She reminded me of those aristocratic women who used to seek consolation in their faith, back in the days of religious upheavals when the world was so godless that only mystics still believed in a paradise, which they placed in their own hearts. After I returned to Vienna she wrote me several letters, in her touchingly childlike hand, telling about her girlhood. Her husband was not kind to her. I was amused that this over-sophisticated gentleman wore lace cuffs, like a cavalier at the court of Louis XIV.

One day Loos arrived and took me to Yvorne, to meet the famous scientist

Auguste Forel: I must paint his portrait, as Loos put it, for all eternity. Loos, though then quite unknown in Switzerland, had written to him in advance, and introduced me with the words: 'I have a young genius here; you must be painted by Kokoschka.' Forel said that he didn't want to be painted; he had no time, and in any event painting didn't interest him in the least. But Loos with his compelling eloquence succeeded in persuading, I almost said forcing, the old *savant* to give in. Since during the day he was always too busy with his experiments, a compromise was reached: I could see Forel at dinner. So every evening I went to Yvorne and watched Forel and his family – wife, daughter and future son-in-law – eating their dinner. He was a vegetarian and kept next to his place a little pair of scales on which he carefully weighed out just so many raisins, nuts, almonds, a little apple perhaps, as he needed for his calorie quota. I painted him by the faint light of a table lamp, often able to see only his back. His family talked to him meanwhile. I felt rather embarrassed, as if I ought not to have been listening. They spoke French, and it seemed to me that terribly intimate family matters were being discussed: sexual problems, definitely not for my ears. It was a long time before I realized that they were discussing the behaviour of ants, Forel's special field of study. As well as concerning himself with the brain and the problem of hypnosis, he was the first scientist to work on the social behaviour of ants. His standard work, published in 1921, has the title *Le Monde social des fourmis du globe comparé à celui des hommes*. At that time the world of the anthropologists, palaeontologists, and biologists in general, underwent a revolution; a German naturalist, and then a British scientific ornithologist, had made the discovery that in the animal kingdom the male does not fight for the female but for his territory. For living-space; for property, in fact! This was a blatant contradiction of Freud's theory of sex, and indeed of Marxism. It must have bothered Forel quite a lot, too.

He and his wife refused the picture I painted. Loos had to take it away with him. Forel thought it looked as if he had had a stroke. And while bending over a microscope two years later, he did have one. Loos was convinced I had X-ray eyes.

In 1904 Loos had built for a Viennese doctor the famous Villa Karma near Montreux. It demonstrates how progressive Loos was seventy years ago, for the house is still as modern as if it had just been constructed. What is more, such good materials were employed that nothing, not even the electric wiring, needs replacing or repairing. It will be hard to find a house built today of which the same can be said in seventy years' time. Bessie Loos had moved to a *pension* at Les Avants, above Montreux, where it was cheaper, and Loos arranged for me to stay at the Viennese doctor's villa by the lake. The doctor's wife was there alone with her small son, and I was to paint her portrait in order to take her mind off the fact that her husband had been accused of a sexual offence and was in custody in Vienna. Although Loos tried to convince her of the falsity of the accusation, she had started divorce proceedings. Despondency, and the fear that if her husband were acquitted the court might award him custody of her child, had reduced her to a state of total disorientation, like a hunted animal. She spent sleepless nights, and once appeared in my room in a thin white garment, playing the part of Niobe threatened with the loss of her young. She forced me to call the police, and then in a frenzy of gratitude tried to hurl herself into my arms; I fended her off with some difficulty. I can remember that my hands were smeared with prussian blue because I was still working on the picture. I also remember surprising myself by the unconcern with which I gazed admiringly at the silver ceiling of my room, as I escaped by letting myself down out the window with the aid of a rolled bedsheet. The ceiling, as was confirmed to me many years later, is covered with little plates of mother-of-pearl. In the tumult when the police arrived, my escape went unnoticed.

I hied myself to the railway station in a blizzard. The whole incident had taken away any interest I might have had in completing the picture. Nor could I, from the absurdity of my own position, shed any tears over the poor woman's fate. For as I took out the gold coin that my mother had wrapped in my handkerchief, in order to change it to pay for my rail ticket I dropped it in the snow. Inanimate objects often take on more meaning than living ones. The bystanders helped me look for the coin and, in the process, trod it irretrievably into the snow. A kind saviour eventually paid the fare for me.

And so I was able to take refuge with Bessie Loos. The next day the lady from the Villa Karma turned up on horseback, complete with riding-habit and feathered hat. I watched but kept well out of view. She demanded that I should return to her, and nearly used her riding-crop when Bessie, who clearly felt a great deal of sympathy for her in her madness, nevertheless steadfastly denied that I was there.

I have no words to describe the anguish that this whole affair caused me. I must have been pale as death – I certainly felt a cold chill in my stomach – when from the window I watched that solitary maenad galloping off down the icebound, winding road, lashing her horse to make it go even faster. I learned later that the doctor had been unjustly suspected and was acquitted and that his wife had poisoned herself at the Villa Karma. It upsets me to hear such stories, whatever their outcome, though people love to tell similar tales. All things, when regarded closely and simply, are but events, and the judgments people make of them are idle chatter, nothing more.

My stay in Switzerland was not however without its happy moments. One spring day while I was out for a walk among the vineyards on the slopes above Lake Geneva, I saw on the low wall between the vines a young, half-grown girl who lay sunning herself like a lizard. I approached unobserved and then words failed me. I could only ask her name. 'Virginia,' she said – nothing more – and looked up into the sky again. The encounter had no significance: it was beautiful – the country, the lake, the girl on the wall – and that was all. But I have never forgotten that moment. And one icy winter day in Berlin I told the story of the girl Virginia to a friend. Words did not fail me then.

Berlin

It did not matter to me where I went, as long as I could get out of Vienna! Luckily, I had the third-class compartment to myself for a long time. I sat in the window seat, my suitcase tucked under my legs, my face reflected in the window-pane. There were dark shadows waving the travellers goodbye, but nobody waved to me. I hoped it would stay that way. I was due to arrive in the morning at Munich, the centre of the German art world, where I hoped to find a publisher for my drawings. For the first time I was travelling abroad on my own. All I wanted was to avoid having to talk to anyone about where I came from and where I was going. I was unhappy, but did not know why.

In Vienna, a few days before, I had gone with Kraus and Loos to watch a Canadian snake dancer at the Tabarin, and afterwards had visited her elegant home near the Hofburg. Loos had talked her into letting me draw her, but she might have had second thoughts when she met me, young and hungry-looking as I was. With beating heart, I plucked up the courage to ring her doorbell, still thinking of the erotic wrestling-match I had seen between this powerful woman and a python. If the serpent is supposed to have been Lucifer himself, then the tempter must have had staying-power; for at every performance she had freed herself from the python's coils. I rang again. Out of the door burst a giant of an Imperial-Royal gendarme, in his gold-braided crimson tunic, bulging white doeskin breeches and high boots complete with spurs, cramming his helmet with its flowing white horsehair crest down over his red face. He was as taken aback as I was, when he saw the youth who was to be his successor. He glared at me briefly and rushed down the stairs. I had to pull myself together when I stepped into the flat and saw, reclining on the divan, the very incarnation of the evil eye; she was not unlike a giant snake, limp, relaxed, refreshing herself with damp towels as if after a hard fight – and clearly in expectation. To me it seemed indecent. How could I stay, with the whole abyss of love unveiled before my eyes like this? Even

the vision revealed to me at the Opera by Mahler's performances of Isolde's
'Liebestod' would have estranged me then. My mood was broken, and so was
the dancer's. Love is not simply a temptation to sin, I thought; it cannot be
born from a sexual disguise. Experience is the only way to learn this. I kissed
her hand, wanting to wring her neck, then took my leave and went straight
to wash my hands.

It would be a good thing sometimes to find out whether one wants to be
struck by the right or left hand of fate. It makes no difference, of course, but
one would at least have the choice. Without this freedom of choice one is
like the virgin I had seen sold off to the highest bidder in the famous salon of
Madame Rosa in Vienna, where Loos and Kraus had dragged me. I did not
wait for the end of the auction, not wanting to witness an act which must
result in the girl's ending up as either a tuberculous seamstress or a syphilitic
prostitute. Why had I gone there?

I fell asleep, and awoke on the far side of the night in Munich.

Munich seemed endless: houses, streets, the smell of malt, which I cannot
stand; perhaps it was also the brown coal. In an access of panic I felt utterly
forsaken. Vienna was left behind, beyond all memory. Soon, with a sense of
expectation, I pulled myself together. I realized I was a beginner once more:
everything depended on my own power of decision. The world lay wide
open around me, and I felt a kind of euphoria, free from the confines of
everyday routine, free to enjoy life to the full! I was directing my course: life
had to be begin anew.

I tried to get my drawings published by the magazines *Simplizissimus* and
Die Jugend – but in vain. I had a letter of introduction to Gustav Meyrink, the
author of some satanic short stories that I had found amusing, recommending
that he sit for me. It was odd, in the city that since the victory of 1870 had
become the Valhalla of the brewing industry, to find a grown man occupying himself with occult matters, secret Indian lore and auto-suggestion.
Munich seemed little like an artistic 'Athens on the Isar' to me. Rather, in
those days after Wagner and Nietzsche, it appeared that a bank-holiday
feeling had taken over: reality was a matter of living and earning well.
Everywhere – in the gleaming spikes of the reserve lieutenants' helmets, in
the coveted title of *Kommerzialrat*, in the ostentatious life-style of a factory
director – were barriers excluding from society anyone who did not belong.

Perhaps Munich was not quite far enough away from Vienna. My self-
confidence was somewhat the worse for wear. My balance was preserved by
the fact that I had never properly loved anyone, just as on a bumpy track you
have to press both pedals at once to avoid falling off your bicycle. I wanted

to become a man and to put an end to the melodramatic history of my youth, which was of interest to no one but myself. I needed to get a clear picture of my life. How long would it take for me to find myself? Not everyone who goes out in search of Man is given the lantern of Diogenes to take along. I needed a confrontation with new people. I thought of Berlin. How would it be if there, in the Empire with all its golden promises, one were to try to win acceptance for one's work, cutting through all the groups and cliques, just like the writers, politicians and industrialists who were the pillars of the competitive economy?

In my Munich boarding house I made friends with a very likeable young man whose professional name was Alastair. Half German, half English, he was alleged to be related to the German Kaiser and the English royal family. His great enthusiasm for Beardsley's graphic work appealed to my early love for English art and literature, but Alastair, unlike me, was an aesthete. He had dedicated himself to the Mind and the Cult of Beauty, and he regulated his life accordingly.

I ran short of money and had to leave the boarding house. Out of indolence, I had gone on deferring all decisions about the future. Now I had had enough of letting Providence act as my guardian, deciding the course of my life. I went to the station and bought a ticket, not to Vienna, where Adolf Loos had so long taken my decisions for me, but to Berlin. Once I had chosen, I was free. I had taken everything on myself, whichever hand of fate it might come from. I resolved never again to be dependent on others.

The train was crowded, and I had trouble finding a seat. It was too early in the morning to be able to see the outlines of the towns flashing past. I retain only the impression of dewdrops on the windows drying in the warmth of the rising sun. A disturbance rippled through the train. An elderly man, whom I could see coming down the corridor from a long way off, through the open doors between the carriages, was going from one compartment to the next, handing out slips of paper to the passengers. Some accepted them, some refused. I kept the man under observation; dressed in a blue city suit, a beret on his grey head, he was strongly built, with a drowsy Jewish-looking face. He held a handful of slips and a pencil. He reached our compartment. You were to read the questions on the slip and write down the answers, hiding what you had written, so that he could not see it. He wiped his eyes with a coloured handkerchief and told each passenger, as if it were the most ordinary thing in the world, exactly what they had written: their name, date and place of birth, marital status, occupation. Many of the subjects could not believe it; they took the slips out of their pockets, unfolded them and went through the answers. He was right! Breathing heavily he left the compartment. He had not approached me. I felt that his sort of prescience was unwelcome: it represented the dead hand of fate, from which I wanted no revelations. No light yet burned in the future for me, I knew: and in the grey dream of the past I wanted to sleep no longer. Perhaps the present was not particularly hospitable, but it was clearer than anything that came before or after, clearer than all that one had imagined or would imagine.

Cabbages could now be seen in the fields; factory chimneys came nearer; we were in Berlin, quicker than I had expected. My heart was full of golden hopes, like a laden apple-tree.

I had arrived in the capital of the German Empire, and also at the watershed between past and future. To appear there as a new man, I went at once to a barber's shop near the station. He cut my hair, washed it and put a hairnet on me. At the same time, with the ready tongue of a true Berliner, he talked me into buying pomade, toilet water, a brush and a comb. When I finally escaped from his solicitous clutches, I was carrying a sizeable parcel. It was a fine, warm day, and I did not feel like carting a package around with me. So as soon as I thought myself unobserved I dodged into a doorway and left it there. Unburdened of my load, but also of my small store of cash, I went on my way like a plucked chicken. One has to pay for one's lessons in life; and I was the richer by one lesson since arriving in Berlin.

Consulting a street plan I found my way to the editorial office of Herwarth Walden's publishing firm in Halensee, in a house that stood out among the prosperous new buildings around it like an island of poverty. I caught my breath when I stood before the door with the brass plate saying VERLAG DER STURM. Not because of the five flights of stairs, but because perhaps no one was in, or perhaps Herwarth Walden would not remember me. But ultimately it was all the same. The sooner it was settled the better. I was penniless.

Can one never escape from a certain degree of dependence? First I would have to learn what it means to be lost amid millions of people, lost in what seemed to me an antheap, where I could not find my way through the tangle of streets.

I knew Walden slightly from Vienna, where he had come to arrange with Karl Kraus for the publication of *Die Fackel* in Berlin. Berlin in Kraus's view was a morass from which journalistic decadence was spreading to Vienna. He wanted to destroy the corruption at its source. To cover the costs of distribution in Berlin, Walden was to receive a regular financial contribution. At the same time Loos had given him a lot of my drawings, some dating back to the period of the first Kunstschau, plus the illustrations to the play *Mörder, Hoffnung der Frauen*, and a good deal more, not all of which appeared in *Der Sturm*. Much later, after the Second World War, many of these drawings were lost in transit between an exhibition in Munich and another in Hamburg. Before starting *Der Sturm*, Walden had run two or three other short-lived publications and, as secretary of a society called the *Ansorge-Verein*, had edited a two-page modern musical broadsheet. Thanks to Kraus's financial support, *Der Sturm* now appeared as a weekly art magazine. In May 1910 it reproduced my drawing of Karl Kraus, and soon afterward that of Adolf Loos, followed by my drawings for *Mörder, Hoffnung der Frauen* and the text of the play itself.

From then until the end of 1910, drawings of mine appeared almost every week. It is possible to say that in its first year, and to some extent in its next two years, the character of *Der Sturm* was largely determined by my contributions. In addition I acted as assistant editor, writer, reporter and delivery man. During that year I lived and worked with Walden, we had only the bare necessities of life; during the week we survived almost exclusively on biscuits and tea, and on Sundays we went to one of the new Aschinger popular restaurants, where for a few groschen one could eat meatballs and as much bread as one dared.

The paper became known. It was bought by the intellectuals, and soon by the *nouveaux riches* as well. But every week there hung over us, like the sword of Damocles, the problem of where the money for our print bills was coming from. To give the Berliners their due, it must be said that even cab-drivers and bartenders occasionally came to our aid. From Berliners you have to expect the unexpected, as in a game of chance; they are incapable of enduring boredom. If something is the way it is, why can't it be changed? In this attitude, Berlin differs from Paris, London, Rome, and (in another sense) Vienna, where you hear a lot about tradition even though the tradition itself is now completely empty.

In a few years Walden, this haggard Berlin Jew, vanquished the better-financed rival art magazines – in a contest reminiscent of capitalists for markets – and won a total propaganda victory for *Der Sturm*. It was a miraculous achievement; but then, even Krupp, Hugenberg and Stinnes started in a small way.

For a time Herwarth Walden was a dictator in matters of art: he was dynamic and completely disinterested. As the uncompromising spokesman of modernity, he succeeded in establishing his own view of art in Germany to the extent that all the variations, all the 'isms', of modern art came to be taken seriously. Walden had a special gift for detecting rising talents, artists who were completely unknown even in their own native countries, whom he turned into contributors to *Der Sturm*. I never knew most of them, because I went my own way. But I am proud to have drawn attention to the youthful Umberto Boccioni and to Alexander Archipenko, who were responsible in my opinion for the Cubist trend in art at a time when the School of Paris and most of the German painters were following the decorative fashion of Matisse, which stood for a two-dimensional approach. Cubism, if it is understood aright, leads to three-dimensionality and to the dynamism of space: back, in fact, to the art of the Baroque.

Walden was a writer, an editor, and also a composer. By training a musician, he was a theoretician of modern music, and when he improvised for his friends at the piano, with his blond mane flying, he reminded me of the descriptions of Liszt. He composed, among other things, settings of poems by his former wife, Else Lasker-Schüler, and by Arno Holz, Richard Dehmel and August Stramm. For one song, 'Die Judentochter', to words from *Des Knaben Wunderhorn*, I drew him a title page. Else Lasker-Schüler was a Bohemian poetess who lived in the belief that she was the Prince of Thebes. Although she wrote about my pictures in fulsome terms – perhaps because of it – I never really understood her and could never draw or paint her.

All the same, I once went on an unforgettable trip along the Rhine with her and Walden. We set out with a huge package of copies of *Der Sturm*, to publicize the magazine. We put copies through the letterboxes in all the towns where we thought we were likely to get a response. We must have presented a fairly strange spectacle, like a circus troupe. Else Lasker-Schüler as the Prince of Thebes in voluminous oriental trousers, turban and long black hair, with a cigarette in a long holder; Walden no less Bohemian than his wife, peering around sharp-eyed through his thick glasses, with his birdlike head, his great hooked nose and his long yellow hair, wearing a worn frock-coat, the inevitable stiff upright collar, and pointed yellow shoes. I was clad, no doubt with equally comic effect, in a suit made by the Imperial court tailor in Vienna. Thus attired we passed through the streets of Bonn, and were of course laughed at and insulted by onlookers, cheered by children, and very nearly beaten up by angry students.

Because we had little money, we went only as far as Else Lasker-Schüler's home town, Elberfeld, where she had not been since she was a girl. Nevertheless, our journey was something of a success in bringing new subscriptions.

By the following year *Der Sturm* had a very wide circulation; it had made its way in Paris and in Holland, and was in demand among artists.

I first painted Walden's portrait shortly after my arrival in Berlin. In 1954 this portrait was sold from the collection of his second wife, Nell Walden, for what was then a spectacularly high price; and when, in the ensuing decade, the price doubled several times over, I could not help thinking back to the days in Berlin with Walden. At the time of the 1954 sale, I was interviewed on the radio, and asked what I had received for the Walden portrait in 1910. The truth was that I had simply left it at Walden's place, together with a lot of my drawings; he had nothing except his small subsidy from Karl Kraus, and neither he nor I owned a thing.

I lived and worked in an attic above the office. I hardly ever went out into the city; if I had, I would have got lost. My room was small, with sloping walls and a cast-iron stove which took a lot of stoking. The furniture consisted of an iron bed, a chair and a table. I was thankful for the fairly large skylight which usually admitted just enough light for me to draw or paint all day. Here I also did the portrait of Rudolf Blümner, a friend of Walden's, an actor who gave readings from modern poets at many *Der Sturm* events and also reported on the newly fashionable art of Cubism. He was a tireless fighter in the cause of modern art as promoted by Walden. He struck me as a sort of modern Don Quixote, hopelessly engaged in battle against the entrenched prejudice of his times, and this was reflected in my portrait of him.

When it became colder – it was an exceptionally severe winter – we were often at a loss how to keep warm. We wrapped ourselves in all the blankets we owned, and continually made tea. Food was scarce. No large selection of comparatively cheap tinned goods existed in those days. When I descended from the fourth floor of the house where *Der Sturm* had its editorial offices, I was always at pains to avoid meeting any of the other tenants who would greet me with hostile stares.

Today, I remember that period as something out of Gorky's *The Lower Depths*. It never stopped snowing. From the little window I saw the snow piling higher and higher in the courtyard, and wondered when it would reach the point where the doors could no longer be opened. Also, I needed light to work by in the winter afternoons, but the sun was pale, and often I didn't have a groschen to put into the gas meter. This gave only one hour's light per coin, and we were often left freezing in the dark, alone with our thoughts.

At those times Rudolf Blümner and I used to console each other by telling stories. One of them I wrote in my book of short stories *A Sea Ringed With Visions*. It is a fantasy version of my seeing the dream girl Virginia one spring morning on the slopes above Lake Geneva – the girl of whom I knew nothing but her name. That winter, in the attic in Berlin, she became our adoptive daughter, whom we had to protect and provide for. We spun out the dream by turns, in order to bring a little beauty and warmth into our life amid all our hardship and isolation. I used to look at Blümner's face, glimmering a little paler in the reflection of snow from the roofs, and remember the gun he had kept from his cadet days; Blümner was capable of anything. I preferred to remember the beauty of summer in Switzerland, which now appeared in the light of a lost paradise, and the unknown girl on the banks of the lake.

In that year I painted many other members of the Walden circle. William Wauer was one, a corset manufacturer until Walden discovered the sculptor in him. His sculptures of that period corresponded roughly to the later Expressionist-Cubist figures of Rudolf Belling. He also had his say in *Der Sturm* about the theatre, both direction and playwrighting, and later even about the possibility of a new religion. I did a drawing of the poet Paul Scheerbart. He was a heavy drinker; his pet project was for turning Mont Blanc into a sculpture, shaped like a crystal. I painted the portrait of Peter Baum, another poet, who contributed to *Der Sturm* in its earliest period. Always suffering from toothache, he wore round his head a large handker-chief with the ends tied on top, which made him resemble a rabbit, and that is the way I painted him. In 1916 he was killed in action. Walden characterized him in his obituary: 'A giant soul in a giant body. And yet as gentle as the touch of a child's hands.' My portrait of Baum somehow found its way to Paris, and was discovered there, in an antique shop after the Second World War, by the collector Willi Strecker who recognized it and brought it very cheaply. Someone had written a bogus certificate on the back: 'Certifique avoir vu ce portrait de LENJN paint par un artiste russe en 1910 Kamifof? M. Ortiz Paris 1924 OSCAR KokoschkA VieNNA'.*

Hugo Caro was another member of the *Sturm* circle whom I knew and liked. A lawyer, he lived in a slum area of Berlin and devoted his life to the poorest of the poor, the prisoners and the homeless. He looked like a figure from a Dickens novel. I painted him too. He ended up by committing suicide. I did a portrait drawing for *Der Sturm* of the great poet Richard Dehmel, with his skull hewn out of granite and his deeply furrowed features. He was still little known. He could usually be found in the beer-gardens and cafés of the Berlin suburbs, places where customers used to bring their own food. There, in front of all the *petits-bourgeois,* Dehmel would sometimes leap on to the table in a moment of inspiration and recite his poems to a generally not very attentive audience. His lyric novel in ballad form, *Zwei Menschen*, I found unforgettable. I drew the then fashionable art critic Alfred Kerr out of sheer malice, because he kept two seals in his bathroom, which I considered outrageous. And I drew Yvette Guilbert, then at the end of her career, who was appearing in a Berlin music-hall. I had gone as a reporter, and was overcome to see the female sex symbol of the 1890s, made world-famous by Toulouse-Lautrec, now an old woman, capering behind the footlights in a modern incarnation of the twentieth-century Dance of Death.

Der Sturm received complimentary tickets for music halls and circuses. I would have liked to spend every evening in the famous Wintergarten variety theatre. There I drew a man who used to walk up one wall, across an endless expanse of ceiling, and down the other wall; presumably he wore extremely powerful suction pads on his shoes, but it was still an astonishing performance. I also admired Rastelli, the greatest juggler I have ever seen. He threw balls far out into the auditorium, over the heads of the astonished audience, and they came back obediently into his hands like tame birds. This magical feat will never be done again. I admired him so much that I followed him round to several other towns and later in Italy went to see his grave. I was also friendly with an animal trainer who stayed in an elegant suite in the Hotel Adlon with seven trained chimpanzees. When I went to visit him I was rather taken aback to be greeted by the apes drumming in unison with their hands and feet. On the stage they wore clothes and looked ridiculous.

I was very close to Walden. In 1910–11, the first two years of *Der Sturm*'s existence, a total of thirty drawings of mine were reproduced. And in March 1912, when Walden finally reached the point where he could mount exhibitions of his own in a rented villa in the Tiergartenstrasse, I was represented in the first show, along with pictures by Munch, Hodler and the Blaue Reiter group. Even years later, when I no longer lived in Berlin, I exhibited my graphic work and paintings as part of the continuing series of *Der Sturm* exhibitions, in which Walden assembled the entire élite of modern art, from France, Holland, Italy, Belgium, Scandinavia and Russia.

For one early number of the magazine I designed a poster, a self-portrait with a red background, which I used again, with a different text, for a lecture I gave in Vienna on 26 January 1912. The poster shows me with head shaven, like a convict, and pointing at a wound in my chest; it was intended as a reproach to the Viennese, but a few years later, in the war, a Russian bayonet went through my lung at exactly that place. I can remember that lecture in 1912, in the hall of the Wiener Ingenieur und Architektenverein in the

Eschenburger Gasse, because I read from a script, which I do not normally do. The hall was half empty, and most of the people there understood nothing; but one man, Berthold Viertel, a writer, and later a theatre and film producer, was so excited by it that he asked me to lend him the script. This was my only copy, and of course he promptly lost it on a tram-car; so I had to rewrite it from memory. It is a miracle that I succeeded, because I have no memory to speak of. Later I tried to make improvements when it was translated into English, but could not. I still stand by every single word of what I said to those unprepared hearers 'On the Nature of Visions'.

Through my work in *Der Sturm* there came an unexpected change in my circumstances. Paul Cassirer was responsible. He and Walden belonged to different worlds, but Cassirer had kept his eyes open, and he saw that in the *Sturm* group there was suddenly a young artist going his own private way. Cassirer belonged to the milieu of the Herrenklub and the Jockeyklub. He owned a smart villa, with a picture gallery, in the Viktoriastrasse, and was a close friend of the great painter Max Liebermann, president of the Berliner Secession, of which Cassirer himself was secretary. Liebermann was the dominant influence in the artistic life of Berlin; he had been responsible, among other things, for organizing major exhibitions which made the French Impressionists known in Germany.

Cassirer commissioned me to paint his fiancée Tilla Durieux, an actress in the Staatstheater. He went with me one morning to her flat, and I met her first in her dressing-room where Cassirer and I – he acting the high-spirited suitor, in straw-hat and carnation – at once set about helping to lace up her corset – the sort women still wore in those days. The scene reminded me strongly of Manet's famous *Nana*, a painting too well done to be repeated. I painted her in another fashion; but she had considerable powers of seduction, and I don't believe I ever finished the picture. It was left behind in her flat together with my paint box.

My first meeting with Paul Cassirer had already led to an exhibition at his gallery in 1910, but not as yet to a lasting contractual arrangement. Cassirer told me later that Max Liebermann was so jealous that he wept when Cassirer spoke to him about giving me a contract. The contract was later signed, and several times broken off and renewed; fundamentally it remained my only contract with a dealer. I was to receive a sizeable yearly sum, and it was entirely left to me how many pictures I painted. The only condition was that they must be equal in quality to my previous ones.

I was now in a position to send money home. Pictures of mine, formerly worth nothing, had now a commercial value, thanks to Cassirer. My prices soon rose like shares on the stock exchange. The first exhibition at Cassirer's, hung by Liebermann himself, aroused a great deal of interest among progressive circles in Berlin – and a more favourable interest than in Vienna. People saw in my pictures a rejection of Impressionism, and this engendered a whole new attitude. I had not consciously set out with such an intent: I simply painted the way I had to paint. Certainly I was not thinking about sales on the art market.

Liebermann's greatness included an ability to master his own feelings. I had touching evidence of this once, when Cassirer gave a banquet on his birthday. There were a lot of guests. Liebermann presided, and I sat at the other end of a long table. When the toasts came I wrote an admiring tribute to the 'king of modern painting in Germany' on a menu card and passed it along the table to him. I was deeply moved to receive, in return, a message in which he, with equal respect, addressed me as 'the crown prince'.

To me, the uniqueness of Berlin was its violent movement which whisked the ground away from under your feet as you walked through the streets. In my memory Berlin seems like a network of underground railways, elevated railways, surface railways and tramways, columns of carts, motorcars, motorcycles and pedal cycles, along with rotating advertising signs, flickering giant picture palaces, loud-speakers and café orchestras. Maybe even six-day bicycle races – I can't remember. And the scraps of newspaper fluttering across the streets! It all kept the senses alert day and night. In an Impressionist painting, the scattered flecks of colour do not add up until one sees the picture from a certain distance; in the same way, only when looking back from a distant vantage-point in time could I give others my idea of Berlin, the old Prussian city, whose inhabitants, to their own astonishment, had become cosmopolitans virtually overnight. For a long time this accumulation of millions of people struck me as an ant-heap; it is hard for me now to convey my first impressions uncoloured by later memory. For perhaps the first time in history people saw the key to survival in a metaphysical belief, the belief in progress, and so ignored the lessons of history. The catastrophe of the two world wars destroyed not only Berlin, the imperial capital, but the Reich itself. It is a paradoxical thing to say, but now that 'Time's fell hand' has defaced pre-war Europe once and for all Berlin stands revealed as a symbol of the ideology of industrialization: an improvisation, on the part of twentieth-century technology, which broke the dam of the traditional production economy, and led to the discarding of a centuries-old tradition.

At first this unreal atmosphere in Berlin made me doubt my own capacity to adjust. In Vienna, people had forgotten what life was all about. The social and political process of the technological revolution had not yet got under way in idyllic Austria, as it had elsewhere; the fundamental difference between the nineteenth and twentieth centuries could still be ignored just by turning a blind eye. Through intermarriage, the ruling class of nobles and landowners had concluded a frivolous, short-lived truce with the class of financiers and industrial managers, whose origins were so different from their own. The common people were not yet governed entirely by the routine of modern life: they were not yet urbanized, industrialized, mechanized. Austria had as yet been spared the transformation of the masses through power politics and the exploitation of natural resources.

Berlin, however, was in a twilight zone: the past had already lost its character, the future had not yet acquired one. People had not learned to fear the transformation of society into an incoherent, undifferentiated mass, nor could they foresee that this would be the inevitable result of releasing the latent energy in great urban populations. They believed in a coming superabundance of industrial products, and they aspired, with Bentham, to the greatest happiness of the greatest number. Ideas of industrial revolution, world production, world trade, world politics, world domination, Lebensraum, unified the various parts of the post-Bismarck Reich more firmly than all the traditional ties such as ethnic origin, language, or national culture. These ideas gave contemporary Berliners a faith – shared even by the mass of workers, who already possessed their own organization within the state – that they would succeed in the struggle for existence. No subsequent ideology has been able to generate an equal self-confidence. But there had not yet been a world war, and no one could tell from experience where the ideology of technological progress leads or ends: in collective suicide. The machine has neither soul nor imagination. The map of the world still seemed large enough to permit a great leap in the dark: the leap that abandons reason and embraces metaphysics – an idea. And the lesson of history is still not heeded. Icarus burnt his wings, but that did not prevent a German, in spite of the catastrophe that had overtaken his own country, to further the cause of Lebensraum by inventing the space ship – just in case life on earth became totally impossible.

On my first day in Berlin, in the midst of all the din in the streets, I had listened to a blind man playing a barrel-organ – the same folk-tune over and over again – until a policeman told him off for causing an obstruction and he wheeled his barrow into a side-street. I learned my lesson from him and submitted to the prevailing order. There must be no excuses, no trying to evade what Fate has in store: one must recognize facts for what they are, and go out to meet them as Olympic athletes go out to compete. No dodging away from life.

Herwarth Walden was a kind of Mahdi, who preached a lofty doctrine of Progress as a path to a more exalted spiritual existence in a new and better world. He was a fanatic in the cause of Expressionism. What is nowadays labelled Expressionism could have come into existence only in Germany, where there was a desire to carry art to the masses, to the 'new man', as a reaction against Jugendstil or Art Nouveau, which set out only to beautify the surface and made no appeal to the inner life. Expressionism was a contemporary and rival of Freud's development of psychoanalysis and Max Planck's discovery of quantum theory. It was a sign of the times, not an artistic fashion.

The term 'Expressionism' is also erroneously applied to the work of a German avant-garde which congregated around the Blaue Reiter group in Cologne, and which was really much more under the influence of the French Fauves, an 'art for art's sake' movement concerned with sensual, decorative effect. But German and Russian Expressionism was meant as a moral and cultural awakening of the true nature of man, and as a political commitment. Essentially, Expressionism must be seen as a revolutionary movement, a compulsive need to communicate with the masses. Not only painters and sculptors, but also musicians, architects, writers and complete non-artists, in their theories and hypotheses, were striving for a transformation of intellectual life. New 'isms' were springing up everywhere. Borrowing from African art and other prehistoric, anti-classical, anti-rational stylistic modes, each laid claim to consideration as a definitive creative statement and carried on a running battle with all the others. Walden, in *Der Sturm*, managed to hold these factions together, with enormous difficulty, until the National Socialists and the Soviets, within their respective jurisdictions, brought the spiritual disquiet of the younger generation to an abrupt and tragic end. German Expressionism, coming as it did at a fateful moment in the history of civilization, recalls the Children's Crusades of the Middle Ages and the destruction of images in the Wars of Religion. Speaking as an historian, I should say that no one's moustache – not Kaiser Wilhelm's, nor Stalin's, nor Hitler's – is equal in historical importance to the artistic movement of Expressionism in the civilized nations of Western Europe and Russia.

Although Expressionism was taken up everywhere only by a minority, for Europe it held a chance of spiritual survival which remains unrecognized to this day. In Germany, Expressionism was the first art to be declared 'degenerate' in those years when humanity itself was trampled underfoot. By then Herwarth Walden was dead. As a Jew, he fled from Germany only to be killed by the Communists in Russia. There Expressionism is still condemned as the ultimate stage in bourgeois decadence and corruption. What Expressionism lacked was a sense of humour – the gift of making its enemies look ridiculous.

I knew few of the artists of the *Sturm* circle personally, and took very little interest in their formal problems or in their moral ideas. I contributed no manifestoes, not even a signature. I was not going to submit my hard-won independence to anyone else's control. That is freedom, as I understand it.

Back in Vienna

In 1911 I returned to Vienna, mainly in order to see my father, who was getting old. I probably bored him with accounts of my successes: how I was to have a one-man show with twenty-four pictures, organized by the Hagenbund, and so on. He let me go on boasting, but he was a sceptic and saw right through me. Having been tested by a hard life, he was wiser than I. He knew that free will is mere sophistry; there is no such thing. I felt the same, but I was not yet willing to admit it. We were alike, my father and I. He had visibly aged, but was still working as hard as ever.

I had a new exhibition in Vienna, which of course was slaughtered by the press again; but there were invitations to other exhibitions in Germany. One came from the Sonderbund in Cologne, in which the 'Brücke' artists from Dresden were taking part along with a number of aspiring young talents from abroad to whom attention had already been drawn by *Der Sturm*. I was represented there by six pictures.

Before leaving Vienna, I had met through Loos Dr Eugenie Schwarzwald, whose house was a centre of intellectual and artictic life, a meeting-place for cultural and political figures from Austria and elsewhere. It was at this time that I painted my first portrait of her husband, Dr Hermann Schwarzwald. I painted him again when I came back from the war, and again in 1924.* On the last of the three paintings I was asked to write his motto: 'Seulement la paix!' A senior Government official who had risen to become Finance Minister, he was in close touch with Jean Jaurès, until the latter's assassination, and with those other leading politicians in France and England who were working for world peace. I thought all this was just utopianism. In the Schwarzwalds' house I also did a drawing of Dr Schücking, who took a decisive part in the peace conference at Versailles after the war. And it was there that I heard Rudi Serkin playing the piano as a little boy; we have remained friends ever since.

After the Second World War, while she was in exile in Switzerland,

Eugenie Schwarzwald published in the *Neue Zürcher Zeitung* a series of anecdotes concerning me. I am described as a taciturn guest who would suddenly stammer out some sibylline aphorism, such as 'My knowledge is like the lonely pagodas in the Gobi desert.'

Eugenie Schwarzwald ran a private school for girls, based on progressive educational methods. I made repeated attempts in Vienna to earn my living at various public institutions by teaching evening classes in lithography, bookbinding and printing, but as a result of the continuing press campaign against me I was forced each time to resign. Finally I took the position of drawing-master at Eugenie Schwarzwald's private seminary, where the authorities and the Press had no business to interfere. I have pleasant memories of that period. More than half a century later, several of the girls I taught then wrote enthusiastic letters from America, where as Jews they had emigrated, telling me what important and significant experiences those lessons had been for them.

The poet Albert Ehrenstein, first published by Karl Kraus in *Die Fackel*, became my lifelong friend. Ehrenstein was a good, kind-hearted man; he bore the sins of the world on his shoulders as if he had never heard of the fashionable poets from Prague and Brno who were trying to set themselves apart from the herd by means of the newly popular message 'Man is good!' I painted and drew Ehrenstein, and illustrated his 'Tubutsch'. He wrote a beautiful poem about me:

> *Du bist einer von den Lichten,*
> *von dem Aufgang roter Sonne,*
> *was noch schwarz im Dunklen geistert,*
> *weicht von Dir zur Wolkenwende.*
> *Ruhe schwankt zur Bank der Fäulnis,*
> *Chaos misst der Berge Abgrund,*
> *Leben ist im Niedern trächtig,*
> *Liebe giert und wird nicht schwanger,*
> *Schaffen nur gibt Dir die Schöpfung,*
> *schwebend in des Lichtes starken Stürmen*
> *rein im Atem den Äther schirmen!*

Wherever he was – in Vienna, Prague, London or New York – Ehrenstein usually lodged at a jobbing tailor's. He drifted with the current, never pursuing any fixed objective, always making sure that the long cotton-wool plugs that sprouted from his ears like corkscrews did not fall out – partly in order to distinguish him from the merely successful poets of his time, who were not worthy to lace his shoes, but mainly in order to protect himself from the cold. In New York, after the Second World War, together with another lifelong companion, Robert Freund (who died not long afterwards, and whose portrait by me had been slashed to pieces by the Vienna police under the Nazis), I saw to the cremation of my dear friend Ehrenstein's body. He left behind few works of his own, unfortunately; but he never ceased helping younger talents. Among those he discovered was Kafka.

On my return to Vienna from Berlin, I went back to live with my parents. My mother had rented for me an empty workshop in a garden not far from the house, where, when the wind blew, an elder bush tapped against the window-pane and kept me company. It was a rare pleasure, after the turmoil of Berlin and every other place where I had painted, to work in such tranquillity. No longer confused by external activity, the eye could turn inward, illuminating my inner self. It was like a gift from God, allowing me to see everything in an entirely new light. I painted for myself. Feeling it would be presumptuous to have a model, I turned to small compositions: *Knight, Death and Angel, The Flight into Egypt*, a *Crucifixion*, an *Annunciation*, a *Temptation, The Merchant of Venice*. One day the caretaker's daughter, a gentle, shy girl, came to clean the windows, which had been gathering dirt for months. Her name was Veronica. I painted – the favourite of all my religious works – *St Veronica with the Sudarium*, a theme derived from those medieval painters whose faith allowed them to conceive of capturing the image of dying Godhead upon a linen cloth.*

This reawakening of my religious past was connected to an episode in my childhood, itself revelatory of my early desire to become a priest. At some point during my first years at school I contracted a disease, smallpox or measles, I think. But I must explain all the circumstances. I was often invited to go for walks in a certain park with two little girls, whose mother was a titled lady. On one such occasion, in order to give the girls an idea of the burning of Troy, I set fire to an anthill. Unfortunately their mother found out, and I was permanently barred from the park. The childhood Eden of my dreams was lost behind a locked park-gate.

As a consolation my mother took me to the circus, where I saw a clown. Clowns are the prototypes of those who suffer a fate they don't deserve. This particular clown had had the bright idea of bringing his own garden-gate with him. Laboriously he set it up in the ring and then unlocked it carefully with a large key in order to pass through. Even I could see that there was no need to go to the trouble of bringing the garden-gate along, except to elicit laughter. But the jest had given me an idea: why should a silly park-gate keep me out of the garden? I felt that I must at all costs look upon Eden once more, if only from a distance. I could still get in from the back unseen, at a spot where the local people used to tip their rubbish. So one day I started boldly to climb up the tall fence. At the top I found no further foothold. I could not hold on just with my hands, as the wooden slats of the fence were studded with rusty nails. My strength began to fail. I confess that I now forgot my longing for the lost paradise; my state of mind was less elevated than my physical position. I felt an irresistible downward pull and fell on a heap of filth, a midden full of broken crocks, crawling with unimaginable, insatiable life. A stinking yellow liquid spurted up. There was a long-dead, putrefying pig, from whose swollen carcass rose a cloud of flies.

My mother came out to look for me, and found me unconscious. The doctor had to be sent for. I had a fever and an inflammation of the eyes, and spent a long time in bed. During my fever I could not open my eyes, nor close my mouth. At the root of my tongue sat a fly, which constantly turned round and round, laying its grubs in a circle. It cut into my parched throat like a disc of iron. My tongue had grown short and thick, and I could not move it. The fever squeezed all the fluid from my pores. My mother nursed me day and night, and continually gave me soothing milk of almonds to drink. The violent pounding of my heart against my ribs made her imagine I would not recover. The doctor seemed helpless. She sent for the catechist who gave the religious instruction at school, and who had taken a particular liking to me. He laid a little picture of *St Veronica* with the Sudarium of Christ over my face, knelt down and prayed. Soon, as if by a miracle, the eruption of my eyes subsided.

My mother believed, and I cannot help thinking so still, that the priest's faith wrought the miraculous change, where medicine had been powerless. Sometimes, even today, I am inclined to believe – as at those moments when one wakes from a dream, rubbing one's eyes – that that childhood world still holds me fast like an anchor, while curiosity, restless endeavour, ambition and desire fill the sails which drive my life forwards. Two opposing impulses out of which my inner conflicts spring.

Carl Moll, a painter friend of Klimt's, was so impressed by my first collective showing, at the Hagenbund exhibition that he asked me to paint his own portrait. He was a pupil of Emil Jakob Schindler, a painter of sensitive land-scapes, now little known; the two were inseparable, and after Schindler's death Moll married his widow. He lavished almost more devotion on the upbringing of his two stepdaughters than he later did on that of his own daughters. Moll was no genius, but he was a cultivated man. As buyer for the long-established and respected Viennese art firm of Artaria, he was the first to bring Impressionist paintings to Vienna; they were acquired by the Moderne Galerie. He had a true eye for the quality and the content of a work of art; once he discovered an important El Greco in a little provincial chapel in Spain where it was being used as a floor mat. But for his sharp eye, the picture would have been lost. His discovery had taken place just about the time that, in Germany at least, El Greco was being rescued from oblivion by Julius Meier-Graefe, and the picture was, I think, bought by Marcel von Nemeš of Munich, who owned a famous collection of Spanish art. Nemeš, whose portrait I also painted, restored,* his own pictures, a service I believe he also performed for this filthy and battered El Greco.

I painted Carl Moll in his patrician residence, with its neoclassical mid-Victorian décor, on the Hohe Warte, a district favoured by the prosperous Viennese bourgeoisie. I was often asked to stay to dinner. I liked the atmosphere of the house, although its slightly oriental magnificence was less reminiscent of Schindler's time than of the age of Ingres and Delacroix (or Makart, whose pupil Moll had also been): Japanese vases, great sprays of peacock feathers, Persian carpets on the walls. The table was elegantly laid; there were always flower arrangements, gleaming silver, sparkling glass – and good wine. The concertmaster of the Vienna Philharmonic, Arnold Rosé, and his family, were close friends of the Molls, and there were often chamber recitals. The table talk was usually about art, especially after Moll's stepdaughter, Alma Mahler, returned from abroad. She was the widow of Gustav Mahler, the director of the Opera, who had died a year before. It must have been very difficult for her to take leave of the little man on his bier and to find herself suddenly removed from the atmosphere of fame and consequence that she had shared with her husband. What had bound her to Mahler was perhaps not so much a great love as a great passion for music. In the last years of his life there had also been the excitements, intrigues and feuds of a small section of Viennese society, the sort of thing she revelled in all her life. How often had he appeared in the great Opera House and reduced a garrulous Viennese audience to silence with a flash of his hypnotic eyes!

Following Mahler's funeral she had cut herself off for a time from everybody; but she was young, and now she wanted company again. She was curious to meet me.

After the meal she took me to the piano in the next room, where she

played and sang – for me alone, she said – Isolde's 'Liebestod'. I was fascinated; she was young and strikingly beautiful in her mourning, and lonely
in spite of all the people she saw. When she then proposed that I paint her
portrait at her home, I was at once overjoyed and perturbed. For one thing,
I had never before painted a woman who seemed to have fallen in love with
me at first sight; and for another I felt a certain shyness and apprehension:
how could one man find happiness where another had so recently died? The
portrait of Carl Moll came much more easily to me; there were no complications there, and I painted him with love and gratitude.

Now began an exceedingly passionate relationship, which lasted three
years. Lately I have been looking for the first time through Alma Mahler's
biography, and I see that she never forgot me. I admit there were times for
me, too, when I could not imagine living without her. I was an immature
youth with a tendency to run full tilt at brick walls, and she a woman of
thirty, accustomed to luxury and always surrounded by men, who had
learned in her childhood, accompanying her father to one great house after
another, that in order to survive an artist needs patrons. I can see now that a
person to whom social life is absolutely vital will be prepared to pay almost
any price to gain material independence. Circumstances of this kind create
a single-minded character.

I read in her book that she accuses me of power mania, and complains that
I treated her like a prisoner and prevented her from seeing other people. In
my own defence I must say that her complaints seemed to me then utterly
insignificant and trivial. And she cannot really have felt very different herself,
or she would not have remained, as she did, passionate in her devotion to me
until the moment when I enlisted at the outbreak of war. She writes that I
fulfilled her life and at the same time destroyed it. The latter was certainly
not my intention. She writes that she saw me, after leaving her, pacing up
and down outside her window until first light; but I did not do that in order
to spy on her.

To begin with, we went together to Naples, where I painted a large landscape with Vesuvius in the background; it was destroyed in the Glaspalast
fire in Munich in 1931. We travelled to Mürren, and later to the Tre Croci
pass in the Dolomites, where I painted another landscape and did some drawings. I also painted several fans for her.* She writes that I sometimes gave
pictures away, or sold them twice over, because I had no sense of reality.
I cannot remember behaving like that as far as she was concerned.

When later, after we had parted, I was severely wounded in the war and
my death was announced in the Viennese papers, Alma did not scruple to

have sackfuls of her letters carried off at once from my studio, to which she still had a key. War hardens people. To me it seemed cold-blooded and out of keeping with her passionate nature. In contrast, I think of the pounding heart with which I waited every morning for the postman to bring me the longed-for daily message of love! It mattered less to me that she also took hundreds of sketches and drawings I had left behind, foolishly believing that the war would not last long. When she remarried in 1915, she is said to have given these away to young painters, by whom they were unfortunately ruined in attempts to complete them and render them saleable. Perhaps she was trying to appease pangs of conscience, or liquidating an unsuccessful enterprise. She always was ready to help out an artist. Naturally she did not know that someone taken for dead may still come back alive. That was how I explained it to myself afterwards. While I was at the Front I forgot for a time that she existed.

Word of her second marriage reached me in hospital in Vienna. I received the news with a certain malicious pleasure, and tried to guess how long it would last. I was not sure I myself was going to survive; morality, composure, belief, were overwhelmed by the anarchy within and without. Nothing mattered except the daily death-rate announced in the war bulletins. I could not think of love or happiness any more. Still, some people must have had quite a good war, judging by the birth statistics.

It was also in hospital that I heard she was pregnant. I can no longer say what possessed me, but I sent my old friend and patron, Adolf Loos, who was deeply distressed by the seriousness of my condition, to ask if she would come to my bedside. Too late, too late! Really, I knew that any attempt to recapture the past must be in vain. The dying Tristan sent the faithful Kurwenal to Isolde; Alma Mahler, who had sung me Isolde's 'Liebestod' so often and with such an ecstasy of grief, now not only turned Loos away but wrote him a letter to say she regretted ever having shaken his hand. She admits this herself, in her diary.

Helped by a strong constitution, I recovered from my war wound, but I had lost all desire to go through the ordeal of love again. Nevertheless, for some years I derived pleasure – and this perhaps does not deserve forgiveness – from raking the ashes of a dead grief, without asking myself whether Alma's psychic wounds had healed as well as my physical ones. Time and again, I found opportunities to try her. For instance, I would suddenly write her a hypocritical letter offering to forget the past, to wipe the slate clean; or a telegram full of devotion and without a trace of reproach or recrimination; another time it was flowers, and finally an invitation to the première of my play *Orpheus und Eurydike* in Frankfurt. I had put into that play, as near as I could get to it in words, the experience whose burden I had inwardly borne. We met once, by chance, in front of some pictures of mine at the 1922 Venice Biennale; I promised to see her the next morning at the Café Florian. I did not turn up; I wanted no explanations. Something within must have warned me of an impending disappointment; sometimes a pounding heart is enough to establish a self-diagnosis.

My mother was very firmly against any *rapprochement* with Alma Mahler, and wrote threatening to shoot her if she attempted it. When I returned to Vienna, my mother learned from Loos – his steady opposition to the affair had led to a cooling of our friendship for a time – that I had met Alma again. She paraded up and down outside Alma's house for several hours, one hand ominously in her coat pocket. She glimpsed Circe, as she called her, peering out of a window, and told me afterwards how she had given the poor thing a fright. We both enjoyed a good laugh, for of course my mother had no revolver.

An experience of quite another order belongs to this same period. One day a few months before the outbreak of the First World War, Carl Moll returned from Italy with a painting by Titian, which he left in my studio to be hidden from the public eye. The painting, *Venus with Organ-player*, had belonged to a Prince of Orleans, of the Italian branch of the family, and had been brought secretly over the frontier. After the war it was purchased by the Kaiser-Friedrich-Museum in Berlin where it remains, as one of the glories of the museum's collection.

The picture dates from the middle of Titian's career when, to replace the classical drawing and local colouring of the Renaissance style, he began his search for new means to convey the luminosity of space. This endeavour culminates in the *Pietà* in the Accademia in Venice, perhaps his last work, where the light transforms and recreates space, and the static Renaissance perspective is broken by a new visual concept: the scene begins to move instead of being read like a page in a book. For the first time, in the *Pietà*, Titian does not present the Passion of the Son of God, but rather an image of the transience of Creation – and thus an image of the modern world as created by man.

The movement of the beholder's eye is no longer directed by the signposts of contour and local colour, but is governed by luminous intensity. This creative achievement introduced into painting the miraculous quality of Archaic Ionian sculpture, where the surface is resolved into tiny facets, and light not only touches it but stirs it into life. Here, the spell of Egypt was finally broken. Henceforth light – and not only cubical mass or volume – distinguishes spatial composition.

Titian remained forgotten for a long time after his death. Poussin, not a great painter but the possessor of an excellent eye, was the first to discover, from an intensive study of Titian, that his work contained a quality foreign to all other painters and far different from the drawing and local colour of the Renaissance: luminosity, the dynamic action of colour. Methodically, by geometrical analysis, Poussin set out to extract this secret from the composition. He broke the surface up into facets of varying sizes, producing a 'space crystal'. He thus struck out on a path which distinguishes him entirely from the classical painters of his time – and from Ingres; for classicists acknowledge only classical drawing and local colour as the expressive resources of their art. But to learn from Titian the triumph of light, the triumph of *lumen* over *volumen*, would have required a mental struggle for which Poussin was not equipped.

Cézanne, in his own way indirectly a pupil of Poussin's, went further by methodically transposing the analysis of the pictorial structure into terms of colour. But Cézanne was the child of a scientific age; he moved away from the dynamism of colour, and towards abstraction. Cubism, which lacks light as a source of movement, carried the process of abstraction still further. In the end, art returned to the static vision, the still-life.

Unfortunately the Titian *Venus with Organ-player* stayed with me only for a few months; the war put an end to my surreptitious pleasure. But, as a result of this game of hide-and-seek with the origin of illumination in space, my eyes were opened as they had been in childhood when the secret of light first dawned on me.

The Titian was hidden in my bedroom. I had a new studio at that time in one of the multi-storey blocks on the Stubenring in Vienna, where I lived by myself, completely absorbed in my work, and where Alma Mahler could visit me undisturbed. Ever since our travels together, a melancholy feeling had taken possession of me, foreshadowing a separation. She could not forget that she had been married to a world-famous conductor and composer, while I was at best notorious – and that only in Vienna – and penniless. I hated the society gossip that made her insecure; consequently I became jealous of every external influence, and tried by all the means at my command to isolate her. She bore this for a time, because she loved me; later, she rebelled. We decided to build a little house not far from Vienna, up at Semmering, where we could live all by ourselves. But it seemed as if the house would never be ready: spring was late, and as winter dragged on there

came a string of delays. Once a fire broke out in the loft through the careless-
ness of the carpenters. Then the foundations were flooded by a hidden spring
because the architect had not surveyed the site properly. The water had to be
drained off. We began to think some evil spirit was trying to spoil our life
together.

One day, just before we were at last to move in, a biologist friend of
Alma's caught some toads in the damp hallway, and probably also in the
boggy earth round the house; he enclosed them in a terrarium which he left
in the bathroom ready to take the next day to his institute, at the Prater in
Vienna. He had made his name there in research, including transplantations.
I secretly hauled the glass case out of the house overnight and tipped the
contents into the nearby stream. I wanted to prevent Alma from seeing it,
because she was pregnant. But the next morning, when we went out, I saw –
and unfortunately so did she – the toads crawling across the field towards us
and mating as they did so, the smaller males clasping the bulkier females with
the mating-pads on their legs, approaching us in a hideous procession. This
revolting cortège of procreation, in front of a woman in Alma's condition,
nearly made me sick. I had never foreseen that our love could be lost in a
quagmire. Shortly before, as a surprise for her, I had painted a fresco over the
main fireplace, showing her and myself rising from the flames. The fresco
was destroyed by the Russians during the occupation after the Second World
War.

Because I am superstitious, I had always insisted that nothing of the dead
Gustav Mahler, not even his bust by Rodin, should be brought into our
house. Perhaps I feared that the child she was carrying might have the
features of the dead man, of whom she spoke too often for my liking. In
particular I had forbidden the introduction of Mahler's death mask, which we
knew was in the post to her. This led to several unpleasant scenes. And then
one day a box was delivered to the Semmering house, and from it she
reverently took the mask, packed in wood shavings. Perhaps this finally
brought the crisis; surely scandal and the advice of friends had been no more
than contributory factors in the decision Alma now took, and which I never
forgave. She went into a clinic in Vienna and had the child, my child, taken
from her. And so, for me, our affair had already ended even before the war.
It is wrong to cut short the process of life merely from indolence. This was
clearly a decisive event in my own development. One must keep awake to
the meaning of life and not be content to vegetate.

Even after the abortion, Alma did not want to be deprived of company
and, although she came to see me willingly enough, she must have begun to

feel like a prisoner. Now too she started to regard me in a different manner, as an artist. With fresh eyes she looked at my work and saw expressed a melancholy – in the lithographs of the two series *Columbus Bound* and *Bach Cantata*, for instance – which, while giving form to an inner experience, lifts it out of the sphere of a commonplace love affair. In one of the *Columbus Bound* prints a death-mask lies on the ground like a warning against unbridled passion. In the penultimate print of the *Bach Cantata* series I am in the grave, slain by my own jealousy, like Hyacinthus by the discus that a treacherous fate turned back upon him.

Such feelings also gave rise to my poem 'Allos Makar'. The Greek title, which means 'Happiness is otherwise', is an anagram of our two names, Alma and Oskar. It begins with the lines:

> *Wie verdrehte wunderbar mich,*
> *seit aus einer Nebelwelt, sie zu suchen,*
> *mich ein weisses Vöglein aufgerufen, Allos.*

and ends:

> *Ein Männchen und ein Weibchen würgen eine Schlange.*
> *Einer sieht des anderen Vorteil bange.*
> *Und eines am anderen die Kraft verlor.*
> *Da windet aus den schreienden Schnäbeln der Wurm sich hervor.*
> *Liess einen Zettel fallen, vom Raufen zerdrückt.*
> *Ich nahm ihn und las ihn, in Staube gebückt.*
> *Lachen die Lippen zur täuschenden Ruh. Allos Makar –*
> *'Anders ist glücklich.'*

I also painted a double portrait of Alma Mahler and myself at that time. But to me, and perhaps to others as well, those lithographs will always remain – in contrast to Art Nouveau, Impressionism and all the contemporary art of the period – a myth, a created symbol, heavy with the essence of meeting, begetting and parting. It was not only jealousy that made me rage against fate. I had a premonition of impending doom. The shadow of melancholy hung over our ecstasies and our love, silencing Apollo's lyre. Later, in my play *Orpheus und Eurydike*, composed in hospital on nights when my fever abated, I tried to depict, with the perspective added by time, this transition from intoxication to cheerless sobriety.

One evening the poet Georg Trakl arrived at my bleak studio, the walls of which I had painted black so that my colours should stand out better. Apart from the big easel on which stood the painting *The Bride of the Wind*

(*The Tempest*), the only furniture in the room was an empty barrel which served as a chair. I gave Trakl some wine, and went on working on my picture; he watched in silence. He had come all the way from Salzburg, and was completely soaked with rain; he loved to walk long distances deep in thought, oblivious of day and night. From the large window of the studio, I could see the pale summer night descending, the moon rising and riding over the long roof and the sea of houses. A wind sprang up, and the air turned suddenly cool. I felt cold; the day was over. In the union of melancholy and silence, I now first grew aware of the passage of time and of the way love had crept out of the azure reflection of the sun and into the realm of shadows. My painting, which shows me, with the woman I once loved so intensely, in a shipwreck in mid-ocean, was completed. Suddenly the silence was broken by Trakl's voice, a voice like a second self, like the brotherly Thou. My colours had not lied. My hand had plucked an embrace out of the stormy shipwreck of my world. The heart needs no more, in order to maintain in days to come an illusory pledge of survival, a memory as if on ancient tapestry.

Georg Trakl wore mourning for the death of his twin sister, to whom he was bound by more than a brother's love. His grief was like the moon as it moves in front of the sun and darkens it. And then, slowly, he began to say a poem to himself: word by word, rhyme by rhyme. He composed his strange poem 'Die Nacht' in front of my picture.

> ... *über schwärzliche Klippen*
> *stürzt todestrunken*
> *die erglühende Windsbraut* ...

With his pallid hand he motioned towards the picture; he gave it the name *Die Windsbraut*. Not long afterwards, at an army hospital in Cracow where he had gone as a medical orderly, he fell into despair over the slaughter at Grodek, and killed himself with an overdose of pills.

War

On 28 July 1914 – it was a hot summer morning – I heard through the open window the newsvendors hawking a special edition: 'Austria declares war on Serbia.' I quickly shut the window, sat down on the edge of the bed, and thought: '*Tu felix Austria nube!*' Now everything was falling apart, as when a family shares out the estate of a dying relative. Although this is not going to interest the younger readers of this book, who are bored by the endless stream of books and memoirs by leading politicians and generals explaining how the war came about, I am going to write it the way I see it. My young readers only have to bear the consequences of that war and the next one, and maybe a third one as well. I will be brief.

I am not a particularly peace-loving person, but I have never killed anyone that I know of. I do not believe in a God of Battles; I just wonder how I could have been sitting on a powder-keg without suspecting that it might go off.

In the following paragraphs I shall sum up what the books and memoirs say. Archduke Franz Ferdinand, the heir to the Austrian throne, was on a tour of inspection in Bosnia and Herzegovina. The Serbian Government was egging on the local terrorists, who had a short time before assassinated the members of the Obrenovič dynasty, and who were carrying on a propaganda campaign among the South Slavs which caused Hungary to feel threatened. The terrorists' dream of a Greater Serbia could be realized only if Serbia gained access to the Adriatic.

Unfortunately Italy, Austria's ally, had also cast covetous eyes on this coastal region, and had even signed a secret treaty with the Triple Alliance, in London, whereby Italy was given certain assurances. But these same coastal areas – former Turkish provinces – had in 1878 been handed over by the Great Powers to be administered by Austria. Great powers are always generous with other people's property.

Archduke Franz Ferdinand and his friend Kaiser Wilhelm II had far-

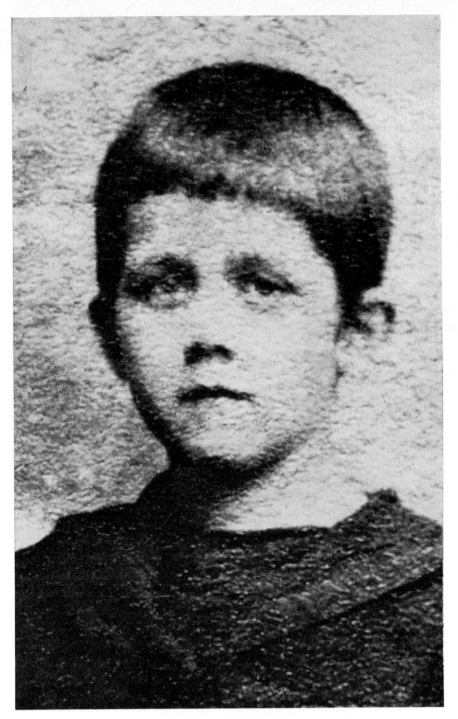
1. *Kokoschka at the age of five*

2. *OK's father, Gustav*   3. *OK's mother, Maria Romana*

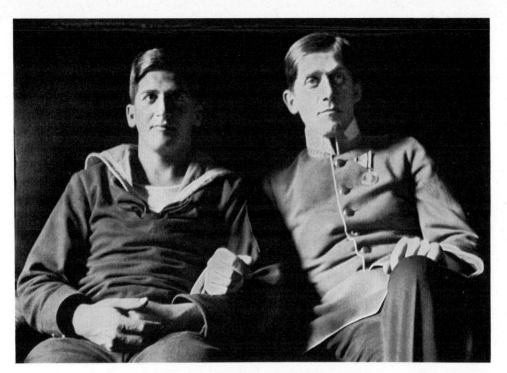

5. *OK and his brother Bohuslav*

4. *OK's sister, Bertha Theresia*

Umfang acht Seiten

Einzelbezug: 10 Pfennig

DER STURM

WOCHENSCHRIFT FÜR KULTUR UND DIE KÜNSTE

Redaktion und Verlag: Berlin-Halensee. Katharinenstrasse 5 Fernsprecher Amt Wilmersdorf 3524 / Anzeigen-Annahme und Geschäftsstelle: Berlin W 35, Potsdamerstr. 111 / Amt VI 3444	Herausgeber und Schriftleiter: **HERWARTH WALDEN**	Vierteljahresbezug 1,25 Mark / Halbjahresbezug 2,50 Mark / Jahresbezug 5,00 Mark / bei freier Zustellung / Insertions- preis für die fünfgespaltene Nonpareillezeile 60 Pfennig

JAHRGANG 1910   BERLIN / DONNERSTAG DEN 14. JULI 1910 / WIEN   NUMMER 20

Zeichnung von Oskar Kokoschka zu dem Drama
Mörder, Hoffnung der Frauen

Mörder, Hoffnung der Frauen
Von Oskar Kokoschka

Personen:
Mann
Frau
Chor: Männer und Weiber.

Nachthimmel, Turm mit großer roter eiserner Käfig-tür; Fackeln das einzige Licht, schwarzer Boden, so zum Turm aufsteigend, daß alle Figuren relief-artig zu sehen sind.

Der Mann

Weißes Gesicht, blaugepanzert, Stirntuch, das eine Wunde bedeckt, mit der Schar der Männer (wilde Köpfe, graue und rote Kopftücher, weiße, schwarze und braune Kleider, Zeichen auf den Kleidern, nackte Beine, hohe Fackelstangen, Schellen, Getöse), kriechen herauf mit vor-gestreckten Stangen und Lichtern, versuchen müde und unwillig den Abenteurer zurückzuhalten, reißen sein Pferd nieder, er geht vor, sie lösen den Kreis um ihn, während sie mit langsamer Steigerung auf-schreien.

Männer

Wir waren das flammende Rad um ihn,
Wir waren das flammende Rad um dich, Bestürmer verschlossener Festungen!

gehen zögernd wieder als Kette nach, er mit dem Fackelträger vor sich, geht voran.

Männer

Führ' uns Blasser!

Während sie das Pferd niederreißen wollen, steigen Weiber mit der Führerin die linke Stiege herauf.

Frau rote Kleider, offene gelbe Haare, groß,

Frau laut

Mit meinem Atem erflackert die blonde Scheibe der Sonne, mein Auge sammelt der Männer Froh-locken, ihre stammelnde Lust kriecht wie eine Bestie um mich.

Weiber

lösen sich von ihr los, sehen jetzt erst den Fremden.

Erstes Weib lüstern

Sein Atem saugt sich grüßend der Jungfrau an!

155

7. OK in 1909

8. *Drawing of Alma Mahler by OK*

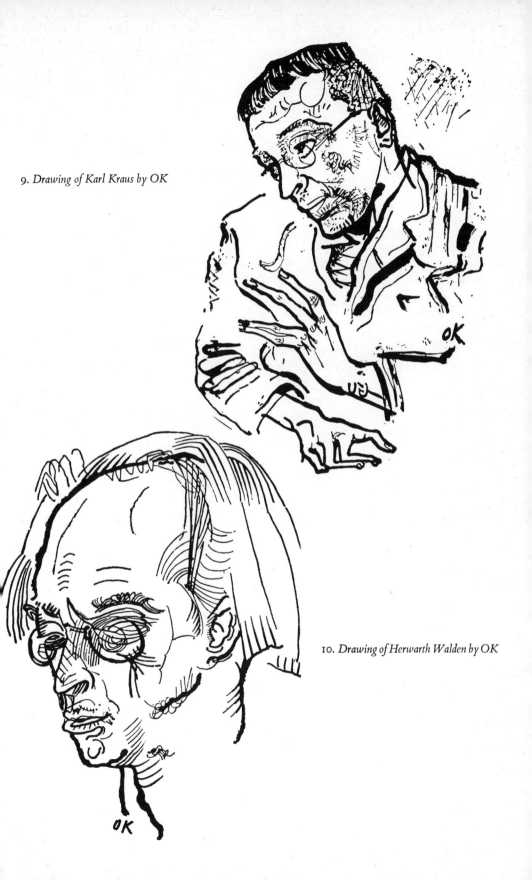

9. *Drawing of Karl Kraus by OK*

10. *Drawing of Herwarth Walden by OK*

11. *Ernst Deutsch and Käthe Richter in the play*, Der brennende Dornbusch

reaching plans for a thrust through the Balkans. With the support of the big German banks, railways were to be built and economic life stimulated, i.e. markets were to be created in the backward Balkans for German industry. This was a thorn in the flesh for France and England, because they wanted to do the same for themselves. England additionally felt threatened by the growth of the German fleet, and France could not forget the loss of Alsace-Lorraine to Germany in the war of 1870–71. And finally, of course, Russia felt compelled to come to the assistance of its Slav brothers in the Balkans.

Germany thus felt threatened on its western and eastern boundaries. France had an alliance with Russia, because the French had taken some of the gold out of their old stockings and invested it in Russian loans. That money was threatened; Austria was threatened by the Russian mobilization; Germany had to come to the aid of its ally. So all the great powers were prepared for a world war; France and England could also count on troops from their colonies in Africa and Asia. America lay low.

And then the French apostle of peace, Jean Jaurès, was murdered in the street; Archduke Franz Ferdinand and his wife had met the same fate a month earlier, during their tour of inspection. Hungary insisted on a punitive expedition against Serbia; an ultimatum was sent to the Serbian Government, and rejected as a violation of the sovereign dignity of the Serbian people. The Austrian and Hungarian senate and parliaments voted for a declaration of war.

Old Emperor Franz Joseph, who had great staying-power, had persisted too long in his efforts to preserve the patriarchal state of affairs in his dominions. Franz Joseph's brother had been shot by rebels in Mexico; France, after offering him the Mexican throne, had failed to stand by him. Crown Prince Rudolf, the heir apparent, had been found dead in a country house. There are still rumours that the old Emperor perhaps kept silent out of political tact when the death of his heir was announced as suicide. The young man might perhaps have represented a promise of a more peaceful future; on his travels round the world he had learned much more than many politicians who never look farther than their own borders. Long before the outbreak of the war, Empress Elisabeth had also been murdered, by an Italian anarchist who stabbed her in the back as she was coming ashore from an excursion steamer on Lake Geneva.

Abroad, Franz Joseph had become rather a figure of fun, because he was so old, and because he held fast to the central position of an Empire whose traditions went back hundreds of years. Living his lonely life in the Hofburg, he rose from his iron camp-bed at six every morning and sat down at his desk. There he examined the reforms proposed by his heir presumptive Franz Ferdinand and by the latter's friend Wilhelm II: those in the economic field, and those concerned with calming national rivalries within the Empire. He disagreed with both. But he was not an absolute monarch, and he had to accept what his parliament decided.

In the age of rationalism, the Holy Roman Emperor's claim to rule by Divine Right had come to be regarded as contrary to natural law, as a consequence of Copernicus' demonstration that the belief in the central position of the earth was erroneous. Since man is no longer the centre of creation, we may well look for new rules of social conduct. The evolutionary theory of Darwin, which proclaimed the survival of the fittest, caused a revolution in men's minds; the dinosaur died out because its brain evolved in a less progressive way than those of the rest of the animal kingdom. Now God had abdicated, and with him had gone the divine order of the *Civitas dei*. Nietzsche had announced this in his *Will to Power*, and had found madness in his own heart. Successive tendencies in the development of thought had robbed rationalism, whose father was not Hegel but Plato, of some of its prestige. Rationalism turned towards metaphysics, without anyone really being aware of it. Before the French Revolution, Rousseau had set out in his *Nouvelle Heloïse* the rationalist idea that man is good, that corruption is simply a result of the loss of his innocence, and also that savages are better people. These ideas are perpetuated even in *Das Kapital*, the Communists' Bible, and are still seen as beacons of truth in our own prosaic age. In place of the divine order, Rousseau envisages an ideal future State which will take over from man himself and bring idyllic happiness, through the rule of human reason, and thus eternal peace. The fact that the *sans-culottes* had to resort to the guillotine was ignored as a mere blemish on the face of the future State; as is the fact that, several generations before Rousseau, Hobbes in his *Leviathan* had given a classic demonstration of the folly of utopianism.

The Habsburg Empire, ruled by the old Emperor in the enlightened spirit of Joseph II, was not an ideal State; but before the First World War summary trials, witch-hunts, torture, public executions, secret death sentences, concentration camps, deportations and dispossessions were unknown there; so were slave labour – Austria had no colonies – and child labour. Antisemitism was a punishable offence; compare Russia's record, or the Dreyfus case in France, with Masaryk's courageous intervention in the Hilsner ritual murder case.

Of course there were crises and social problems, the result of an over-hasty industrialization controlled not by reason but by the productive capacity of new machinery, East and west are still alike in that respect, to this day. But people are always ready to try to cure problems by irrational means. There are always enough prophets in a hurry to set the world to rights, although they cannot agree among themselves about their ideas or their reforms. And the peoples themselves? Since time immemorial the man who tires of following the plough has been happy to take up the sword. In 1914 the police arrived too late; the old Emperor had warned his people in vain against rending the limbs from the living body.

Of course Bohemia would have preferred to keep the income from its ore and coal deposits for itself, in order to build up a heavy industry of its own; the Hungarians wanted to defend their monopoly of pig production against the Serbians at all costs; the Pan-Germans wanted to strengthen their claim to hegemony by joining the German Reich. Every nationality had its own greater or lesser troubles. But what complicated matters was that Russia, which since the expulsion of the Tartars had brought under its rule all the peoples of northern Asia as far as the Chinese frontier, had suffered a painful defeat in a naval war against Japan. In the East the Tsarist empire had lost face; so it began to turn its missionary zeal towards the West. The essence of the Christian doctrine as preached by the Kremlin among the western Slavs had left the Great Powers more or less indifferent; they were, after all, Christians already. For the western Great Powers the doctrines of the Russian Orthodox Church would obviously never have justified a bloodbath of the dimensions of the one they now started. But there was another, more potent idea; the nineteenth-century concept of nationhood, from which followed that of the liberation of oppressed nations. This was propagated in Austria-Hungary, in the guise of Pan-Slavism, by the political agents of Russia, and was approved by the Great Powers. Did anyone stop to ask himself, as armament production became the most prosperous branch of industry, what was the value of, say a nation State whose industry is based on the production of weapons of war – vide Sweden and others today – so that every illiterate, whatever his colour, knows how to use an automatic weapon and also has one of his own? This is the conception of the nation State that best corresponds to that of modern democracy; in accordance with it, mankind has been endeavouring since the French Revolution, with the help of a method of mathematical analysis, to equate human existence with productive capacity. A method which uses mathematical calculations – such as election results – to create on a statistical basis the State organization whose validity it sets out to prove, is virtually drawing conclusions from an irrational premise. The nation State is a romantic, irrational idea which is often confused with the mysterious power of attraction exercised by one's birthplace. A modern branch of biology – ecology – elucidates the instinct which leads animals to secure their territory in order to preserve their progeny and hence the species. In me this instinct had been rather weakened, perhaps as a result of my travels; before the First World War you could travel anywhere, except Russia and India, without a passport.

I had not become as tired of travelling as I am now; and I had not seen enough of the world. On the other hand, I would have liked a home of my own; the tourist never sees the wood for the trees, and the individual who once becomes an alien can never be quite the same again. My case was like that of a lot of men of military age who either had not found the right girl or had become weary of everyday life, and who sought in a cataclysmic transformation of their environment, such as a war provided, to find a new relationship to life – whether for better or for worse.

The newsvendor had disappeared from the street, so I went to the coffee-house to read the newspaper there. A colonel named Redl, on the General Staff, had betrayed the Austrian plan of campaign to the Russians the year before, and now two Pan-Slav parliamentarians had been arrested. So it began. But I was not satisfied merely to regard others as lunatics. One must try to keep one's eyes open, to see how long one remains sane oneself.

In 1914 I was twenty-eight years old, and thus liable for military service. It seemed to me better to volunteer before I was conscripted. I had no wife or child to await my happy return. I had nothing to lose or to defend. I felt melancholy at the sight of the young bank clerks, the little office workers, whom I saw hurrying with their suitcases to enlist, and yet I did not share the doom-laden mood that prevailed on the streets. The air was thick with rumours that part of the army had gone into the field wearing peacetime uniforms, with inadequate weapons and obsolete equipment. There had been no proper rearmament, and sloppiness was the rule in Austria-Hungary. Men took up arms only to die.

I was not robust enough for the infantry, not good enough at maths for the artillery, so Loos managed to arrange for me to serve in the cavalry, where I would at least have a horse to rely on. Friendships between men are dependable; I had been estranged from Loos during the years I spent with Alma Mahler, but now he did his utmost to see that I would survive the war. It must have been a real satisfaction to him, after suffering Alma's hostility, to have made it possible for me to post to one of the most prestigious regiments in the Monarchy – the one in which the upper nobility of all the Crown

Lands, and members of the Imperial family itself, used to serve. And I took all he did for granted, without ever thanking him.

Anyone joining the cavalry as an officer cadet had to provide his own horse, so Loos and my mother went to see the Jewish horse dealer whom he knew. I had recently sold *The Bride of the Wind* to a Hamburg pharmacist; the money was just enough for a horse that, as the Jew promised my mother, would bring me a happy homecoming. He liked her, and the horse fulfilled his promise, more or less. It was a half-breed mare, called Minden Ló (which means All Horses, in Magyar).

Since my kit had to match my status, I was fitted out by Goldman and Salatsch, whose premises opposite the Hofburg had been designed by Loos, and for whom I had painted a child's portrait. I made a wonderful target in my light blue tunic with white facings, red breeches and gilt helmet; the Russians had learned from the Japanese to camouflage themselves in field-grey uniforms and to dig themselves in. We imagined ourselves setting out with trumpets blowing and banners waving, and heroically overrunning our enemy – but he was lying low in trenches.

When I left I asked my mother to keep for me a necklace of blood-red glass beads, a memento of Alma Mahler. My mother put it in a flower-pot to avoid having to look at it, because it made her think of blood. I promised before I enlisted that I would come back when I had seen all there was to see. I kept my word.

But first I had to learn how to ride. Towards the end of my training I was very nearly put in irons for some act of insubordination, which would have meant missing promotion to officer rank. Then a great passing-out parade of the cavalry regiments was ordered. Losses had been so great that regiments from the reserve were needed at the Front. The General Staff, their horses restless in the midday heat, reviewed the parade from a command point on a hill. I had an idea: when almost all the detachments that were going to the Front had been called out from the various regiments, I galloped up, planted myself in front of the astonished General Staff, and volunteered for active service. The Chief of Staff said dismissively: 'You can't even ride a horse properly yet!' But one of the generals, a Spanish marquis whom I had always smartly saluted in barracks, took my part and said 'Stick the pine twig on your helmet and come with us.' He used the familiar pronoun *du*, which was customary in those days among the officers of the Austrian regiments, and among candidates for a commission (although one did well to use the formal *Sie* to an officer senior to oneself, and to address him correctly by his rank). And so I escaped the guard-house – and gave a boost to my self-confidence. I took leave of my officer in the training squadron, and of course he let me off when he saw the pine twig on my helmet.

I crave indulgence for mentioning my private life, which in the context of a great catastrophe may not strike my readers as particularly important; but then I doubt whether anyone who has lived through the twentieth century really has anything important of his own to relate. The whole godforsaken century can only be seen as one long nightmare, although it began as the 'century of childhood'.

For example, my dear brother Bohuslav, who had hardly left school, was called up for the navy within days of the outbreak of war. When he went, he showed me, laughing, a hollow piece of bamboo about a metre long, issued by the Government: it was to breathe through if your ship was sunk in the Adriatic, where the waves were as big as houses. In those days hardly any town child knew how to swim; and the speculators had clearly shown no more forethought than the military leadership. Not that my brother had anything to fear; everyone knew that Italy was Austria's ally.

I had no fears, either, for my younger sister Bertha. She had married a few months before war broke out, and had gone to live at the Austrian naval base of Pola with her husband, a Czech officer in the legal branch of the navy. My father and I had provided her trousseau between us; I had contributed a piano as well. It had given my father and me a good laugh when, in our top hat and tailcoats, we stopped outside a wine-bar after the wedding guests had seen the bride and groom off; we felt in need of a little something to strengthen us, but emptying our trouser pockets we discovered we had not a penny between us.

After the war my sister and her husband moved to Prague; but, upon the passing of Masaryk's enlightened regime, the Czech New Jerusalem turned into a travesty. This was already evident under Masaryk's immediate successor Beneš, who eventually had a quarter of the population, those who spoke German, expropriated and driven out as aliens, although before Hitler they had overwhelmingly voted for Beneš himself. Nobody reflected how much their forefathers had contributed to the culture of the country. Beneš's example was followed by the other liberated nation States, all of which, after a brief period of independence, were swallowed up by Russia – or are still being swallowed up. In his memoirs Churchill wrote that none of the peoples of the old Habsburg Empire was spared the torments which in the Middle Ages poets and philosophers invented for the damned. Even Masaryk had been of the opinion, until shortly before the First World War started, 'that the preservation of Austria in the form of a multi-national State was far to be preferred to its dissolution into a number of nation States, because this great Central European empire could offer the nationalities the best prospects of economic and cultural development – provided that it could successfully be transformed into a State composed of equal nations'. That is what we are told by the Communist historian Eva Priester in her *Kurze Geschichte Osterreichs*.

To me the political history of the world resembles those novels in which error and tragic guilt achieve their resolution at the end. In novels, however, as soon as tragic conflict is resolved, the book gets tossed into the wastepaper basket. Political history is different: when one gets tired of it one cannot just go home as if returning from a walk. Perhaps it is for this reason that the whole world is presently falling to pieces.

Basically all this did not bother me at the time. Where the Habsburg Empire had been there was a vacuum and into it, after the fall of the Weimar regime, Hitler moved, overrunning all Europe in a second great war and hence perpetuating, together with Roosevelt and Stalin, the same vacuum. There is still no end in sight.

Since I had done no service previously, my training in the cavalry school at Wiener Neustadt lasted several months. The final theoretical and tactical exercises for all the regiments took place at Mährisch-Weisskirchen (now Hranice na Moravĕ). I had turned into a good horseman. However, my horse, though it did not balk at any obstacle in the open fields, refused every time it came to taking hurdles in the riding-school. My captain, a Swedish volunteer, could not believe this until he tried himself and failed. This last problem was solved by Prince Sapieha who lent me one of his four horses for the final examination. On Sapieha's horse I sailed over the hurdles and passed with ease.

We made the endless journey to the Eastern Front in cattle trucks which also transported the horses. When we left Hungary, girls in colourful costumes brought us Tokay wine and cheered us; I lifted one girl on to my saddle. How proud I was to be on horseback! People in Galicia, the Austrian part of Poland, threw flowers and rejoiced in our coming; we were welcomed like liberators. Riding beside the commanding officer of my regiment, Brigadier von Bosch, who always rode at the head of his men, I was the first into Przemysl, which had just been liberated from the Russians, and into Grodek, Lwow and Wladimir-Wolhynsk.

Beyond the Russian frontier the countryside was suddenly deserted. The Ukrainian population had been evacuated by the Russians after the Galician offensive, for which the Austrians had already had to call in German re-inforcements. Later we came upon groups of Russian prisoners, escorted by German military police, and saw hanging from the trees the bodies of those who had openly collaborated with the Germans. In the marshy woodland it was hard to get the horses through the mud. Our cavalry was protecting the flank of the infantry and artillery of the Austro-German army corps. I thought of Dürer's sombre picture *Knight, Death and Devil*.

I had done all my examinations, but did not understand much about tactics, and I always volunteered to ride the advance patrol, with an experienced sergeant. I would never have lasted if I had stayed with the regimental staff; the gaps in my strategic knowledge would have shown up too obviously. So although I was the officer, my sergeant was in command of the patrol. At the beginning, we were not wearing field-grey. Our uniforms, red, blue and white, stood out only too well, and as I rode out, I felt spied upon by an unseen enemy in the dense, dark foliage of the forests.

The first dead that I encountered were young comrades-in-arms of my own, men with whom, only a few nights earlier, I had been sitting round the camp-fire in those Ukrainian forests, playing cards and joking. Not much more than boys they were, squatting there on the moss in their bright-coloured trousers, a group of them round a tree trunk. From a branch a few paces farther on a cap dangled, and on the next tree a dragoon's fur-lined blue cloak. He who had once worn these things himself hung naked, head downward, from a third tree. The horses lay in the forest with their hooves in the air, swollen-bellied, swarming with flies. At the sight of this huge dung-hill my own horse reared, so that I had to dismount in order to quiet her. My patrol had been sent out to relieve these friends, who now sat there together as peacefully as if they were picnicking. Only now they would never speak again, and when I thrust my hand into the hair of the youngest among them, his scalp slipped sideways and came off in my hand.

The next moment I was ambushed for the first time in the forest. My patrol had ridden on ahead. As in an old oleograph there was a flash of sulphur-yellow from the Russians' rifles. My horse reared and whirled round, and I could not help mentally comparing myself with the equestrian monument to that glorious King of Italy, Victor Emmanuel, which I had seen not so very long ago in Naples. Like him I flashed out my brand-new sword. What did not seem to belong to this picture at all was a wickerwork chair by a tree, on which the Russians had fixed up their field-telephone. I had no chance to get a closer look at this, for my Hungarian mount was already settling into a gallop, and she kept the lead in that race, leaving the little

Russian horses simply nowhere. When I looked round and saw with relief
that the distance between us was rapidly increasing, I expected to see the
Cossacks at their equestrian acrobatics as in the circus. I was not yet ripe for
war, though to be sure I was already crawling with lice.

Our advance had come to a halt long before the famous communiqués
from headquarters ceased to reassure those at home. The armies dug themselves in, and to a large extent troops were put into the field-grey uniforms
the Russians had worn from the beginning to make themselves invisible, and
on account of which we had sneered at them for cowardice. I was surprised
that the Russian dead, lying in front of our trenches, looked so fat. They had
been out there for several days. The contents of their pockets were investi-
gated by experts, with a view to establishing the strength and tactics of the
enemy division opposite. Generally the enemy dead looked rather amiable,
like peasants. On the earth lay crumpled photographs of their wives and
children, which were of no military interest; but obscene postcards were
handed round among us. Our cavalry regiments were now partially equipped
with spades, by way of experiment; but once again it appeared that the
Russians had more experience with the spade. Later not even gas-attacks
could establish definitely where a whole army had dug itself in, with mole-
burrows and stinking underground passages in all that burnt, bombed filth.
If it had not been for the barbed wire one might have thought there were
armies of rats dug in there. For the first time I heard heavy artillery fire. We
learnt to distinguish the explosions of shrapnel, the cloud of pink smoke
from the enemy's side from the grey of our own. There was a weak point
where my cavalry regiment was moved up. The cavalry, accustomed to
being in the van, considered it anything but heroic to be led through the rain
at night, in Indian file, up to the trenches. We had to go on tiptoe in order
not to make a noise, for the clatter of spades or carbines would have betrayed
our presence to the enemy. It was said that a murderous battle had taken place
near by. The previous day we had passed the newly made mass graves of the
Tyrolese Rifles. It was no empty rumour that those mountain troops had held
the Ukrainian marshlands and forests to the last drop of their blood, never
having yielded an inch.

Then we advanced upon a Russian town that the Germans had already
taken but had had to relinquish. Only the indispensable Jews were there
again. Since the days of their forefather Joseph these strange people from the
ghetto, who also have their uses as a scapegoat whenever a government has
to massacre somebody in order to divert public attention from domestic
difficulties, have regarded war as a typical Christian amusement – *goyim*

naches. But since the days of the Pharaohs they have also maintained their special talent for dealing in grain.

Many soldiers who survived the world war and returned home might not have found their parents, wives, and children still there had it not been for the cunning of the Jews organizing food supplies behind the lines. Not merely in the two last winters of the war, but from the very beginning, everyone in Austria would have starved, while the men were playing at soldiers instead of working and the women were not only keeping house, bearing and looking after children, but working in armament factories. The army itself went to the Jews. In quiet sectors, however, they would be rounded up from the villages and forced to dig graves, which they did not like. They hid like fieldmice in subterranean storage places where they had stocks of corn, hay, bonds and other valuables.

Once our squadron was relieved from its turn in the trenches, and we went back to the horses, which were with the reserve in a little Jewish township on the River Bug. The sergeant handed out billet-slips for the officers, who were quartered in houses, whereas the men slept in barns. I slept in a room strewn with feathers, for a former occupant had gone to bed with his spurs on. There was still a mahogany chair in the room – a miracle that the legs had not been used for firewood. A glass case in one corner of the room had been smashed, but it still contained two coffee cups with painted hearts and initials on them. It was wonderful to sleep in a real bed again! Over this bed there was a framed picture, ingeniously done with hair. It must have been a souvenir of peaceful days: a pair of sweethearts, the girl with dark eyes and the young man in spectacles, with a white cravat made of paper, pasted on. Even barbers have their artistic urges.

My Swedish captain, a mercenary who had joined our army out of a taste for adventure and who now commanded my squadron, was up and about at dawn, searching the house for something to drink, while I was still tucked up in bed. Reveille was not till six, according to daily orders. I heard a woman shrieking and the captain laughing, and I got up, looking forward to having a shave, for it was a long time since I had been anywhere near hot water. In the yard I found the Jewess and asked her for some. She merely looked me up and down. Scarcely opening her mouth, she made a contemptuous gesture and said: 'Fetch it yourself from the river.' I followed her slowly and watched her walking down to the river in her tattered dressing-gown, with a scarf wound turban-wise round her head. There was a ford. She waded in and, paying not the slightest attention to me, lifted her clothing above her waist and patiently washed her body as clean as she could. In spite of everything,

I liked her, for it was a long time since I had seen a woman. I thought to myself: What these women may pick up in the war can't be washed off even with all the water in this river. What a jolly change the war had made even to life in this little township – how right the armchair strategists were at home, talking of a bath of steel! It was some time before our squadron moved on. With my first pips up, I did not have to groom horses any more, only to make rounds of the stables morning and evening. So I had time to go round here and there and find out a little about my landlady, while my comrades-in arms were playing cards on up-ended buckets meant for collecting the horse-droppings. Her name was Jessica.

A bugle sounded – fall in! The horses were out in the street, all saddled, and the stable smell had caused me to drift off into a dream. One of the military police was marching off a group of tousled peasants. Among them was a dramatically pallid, fat Jew with a big black beard, wearing a fur-lined winter coat, one Herr Isaak Borowitcz, who had been blackmarketing in grain and had not wanted to produce it all merely in exchange for a scrap of paper with a rubber stamp on it.

To horse! The bugle gave the signal. Out again, to war! The dashing cavalry – to war! First of all we attended Mass, which was celebrated at a field-altar. Then, when the salute was fired, the horses became restive and swords leapt from their scabbards like a single flash of lightning. Officers to the front! Silence. My horse stood two paces ahead of my troop, dead straight in line with the other cadets. I was lucky; my horse stood as quiet as a statue, man and mount cast in bronze. The regiment ceased to breathe. The Prussian Field-Marshal von Mackensen, the chin-strap of his shako, the shako of the Death's-Head Hussars, martially pushed up on his chin, his dolman – bordered with leopard skin – decoratively flung back over one shoulder, and mounted on his high-bred Arab dapple-grey, came riding along our lines there on parade, his entourage following him. Mackensen himself gave me an order – and I, lost in admiration of the splendid spectacle, which reminded me of my boyish enthusiasm for Napoleon and his generals, did not hear it properly and promptly forgot it. They said he always had a French chef with him, for he liked to give magnificent dinners in his temporary headquarters, which was also the headquarters of our own troops since we had suffered our great strategic set back. Beside the Imperial German helmets, eagle-crowned, gold and silver braid, glittering orders and stars, the Imperial-Royal Austro-Hungarian generals held their own with the gleaming blue plumes in their cocked hats. On either side the staff officers could be recognized by the red stripes on their trousers. I had to take a message to the staff mess, where the table seemed, so far as I could see, to be plentifully provided, and where, modestly separate from that of the loftier war-lords, there was also a table for the chaplains. The latter all wore black, most of them with a large cross bobbing on their breast. The war of religion between the seven confessions represented in our army, the Gospels' message of love for one's neighbour, seemed to be settled over the wine and the not entirely dry bread for the shepherds of souls – which set my mind at rest. An equal, a peer among his peers, there was the rabbi among them too, with his own personal reasons for rejoicing. The German Supreme Command had sent a special call to Jewry to make common cause with the Germans. 'To my beloved Israelites!' Ah, the darling man, General Ludendorff! A heart of gold! What goodness came gushing forth from the source of German strength and joy!

Then it was war again. The cavalry was to cover the flank of the retreating army. Each of us tried to work out how to correct the strategic disaster of which we could speak only in whispers. If it came off, there was the order of Knighthood of Maria Theresa; if it didn't, court-martial for insubordination. Passing through abandoned villages, we saw swarms of bees in tree trunks, not in proper hives, as at home. In a clearing in the forest we spied a stray pig. Before the words 'Catch it!' had passed from man to man, the pig had breathed its last sigh and was chopped into as many slices as the troop had horsemen. Every trooper found room in his saddle-bag for his allotted portion. We were thirsty for fame, but we were hungry as well; all we got our fill of was rum. Once our field-kitchen ventured as far out as the forward patrols and even had an independent skirmish with the enemy.

In one of the hutments in the forest, in tumble-down thatched cottages, our cholera patients had been housed during the retreat and most of them died there too. We grew used to sleeping on the same straw palliasses from which we had just seen the dead being carted off. We were too tired to care. One night in an abandoned village, to which I had ridden over felled tree trunks instead of along a track – the place was so swampy – I was wakened by a sound. An old peasant with a long beard and the staring eyes of a madman was bending over me. The sound was a faint one, like that of a knife being whetted. His bleached hair lay like a thatched roof over his wrinkled forehead. The dirty coarse linen shirt he wore hung down over his trousers. 'You shan't slit my throat like a pig's!' I yelled, making a jump at him as he disappeared into the darkness, nimble and soundless on his bast-soled shoes. I managed to do no more than knock over the spinning-wheel, which looked like an old man in the light of the dying fire. Perhaps I'd been mistaken?

Was it my own heart beating so loudly? After that I couldn't go to sleep again, so I looked round among the old-world domestic utensils by the light of a resin torch. Everything was made of wood, as in those villages built on stilts, except that here there was an ikon hanging under an oleograph of the Tsar in one corner of the room.

There was something stirring at the edge of the forest. Dismount! Lead horses! Our line was joined by volunteers, and we beat forward into the bushes as if we were going out to shoot pheasant. The enemy was withdrawing deeper into the forest, firing only sporadically. So we had to mount again, which was always the worst part, for since conscription had been introduced the requisitioned horses were as gun-shy as the reservists who had been called up were wretched horsemen. After all, most of them were used to sitting only on an office chair. In the forest suddenly we were met by a hail of bullets so near and so thick that one seemed to see each bullet flitting past; it was like a startled swarm of wasps. Charge! Now the great day had come, the day for which I too had been longing. I still had enough presence of mind to urge my mount forward and to one side, out of the throng of other horses that had now gone wild, as if chased by ghosts, the congestion being made worse by more coming up from the rear and galloping over the fallen men and beasts. I wanted to settle this thing on my own and to look the enemy straight in the face. A hero's death – fair enough! But I had no wish to be trampled to death like a worm. The Russians had lured us into a trap. I had actually set eyes on the Russian machine-gun before I felt a dull blow on my temple.

The sun and the moon were both shining at once and my head ached like mad. What on earth was I to do with this scent of flowers? Some flower – I couldn't remember its name however I racked my brains. And all that yelling round me and the moaning of the wounded, which seemed to fill the whole forest – that must have been what brought me round. Good lord, they must be in agony! Then I became absorbed by the fact that I couldn't control the cavalry boot with the leg in it, which was moving about too far away, although it belonged to me. I recognized the boot by the spur: contrary to regulations, my spurs had no sharp rowels. Over on the grass there were two captains in Russian uniform dancing a ballet, running up and kissing each other on the cheeks like two young girls. That would have been against regulations in our army. I had a tiny round hole in my head. My horse, lying on top of me, had lashed out one last time before dying, and that had brought me to my senses. I tried to say something, but my mouth was stiff with blood, which was beginning to congeal. The shadows all round me were growing huger and huger, and I wanted to ask how it was that the sun and moon were both shining at the same time. I wanted to point at the sky, but my arm wouldn't move. Perhaps I lay there unconscious for several days.

I returned to my senses only when enemy stretcher-bearers tipped me off their field-stretcher as a useless burden, beside a Russian with his belly torn open and an incredible mass of intestines oozing out. The stench was so frightful that I vomited, after which I regained full consciousness. Hadn't I promised my mother to be home by a certain date? Can't remember what date it is at all! I kept on trying to work it out – yes, well, it must be about the time. One, two, three, four, five I counted on my fingers, and there was that little round hole in my head. Was I actually still alive? Oh, definitely. After all, when I said goodbye to my mother I gave her a necklace of red glass beads to keep, which a certain lady had given me. Only I could know that. But what horrified me most was that I couldn't scream, I couldn't utter any sound at all, and that was far worse than suddenly seeing a man standing over me. I opened my eyes wide, which hurt, because they were all sticky, but I had to see what he was going to do to me. Actually all I could see of him was his head and shoulders, but that was enough: he was in Russian uniform, and hence my enemy. I watched him so long that I thought I should have to wait all eternity while he stood in the moonlight setting his glittering bayonet at my breast. In my right hand, the one that wasn't paralysed, I could feel my revolver, strapped to my wrist. The revolver was aimed straight at the man's breast. The man couldn't see that, because as he bent over me he was in his own shadow. My finger pressed the cock. I managed to do it lightly, and only I heard it, but the sound went right through me. In accordance with regulations, there was a bullet in the chamber. Then his bayonet pierced my jacket and I began sweating with pain. I thought I wouldn't be able to stand the pain, telling myself that it was only fear, while the bayonet came sliding through the stuff of the jacket. A slight pressure of my finger, just such as you, dear readers, exert in order to flick a little flame out of your cigarette-lighter, would have sufficed to bring me back alive to Vienna, home to mother. After all, it's our mothers who bring us into the world and not our fatherland. Now the point was beginning to pierce the skin, was searing into the flesh. My ribs were resisting, expanding, I couldn't breathe. My capacity for endurance was failing. It was unbearable. And still I went on telling myself, as I grew weaker and weaker: 'Just a second more! This ordinary Russian is only obeying orders!' Then suddenly I felt quite light and a wave of happiness – never since then in all my life have I felt it so physically – a sense of well-being positively flung me upward. I was buoyed up on the hot

stream of blood from my lungs that was coming out of my mouth and
nostrils and eyes and ears. I was floating in mid-air. So this was all there was
to dying? I couldn't help laughing in the man's face before I breathed my
last. And the ordeal was over. All I took with me to the other side was the
sight of his astonished eyes. The enemy ran away, leaving his weapon
sticking in my body. It fell out under its own weight.

What happened to me then I do not know. There are gaps in my memory.
It seems that one, two, or more days later they lifted me into a railway
wagon, and there was a Russian conscript who had lost both his feet who
kept trying to push a withered apple into my mouth – but even a surgeon
couldn't have opened it, my face was so swollen. Then they lifted me out,
and Russian guards officers saluted, presumably mistaking the yellow cotton
threads on my collar, the cadet's badge, for real gold. Yes, it was the scent
of mimosa-pollen, that was what I hadn't been able to think of before. It
was mimosa that I used to send to my lady-love in Nice every evening by
express train from Vienna, so that she should have the scent of it before she
encountered it in the flower markets there. And then I was required to write
out my 'particulars' before I died – so one of these friendly people kept on
insisting in broken German. He even guided my hand as I wrote, but the
sheet of paper had not enough space for my name. Several times we poised
the pencil, and I wrote right off the edge of the paper, as if into the sky. I
might almost have ended as the Unknown Soldier of the First World War.
Thanks to this medical orderly and another one who also came along, I was
able to study the white shrapnel clouds mingling with the pink ones over the
railway station, during the hours that the train stood there. On my promising
to protect them, they stealthily lifted me out of the cattle-wagon and stayed
by me that night, while the train travelled eastward. They were both Balts.
I would have promised anything to stop that rumbling of wheels going
round in my head! As often as fur caps came bursting in, asking in menacing
tones if there wasn't some damned German or Austrian there, I answered
only with a smile, whereupon they too remained. After the thunder of the
guns there was now rifle-fire to be heard. It was our troops coming closer.
There was a bugle call! Then, in my own native language, an order to attack
the station. The Russian orderlies raised me up so that I could be seen in the
burnt-out window. They held my arm so that I could salute the lieutenant,
saying: 'Cadet XY, reporting back for duty with eighteen prisoners.' For this
my colonel pinned a medal to my breast, in front of the whole regiment.
And there was a rose that someone had laid on the stretcher. Heaven alone
knows where it had been picked.

An Austrian ambulance – they were still horse-drawn in those days – took me, together with the other wounded, to Wladimir-Wolhynsk, a few miles north-west of Luck. It had been retaken by the Central Powers in August 1915, and a field-hospital had been set up under canvas close to the Front. I was told later that arms and legs had had to be amputated there without anaesthetics. Being subject still to frequent blackouts, I consequently missed most of the excruciating journey, over virtually non-existent tracks, through the heavy soil of the shell-pitted farmland. The other wounded men screamed with pain.

I had to wait many weeks for transport home, always in danger that the Front would be rolled back. I had lost all sense of time, and for some reason I felt spatially isolated as well, as if in a cell. There were flies everywhere. Sometimes I was overcome with memories of the past: I saw the woman from whom I had so painfully parted standing there before me. I felt myself succumbing to her power of attraction, as if I could never part from her. The head wound had impaired my power of locomotion and my vision, but the words of my imaginary conversations with her phantom impressed themselves so vividly on my mind that without having to write anything down I could progressively expand them in my imagination to create whole scenes. My play *Orpheus und Eurydike* grew out of the repeated hallucinations I experienced in the camp at Wladimir-Wolhynsk. I wrote it down from memory afterwards.

Eventually, in a proper hospital train, I reached Vienna where there was a shortage of everything. Hungary was not supplying grain, Bohemia was not supplying coal, the countryside was not supplying vegetables. Over and above all there was the deadly influenza epidemic which by the end of the war was to affect over a quarter of the population of Vienna. The home front presented a horrifying picture. My first outing from hospital – on crutches – was to see my mother. I had left her a year before with her hair still a beautiful brown; now it was white. She lived a lonely life with my father, already an old man. She did not complain; she was steadfast. All her children had left her: my brother was on a warship, my sister in the naval port of Pola. With great difficulty she kept my father going, managing on occasion to obtain an expensive piece of meat for him from the horsemeat butcher. I was still mentally disturbed, unable to adjust; instead of asking right away how she was and what news she had of my brother and sister, I blurted out the question: 'Have you kept my necklace?' Quickly she took the flowerpot with its withered flowers from the window-ledge, shook her head as if to chase away an unpleasant thought, and dropped the pot on the floor. With her bony fingers she pulled out from the mass of potsherds and earth the necklace of red glass beads – triumphantly, as if secretly pleased that she had been proved right. There was the source of all our misfortune! Suddenly I felt cured of my tragic love, and embraced my mother. 'That's all over, I'm alive, I'm back, just as I promised you.' I told her that as far as I was concerned the war was over, too. Unfortunately it was far from over for Austria.

I spent several months in the Palffy-Spital in Vienna, nursed by young ladies of the aristocracy during the day and by nuns at night. Reduced by the enormous losses of the first two years of war, the army was already running short of men and equipment. The process of recovery had to be speeded up by all available means. From time to time there came to the wards a much-hated general, known in the army as 'the hyena of the hospitals', whose job it was to get the wounded back to the Front as quickly as possible.

My lung wound more or less healed in a few months; but the head wound had affected the cerebellum in such a way that I had lost my sense of balance. No one minds a momentary blackout; but imagine falling continually, and having to learn to walk straight all over again! I was like a sufferer from beri-beri, stumbling round in a circle, or like a chicken in a laboratory experiment, set down on a straight chalk line which hypnotizes it.

Medical specialists experimented on me in every imaginable way. I could not walk, but my kind young nurse, Countess Alexandrine Mensdorff-Dietrichstein, used to take me for drives in her pony-trap in the grounds of her parents' country house, hoping to cure me of the panic terror of woods that I suffered from ever since the ambush in Russia.

In memory of my return from the Front I dedicated a poem to her, called 'Zueignung', which I printed a year later in the Bach Cantata portfolio:

> Ungewisser muss ein Kampf bestehen,
> Um mit Rostgedanken, der anklebt, zu rechten.
> Schimmelblüten, um die Stirn gestürzt, ihn um
>   Heitren Anblick brächten.
> Um eine Spanne scheues Licht.
> Siehst ägyptische Nacht gestreift von einem Licht,
> Schnell wie du nicht eilen kannst! Mag bestehen
> Trügerische Decke unter deinen Füssen?
> Wenn die Welt erst sich der Dunkelheit, die aus dir bricht,
> Entwindet, Land, Festland unter Füssen,
>   einer melancholischen Begrenzung Welt
>   Wirst du gerne missen.

In eine Enge Verschlossener zu
Auflösung wechselst du
durch eine Scheidewand.

Though there could be no question of my being fit for further active service, the danger remained that I would be employed at a desk job. This I tried to prevent by every means at my command, not wishing to harm the cause of victory, for which prayers were being said in all the churches. In addition, I found the atmosphere of the home front utterly unendurable. Poverty and speculation, war and destruction: these are the four horsemen of the Apocalypse.

I contrived to get myself sent to the Italian Front as a liaison officer; my job was to escort a group of journalists and war artists – painters and draughtsmen – and hand them over to Army Command in Laibach (Ljubljana), where they would be assigned to individual regiments. Subsequently, to avoid being sent back to Vienna, I seized the chance to attach myself to a Hungarian regiment whose colonel liked me. I followed the example of the gipsy whom the Hungarians kept to entertain them and who played for them to dance. The Hungarians were not bureaucratically-minded; and their trenches were always safe, except when the Italians chose to show their gratitude for a new consignment of American guns and supplies by starting up a bombardment.

The Italians were well off; their positions were on the mountainsides, and they had the latest long-range guns. We were down below in the marshy Isonzo valley. Once, in a calm spell, I crawled out through the barbed wire towards a chapel that stood near by with the intention of taking as a souvenir an artificial flower that some pious person had presented in time of peace; but the Italians spotted me and decided to try out their American artillery. When the dust settled I was unharmed, but the chapel had disappeared.

Driven by restlessness and curiosity, because militarily I had nothing to do, being a guest of the Hungarians, I ventured out another time near the bridge over the Isonzo, a saddle-backed bridge such as the Romans built. At that moment it was blown up, and this time I collected a bad case of shell-shock. My freedom had ended once more.

Stockholm and Dresden

The Hungarians took me to the field ambulance; then I went to the local military hospital, where my identity was established. From there I was returned to Vienna. Again, the endless round of examinations and investigations. Every two weeks I was exposed to an electric current, to create artificial cerebellar spasms, then X-rayed so that the lesions in my cerebellum could be observed. It always took a week for me to recover from the pain and stress of the examination.

I was not far from putting an end to my life. The night nurse, a young and pretty nun, who had to give me pain-killing injections, was very concerned about the salvation of my soul. I had to promise her that I would return to the bosom of the One True Church before she would tell me, with great pangs of conscience, where she kept the sleeping-pills. I kissed her and saw, as her head-dress slipped off, her shaven head. I regretted having so shamefully taken advantage of her childlike piety; so the next morning I did go to the hospital chaplain and make confession. After he had given absolution he offered me the host, as a sign that the lost sheep had returned to the fold, which I had been stupid enough to leave in order to be able to marry Alma Mahler in a civil ceremony.

I was now granted a convalescent leave. For the moment, I was free. I went to Berlin, where, in April 1916, Walden had given me a major one-man show at the Galerie *Der Sturm*, including *The Bride of the Wind*, which had paid for my horse a year or so before. Now I painted a portrait of Walden's second wife, Nell, and another of Princess Mechtilde Lichnowsky.

By this time, Fritz Gurlitt had published my two series of lithographs, *Columbus Bound* and *Bach Cantata*, which I had drawn on stone shortly before the outbreak of war.

But my days of liberty were numbered. Time was running out. The war dragged on. I had to go back. In a dirty, unheated train I travelled from Berlin to Dresden, where I was to report to a convalescent centre before proceeding to Vienna. I was glad to get away from Berlin, that once-confident city, as quickly as I could. The effects of the war had spread from the front line to the hinterland. The dominant atmosphere was one of grey misery: the men were fighting on one front or another, the women working in the munitions factories, the grubby children loitering in the streets. There was no prospect of an end.

In the compartment, conversation started up again as soon as the other passengers had got used to me and stopped thinking I was an informer. I felt the sort of oppression one has before a dress rehearsal. Death seemed to lie in wait for all those who sat there disguised in uniforms: for those thinking of victory or revenge or rebellion, hostile to any kind of government – understandably, in view of the situation; those coming home for a short spell of leave, and those on their way to the Front. They faded from view in the gathering darkness. I fell asleep. Vague memories passed through my mind of seeing my old friend Albert Ehrenstein in Berlin, a man completely without illusions, who expressed with Swiftian humour his opinions about why the world was lying in ruins. He had seen me off at the station.

The train arrived in Dresden, and everyone had to get off. A stranger, an undernourished-looking middle-aged man, came up to me.

'A mutual friend of ours, Dr Albert Ehrenstein, has asked me to meet you on your way through. My name is Dr Fritz Neuberger.'

His face was framed by a dark beard, and his eyes were remarkably gentle. He plucked my sleeve and drew me aside until the other passengers were out of the way. I was too tired, too lacking in a will of my own, to resist. I had no idea of the debt of gratitude I was to owe this remarkable man. 'My train leaves very soon,' I objected.

He took the slouch hat from his bushy crown and swung it to and fro, smiling. 'May I ask where to?'

I answered curtly: 'To my regiment, naturally, on the Austrian Front.'

He shook his head and pointed with a soothing gesture towards a group of reservists, fast asleep on the platform despite the noise of an incoming train; they had been encamped there with all their kit for God knows how long. 'There will be no trains out of Dresden for the next few days; I've just found out from the station-master's office. First you must come home with me and wash and get some sleep; I have a spare bed for you.'

'But why did Ehrenstein send you to meet me?'

'He wrote me a letter saying that you want to put an end to yourself. Our friend often sends me patients like you. I make something of a speciality of them in my medical practice. Even in wartime one must not neglect one's chemistry; a good sleep makes up for a lot of wear and tear. We'll talk about the illusions later. I worked as a chemist once, in Australia.'

Greatly agitated, I stammered: 'So Ehrenstein, my friend, has betrayed me! I can't take any more!' I felt as if I had walked into a trap; the damned Ehrenstein had given me away.

Neuberger laid a finger on his lips and told me to lower my voice. 'Be patient, Herr Kokoschka, we all meet our end when our time comes. I am tubercular myself, but one must act rationally, and not throw oneself into the water unless one can swim.' Pointing to the sleeping men behind him: 'These faces here have already lost their identity, and the war is not over yet. Give yourself time to think things out.' His eyes took on an almost hypnotic power as he drew me out of the station by the hand.

As if to himself, he whispered: 'There may be no truth in it, but there's a rumour going around in the chemical industry that because of the alarming shortage of fat in Germany the authorities are thinking of making soap out of the bodies of the casualties.'

I was freezing cold, in the grey morning light, on the empty street. Bitterly, I said, 'Do go on, you'll make me laugh yet!'

'And you Herr Kokoschka, should make the most of the talent you have been given. It would be wasted in a soap factory.'

'Please leave me alone, Herr Doktor Neuberger. At least I must report to the military headquarters in Dresden.'

'One night more or less makes no difference. Report tomorrow, after a good night's sleep. I live in an inn very near your headquarters. Let's get a tram.'

It was all quite different from what I had imagined. When I saw what lay before my eyes, I felt Dresden was completely unlike other cities, especially Berlin, where a bottomless misery now mocked the fool's paradise of the early years of the Empire. If it had not been for the worn-out tram-lines that screeched at every corner, one could have forgotten the accursed war altogether. For hundreds of years men of taste and refinement had worked on these palaces. In the language of Baroque art, Dresden gave voice to the idea of a tradition-centred community in which life would really have been worthwhile. Unfortunately we have no power to alter fate, and that increased my distress.

Neuberger was warming to his theme. 'Great Power politics only go to prove that man is incapable of making the transition from primitive to modern civilization. The speed of industrialization makes it impossible for him to adapt to the changes in his environment. And meanwhile we've lost the use of our prehensile hands and feet, which would have allowed us to go back up into the trees. In any case, soon there'll be no trees left.'

I was fully awake by this time, and starting to put my thoughts in order. I had got myself into a world war because of a love affair – it had, frankly, been an escape from an apparently hopeless situation. So far, I'd been spared the fate of countless others who had lost their lives. This made all the difference. So I ruminated: It is like a stage play. Someone else gets killed, and when the curtain comes down you are free to return to reality. With the bridges behind one, of past, parents, school, a love affair, hope still remains.

Our tram crossed the Augustusbrücke and we got off outside the Dresden Art Gallery to wait for our connection to Weisser Hirsch. 'Raphael's *Sistine Madonna* is in this collection. But that's not committed art, not like what's done today, now that we've fragmented eternity into segments of time. Look at our shadows, for example, how they follow us at sunrise and seem, as the day proceeds, to hasten on ahead of us. That's the way an artist seeks to create an image of eternity. Consider the Greek philosopher's argument about Achilles losing his race with the tortoise.' At this point we reached the inn where Neuberger introduced me to his friends and acquaintances, some of whose names I already knew through magazines and newspapers. But they could not convince me, these universal reformers, that they were laying the foundations of a new social order. Peace among Nations! Equality! Liberty! Brotherhood! It was all a bit shop-soiled now.

The landlord, a reservist on a short spell of leave, was a shadow of his former self. He told us, while peacefully spooning his soup, how in the last attack he had planted his bayonet in a black man's belly. His wife, a stalwart woman who had kept the business going despite the famine during the third winter of the war, managed at least to offer her guests hot turnip soup on cold winter days; she discharged her duties undaunted, like a sharp-tongued Ceres; but talk like that at her table she would not allow.

Living at the inn, besides Neuberger, were a young actor from Prague, Ernst Deutsch, and the poet Walter Hasenclever, who had enlisted as a volunteer in 1914 but was now a fanatical opponent of the war. Both had been discharged from service through Neuberger's intervention. Käthe Richter, who had just left drama school in Berlin, and was in peacetime to become a great tragic actress, was another resident. She and I were soon close friends, for Dr Neuberger did not allow me to continue my journey. I had no say in the matter. He arranged with Dr Teuscher, the director of the Weisser Hirsch military convalescent home, that my journey to Vienna should be postponed indefinitely.

In that sad winter of 1916–17 I portrayed Neuberger and Käthe Richter in my picture *The Emigrants*; behind them, in a cheerless landscape, I painted myself. Later confiscated by the National Socialists as 'degenerate', this picture was rescued by the Tyrolese painter and collector Emanuel Fohn, who exchanged it with Göring for paintings by the Romantics.*

My early plays *Mörder, Hoffnung der Frauen* and *Hiob* ('Job') were performed in the Alberttheater in Dresden, on 3 June 1917, with Ernst Deutsch and, unforgettably, Käthe Richter in the leading parts. I designed the sets and also directed the plays. Two years later, in 1919, I directed *Hiob* and *Der brennende Dornbusch* ('The Burning Bush') at Max Reinhardt's Kammerspiele in Berlin, to the same sort of uproar as there had been in Vienna. Reinhardt feared that his safety-curtain would not hold back the mob, and the police had to be called in to separate the warring factions outside the theatre. I gave the actor who played Job, Paul Graetz, a removable head mask. When all hell broke loose at the end of the performance, I came on stage, bowed to the audience, picked up the hollow skull of the dead Job, tapped on it and shouted 'Your skulls are just as empty!'

My destiny took a new turn with the decision of the Imperial-Royal Army medical authorities to investigate the latest experimental work of Professor Barany, an Austrian physician in Sweden. It was urgent that results be obtained in the treatment of head injuries. The head is the first part of the body that comes into view over the top of a trench, and the army had to pay a life pension to the war-disabled. This Professor Barany had received a Nobel Prize in 1915 for research into disturbances of the sense of balance. You have to take your chance as they come. I was to be the guinea-pig. After much fussing between the medical commandant of the Palffy-Spital and the Finance Ministry, who objected to the cost, the decision had been taken. An express message arrived from the High Command, Vienna, to my convalescent unit, Weisser Hirsch, Dresden: 'Proceed to Stockholm without delay.' I had to pack my bags. Mission: to obtain an accurate diagnosis. Orders are orders. God knows what would have happened to me if I had delayed. Hence, in the middle of the war – in autumn 1917 to be exact – I found myself in Sweden.

What I remember most about Stockholm is the torment I endured on the Nobel prize-winner's revolving chair. This went beyond even my evangelical patience. 'I can turn you a somersault as often as you like, Herr Professor; the times being what they are, all mankind's standing on its head anyway. But don't give me brain irradiation and then expect an objective statement on whether a weight feels heavier in my left hand than in my right. No doubt it's all very psychological, but any peasant could guess what answer you're expecting. I've had enough experiments. Just put me down as fit or unfit for active service. This waiting around is too demoralizing.'

During the six or eight weeks I was in Stockholm, I lived in a small hotel on my meagre pay as a lieutenant and wore Austrian uniform – without side-arms, of course – as did the English, German, French and American military personnel who were employed in their respective embassies. A lot of spying went on, no doubt. The chance or fate that had brought them all together in a neutral country provided me with the welcome opportunity to see them as human beings in spite of their enemy uniforms.

When I felt strong enough I drew portraits of the astronomer Svante Arrhenius and the poetess Selma Lagerlöf. She lived at Marbacka, in an isolated house whose lighted window guided me and my companion, a Swedish poet, to her door. I recognized at once that the large mural drawings in the house were scenes from her novel *Gösta Berling*, which I had read and loved long before. She was pleased, and, despite the arthritis which made movement difficult for her, she stayed up with us drinking akvavit far into the night.

Sweden too had felt the effects of the war: alcohol was rationed; people had to queue up to get a litre per week. I often gave my ration away. The news-reels had the advantage over those in the belligerent countries; they showed not idealized heroics but authentic shots of the battlefields. Audiences shuddered comfortably and congratulated themselves on their own neutrality.

There were two politicians in the public eye in Stockholm at the time; I met them both, but did not get a chance to draw them. One was Hjalmar Branting, the so-called 'tribune of the people'. A white-maned, leonine figure, he was a Social Democratic newspaper publisher who later became Prime Minister. He was regarded in the German-speaking countries as a man of peace, and was praised in fiery speeches in Germany, while Sweden's war production for both sides rose every day. He received me in his magnificent *salon;* on a polar bear-skin behind his desk stood a concert grand, with a monumental marble bust of Branting himself upon it. I would have preferred to draw him in the old days, when workers' leaders were still puritans and the workers wore cloth caps.

The other politician I met was Camille Huysmans, the Belgian Socialist leader and parliamentarian, who also later became Prime Minister of his country; he was then visiting Stockholm as president of the Provisional Peace Committee.

I arranged meetings with both these exalted personages for three coloured men – an Indian, an Egyptian and an African – who had struck up an acquaintance with me in the street; they had come specially to Sweden from their distant countries on hearing of the arrival of Mr Henry Ford's Peace Ship from America. Now they were waiting, like the Three Kings from the East, and feeling the cold terribly in their thin exotic garments, so unsuitable for the Swedish winter. They cut a sorry figure, especially when Camille Huysmans showed them on a gigantic global map how many problems remained to be solved before the world could be divided up anew on democratic principles. He advised them to be patient and go home, until the Great Powers and the numerous new sovereign nations had come to an agreement among themselves; only then could their problems be examined.

The only politician I did draw was the mayor of Stockholm, Carl Lindhagen, a man regarded with some suspicion because of his anarchist views. Happily, he invited us to a hot dinner – we'd been getting hungry.

In the centre of the city a monolith had been erected, which, instead of telling the time and the weather as such towers usually do, gave the daily exchange rates of the currencies of the belligerent nations. My Austrian money was going downhill steadily; I could hardly afford the bunch of roses I used to send each day to a young Swedish lady whom I very much admired. I had met her at the German Embassy, during a reception they gave when my play *Der brennende Dornbusch* was performed there. The lady, who had been recently widowed, tried hard to persuade me to stay in Sweden. At the Opera she slipped into my hand a little silver case with a rose in it, which I still have. Her mother, an aristocratic lady, favoured the Allied Side, for she still remembered her youth, and to young Swedes Paris is Mecca. Her daughter nevertheless used to sail with me through the shallows, at night, beneath the stars. Our words were like the music of the waves.

A crab can go backwards; but man is supposed to be progressive. When presented with a choice between marrying her and biting the dust, I tended to prefer the idea of an honourable defeat. I had nothing to lose except my life, which I was quite prepared to give up; and anyway I was completely without money. If one has nothing else, there is always one thing left to defend, and that is honour.

That a minor affair in the Balkans had induced all the Great Powers – including ultimately America, driven to enter by the pressure of unemployment – to forget the goal of peaceful competition for markets; that peoples all over the world now faced each other in pure hatred; and that the worldwide slaughter of human beings showed no sign of coming to an end: all this too kept me from deserting. Had I not sworn an oath to the Emperor? His uniform was a new skin, concealing my emotional scars so that others could not see them. And now, when I had barely got over my separation from Alma Mahler, was another woman's wish to be my command? With a final bunch of roses, paid for with my last money, I parted from her. But not yet from life's stage, or from the rhetoric of classical tragedy. She later married an airman, Hermann Göring; she died young, and he built his Karinhall in her memory.

Within, I no longer resembled the man whom others superficially knew, who had worked for a while in the dream-like unreality of peacetime. Reality pounces upon one as if from an ambush. I had no more illusions about love or peace. They are simply polite symbols, as remote from reality as a dove with an olive-branch is from a machine-gun.

I must just mention the bundle of drawings that Dr Ragnar Hoppe (who was then assistant to Gregor Paulsson, the head of the department of prints and drawings of the Stockholm museum) showed me before I left Stockholm. They had been sent to him by the directors of a lunatic asylum, and had belonged to a patient who had died some time previously. The authorities wanted an expert opinion before burning them. They turned out to be the last work of Ernst Josephson, a once highly respected, if eccentric, painter of the old school, who had finally lost his reason. I was able to fortify the two art historians in their resolution to have them published. They were neo-classical drawings, nudes apparently stricken with elephantiasis. This was clearly a case of an artist ahead of his time. How can he have foreseen that after the war the population would start to grow faster and faster? I persuaded the scholars to recognize these obese female figures as symbols of the fertility goddess of those primitive peoples who once paid allegiance to the matriarchal system. Matriarchy always follows a period of male rule, when a war has been lost. The 1914–18 war was a war in which everybody lost. From that moment onwards Hoppe was no longer quite so sure that the Parisian Cubist fashion of the day was the only valid style for the future.

The post-war period showed that he was right. After Josephson's drawings became known in Paris through Paulsson's publication – I had given a copy of the article to my friend Jules Pascin, who showed it around – the dealers launched a fashion for steatopygous representations of the female form.

Whether out of modesty or forgetfulness, in his short memoir of our meeting, Hoppe mentions this, his most important contribution to the history of modern art, only in passing. Also, though he does not remember a large view of Stockholm which I painted from the heights called the Mosebacken, he recalls seeing me in the hotel in the morning, wearing red silk pyjamas.

When the painful investigations carried out by Professor Barany were concluded, I returned to Dresden – once more by way of Berlin. The Nobel prize-winner's medical report must finally have removed any doubt of my unfitness for military service. For me, the war was over. I left the Weisser Hirsch military hospital and moved back into the inn. Under the title of *The Gamblers* (later called *The Friends*), I painted all the people I have mentioned – Dr Neuberger, Käthe Richter, Walter Hasenclever and myself – at a table, and next to the serving-girl a rare guest of the house, a poet, Ivar von Lücken, who belonged to an old Baltic family. A Bohemian in tattered clothes, home-less because of the war, he occasionally turned up, ate a hot meal and left a poem behind. He had learnt the art of living on nothing while still remaining an aristocrat.

Dr Neuberger was out of town when I arrived. After his return Hasen-clever, who knew him much better than I, told me in confidence that he had been on a secret mission in co-operation with the German High Command, indeed with Ludendorff himself: smuggling Lenin from Switzerland across Germany and into Russia in a sealed goods-van. These were not just more empty hopes of peace, as was proved by the mutiny of the sailors at Kron-stadt in July 1917, which Lenin organized – an advance sign of the total collapse of the Tsarist regime.

Within a year the sailors of Kiel and Hamburg had followed this example of rebellion. Better fed than the civilian population, and spared the experience of dodging grenades in trenches for years on end, the sailors wanted to set up a regime of soldiers' and worker' soviets. A secretary of the Social Demo-cratic party had the courage to face up to the rebels, to mitigate their revolu-tionary ardour by means of weekly payments from the depleted State treasury, and to help organize the *Freikorps* from the ranks of the still loyal air force, all with the mere acquiescence of the leaderless General Staff and the Kaiser in Spa. The Berliner Schloss was occupied without resistance. Kaiser Wilhelm had fled.

But the victorious leaders of the Allies had lost their heads, too. Consonant with their ideology of liberating oppressed peoples, they had made use of the leaders of the Pan-Slav movement. But Lenin and Trotsky had other plans. They wanted to carry the Marxist idea of world revolution beyond their own borders, and into the vacuum left by the disappearance of the old Danubian Monarchy. Lenin and Trotsky were served by returning prisoners of war who had been exposed to Communist propaganda while they were in Russia.

At the same time, instead of seeing the Tsarist collapse as a stroke of good fortune, Ludendorff and Hindenburg dragged out the peace talks at Brest-Litovsk and tried to annex the fertile grain-producing areas of the Ukraine. The Allies even attempted to restore the old regime in Russia by supporting *Freikorps* of their own henchmen. Before long the Russians, too, threw off the mask of liberators of oppressed nations. During this time, however, my only concern was for the fate of Austria.

Shortly before Kaiser Wilhelm's flight, the Germany army had threatened to march into Austria, where people were demanding an end to the senseless slaughter and calling for a general strike. The young Emperor Charles had been deposed and a republic proclaimed. But here, at the heart of the Danubian Monarchy, the people had not toppled the Habsburgs merely in order to submit to a Hohenzollern.

In other countries, however, the war on the Home Front was not yet over. Prisons and concentration camps were overcrowded, and entire nations dispossessed. In Austria there had been famine all through the latter part of the war, and the situation was aggravated by the influenza epidemic. Following an exceptionally harsh winter there was a catastrophic shortage of crops which convinced the workers elsewhere in the Empire that it was hopeless to prolong a war against the overwhelmingly superior forces of the whole industrialized world. As Bolshevik teachings spread among the reserve regiments stationed at home, sporadic mutinies broke out in the Austro-Hungarian army, hitherto more or less uninfluenced by Allied propaganda. Nevertheless, the Front held firm, in spite of inadequate supplies and equipment. Even the Bohemian regiments on the Isonzo Front, holding out in the swamps against Italian adversaries armed and supplied by the Americans, refused to withdraw from their positions for weeks after the Armistice. With the exception of the submarines, the Austrian navy had long lain inactive in port. Seamen of Slav origin, heeding the propaganda, began mutinies which were suppressed only with great difficulty. It was different in Kiel and Hamburg, where the German naval forces had initially so perturbed the English; there the war ended in tragicomic farce, as German crews turned their guns against their own ships.

How long it seemed since June 1908, when Franz Joseph's Diamond Jubilee had been celebrated in Vienna, and groups of all the peoples who lived in the Monarchy – Slav, Latin, Magyar and Austrian – had passed along the Ringstrasse in their colourful costumes, cheering, singing and dancing to their own music. It had been a festival of many nations, now almost unimaginable; one has only to contrast it with today's highly organized mass parades,

in which human beings serve merely as stage props. But the old Emperor had
been something of a father figure. In 1908 I was still at the Kunstgewerbeschule,
and was assigned to decorate a cart carrying a group of vine-growers
and several large barrels of wine, drawn by a team of six great Pinzgauer
horses.

But what sort of peace was this? A haphazard collection of delegates from
the Central Powers were forced to sign a treaty modelled on the one Rome
had dictated to Carthage. Wilson was a sick man, pressed by power-hungry
would-be successors. He knew nothing about the thousand-year history of
Austria. The Allies and their protégés, having had a fright, were now to share
out the spoils. And so the world was reapportioned, and Europe's instability
has ever since been spreading to the other continents. From that day to this,
humanity has been like a sleeper in a feverish delirium.

I fled to Berlin for a brief visit. You needed a pass to get across the street.
There was firing from roofs and windows; field-guns were stationed at
strategic points; impotent oaths of revenge were sworn by the returning
soldiers who had been stripped of guns and insignia of rank by the mob.
Homosexual sailors, lesbians, whores, black marketeers, and others who
disliked the light of day, made life somewhat uncertain even when there was
no firing. The street lights were dark because of the coal shortage.

I had taken off my uniform, no longer wishing to be, as I had been in
wartime, mere cannon fodder, a number on an official list. I wanted once
more to be an individual, a naked Adam, infused with the Creator's own
breath! But freedom is not so simple as that. Ever since the Enlightenment,
without our knowing it, we and the whole of nature have been subject to
grand design which closely controls human reactions. We think we are
acting spontaneously, but every movement is intimately determined by cause
and effect. And how would the world get along if we did not believe, like
Calvin, in a determinism which limits our responsibility for our own actions?
What is true of the individual applies as well to society and the State. Since
the French Revolution ousted the Divine Right, the State has been organized
everywhere on more or less authoritarian lines.

People less and less see the historical process as an existential mystery.
Rejecting Schopenhauer and his 'Will and Idea', they have come to regard
reality not as mere phenomena, appearances, but as material fact. What a
difference from the time of Calderón's *La vida es sueño*, or from the world of
the Austrian dramatist Raimund, in which the bourgeoisie might marry into
fairyland! *Tu felix Austria* – you should never have waged a war! The old

Monarchy had grown like any organism, and after centuries of life it died. Such is the law of Nature: become, be, pass on. The end of the Monarchy is history – not a romantic tragedy.

Doubtless as a consequence of my exhibitions and publications in Berlin before the war, I was requested by the student council of the Dresden art academy, the Akademie der Bildenden Künste, to act as a new broom in that institution. But I emphasized that painting and artistic creation could not be taught at a time when the artistic tradition had long since dried up. Further, I tried to make clear my belief that in any industrialized country state-run education aims at producing nothing but human material for industrial production, to aid in the competition for markets, whereas the artist can only try to teach people to see with their own eyes.

I took my example from the humanist Jan Amos Comenius. In the course of his years of exile amid the troubles of the seventeenth century, he had tried in vain to persuade the parliaments of the Great Powers to introduce a system of education designed to improve the human understanding. Now I set out in my turn to open my pupils' eyes. Since then, my pupils have remained faithful to me, in all the countries where I have taught.

One problem, however, remained to be solved. As a State employee in Germany, I should by rights have given up my Austrian citizenship and become a citizen of the Reich. I went to the Saxon Ministry of Education and Religious Affairs, and declared to the official concerned that my allegiance to the country where I had been born, whose history was my history, could not be changed like a shirt, merely in order to get a passport. Years later, at the time of the Anschluss, when I was declared a degenerate artist and lost my citizenship, I began to think differently. But on this occasion the official was helpful and made an exception for me.

At the request of the director of the Dresden museum, Dr Hans Posse, I moved from the inn to his house, one of the old lodges (*Kavaliershäuser*) in the Grosser Garten. There was a housing shortage, and Posse had invited me to avoid having less welcome lodgers billeted on him by the authorities.

Every evening, on the way from the Academy to my new home, I had to cross the Augustusbrücke. One night, both banks of the Elbe were crowded with excited onlookers. Some high official had been thrown into the river. The crowd was cheering, and shots rang out. I could see from the bridge how the man, weighed down by his clothes, was trying vainly to reach the far bank. When he got close to it – the river is very wide – he was driven off by gunfire; he turned back and drowned. Even a dog might have been taken pity on and pulled out of the water when they had had their fill of tormenting him. For all I know, someone in that crowd was looking at his watch, like a referee, until the game ended. I fled, feeling physically sick, but not daring to draw attention to myself. Better to moulder in a coffin or on the battlefield than to fall to the mercy of this rabble, whose hands held guns taken from the returning soldiers. They had forgotten that there is a time for everything, a seed-time and a harvest-time, a time for murder and a time for pity. A direct confrontation with them would have been senseless.

I am not a coward, but then I don't believe in commonplaces like world peace, freedom, equality, and brotherhood either. Nor in statements like 'Man is good', or 'Not the murderer but the victim is to blame': that is all sentimental twaddle. Revolution has its hour, certainly. But even a gift horse should be looked in the mouth to see if it can still deliver the goods. Indeed, not only the underdog was filled with hatred; there was a mob on the other side of the barricades too, led on and hoodwinked by the generals and the politicians. The cause of freedom was in a bad way, I thought, and I wouldn't have taken it as a gift. And so, during the revolution in Dresden, I paid to have a large announcement printed and put up in the main streets. It ran as follows:

'I request all those who intend to use firearms in order to promote their political beliefs, whether of the radical left, the radical right or the radical centre, to be kind enough to hold their military exercises elsewhere than in front of the art gallery in the Zwinger: for instance, on the shooting-ranges on the heath, where human civilization is in no danger. I do not venture to hope that my alternative proposal will find favour, which is that in the German Republic, as in classical times, feuds should in future be resolved by single combat between the respective political leaders – in the Sarrasani Circus, perhaps – with the effect enhanced by the Homeric laughter of the parties that they lead.' I signed it with my full name.

Dr Posse managed to collect forty German newspapers which had printed the text of my statement without comment. George Grosz and his group then published a pamphlet with the title *Die Kunsthure Oskar Kokoschka*, 'The Art Whore Oskar Kokoschka', in which they promised to hang me from the nearest lamp-post when their party came to power. I was not so much indignant because a fairly minor Rubens had been damaged by a stray bullet, as I was concerned to counter hate with derision. If I had wept and wailed about the danger to innocent men, women and children in the streets, no one would have taken the least notice. But now the freedom fighters were provoked. For a time it wasn't safe for me to walk home at night alone through the Grosser Garten.

In the Academy I had at my disposal a spacious studio with a view over the Elbe. For the first time I was set up like a proper painter; usually I prefer to do portraits in the sitters' own accustomed surroundings, and landscapes on the spot, from a carefully chosen viewpoint. I made a daily round of the classes, discussing each student's work with him in detail, after which some of the students might drop by to visit me. I loved this personal contact with them, and I did my best to help with their various personal and material problems. In place of the student–teacher relationship usual in art schools, I preferred an entirely human one, for I think it is personal identity that makes an artist what he is. I would like to quote a letter that I sent to the father of one of my favourite pupils, Hans Mayboden (who died in 1963); the father had asked me whether I could with a good conscience endorse his son's choice of art as a career.

Your letter places me in a difficult position. I cannot honestly pacify your parental anxiety by giving an unfavourable opinion of your son's talent, at least as it has so far manifested itself. And yet I cannot allay your fears about the uncertainty of the objective your son has chosen; on the contrary, I must truthfully say that the dangers from the material and mental point of view can only be endless, and that they will increase proportionally as your son's vocation becomes more profound. For the artist's endeavours can never have his advancement as their objective; rather they impose on him a function in life of which inner satisfaction is the reward, and the promptings of conscience must be the criterion of his own value. It is for this reason that our school gives its pupils no certificates to take out into the world.

Even if your son is willing, as many – myself included – have been before him, to lead a life full of sacrifices, full of battles with the external world and with himself, haunted by the danger of an endlessly renewed threat to everything that has been achieved – even then he may prove to have been prey to a delusion that in the end will break him. But when a human being believes that he alone, among all the thousands who set out, will find his way through to that which the enlightened call the divine, I cannot close the door to him. I must, as a true teacher, encourage anyone who dares to accept the challenge of life, lest the divine imagination remain without a priest, and life without the grandeur of ancient times. The pupil who comes full of reverence is always welcome to me.

I remain, yours faithfully,

Dresden, 31 October 1920   *Oskar Kokoschka.*

The slogans of that period left me, and still leave me, sceptical. 'Democracy' is an idea invented by the ancient Greeks, who did not really understand it themselves for longer than fifty years. Now it has become just another catchword with which people drug themselves while they let the prisons, concentrations camps, expropriations, and liquidations go on undeterred. I myself had rejected out of hand, as far as my own school was concerned, the slogan of 'commitment'; later, under Hitler and Stalin, committed art became the rule, although its only proper place is on chocolate wrappings.

In my walks from home to the Academy I never failed to visit the museum. A number of the masterpieces there became signposts on my way. With the outside world in chaos, I kept my bearings thanks entirely to those artists of the past who had revealed how to order experience as part of the spiritual life. I learned how important a museum can be for an isolated individual.

A museum does not exist to educate the public, or to satisfy the tourist's hunger for sensation; the mob no more belongs in it than do the braying guides – even if the State loses money on entrance fees. Do *they* know, for instance, that in a picture by Van Eyck the spirit of Thomas Aquinas is still alive, expressing the medieval view of man as the creature of a God who has manifested himself in true harmony with existence? The solitary Caspar David Friedrich captured the infinitude of the Alps, their crags, their chasms and their eternal ice. He saw the true fearfulness of Nature and the weakness of the individual – in contrast to the academic, neoclassical attitude, with its deceptive pastoral vision. Rembrandt, in his old age, whether voluntarily or as a result of changes in his circumstances, withdrew from the operatic ceremony of social life and from the false glare of publicity. In his contacts with the Jews of the ghetto, he rediscovered the human face, and found consolation, refuge, and himself. Thus art gives renewed hope as often as the world fails.

Another master well represented in the Dresden collection was Vermeer, the painter of that bourgeois society which created in Holland, after the wars of liberation, an art of self-portrayal, an art celebrating the class that had just come to power. Contrast the classic, 'ideal' art of England and France, at the same period – and also the art of today, the expression of a proletarianized society which does not yet know how to govern itself. The masters of medieval art – Van Eyck above all – had shown the harmony between man and nature in a world created by God; Vermeer, and with him Rembrandt and Hals, saw the human individual in a new light, at home in a bourgeois world. Vermeer created harmony out of everyday things – a house, the view of a garden through a window – and all by means of light. It falls on walls, pictures, a map, tapestry-covered chairs, polychrome faïence jugs, porcelain – so that the woman who is playing the spinet, or sweeping the room, can once more see herself inhabiting a harmonious world, as medieval man once did. Vermeer did not rediscover colour but light: a light perceptible only to a cultivated society, a light that is hidden from the camera.

At that time I painted several views of the Elbe from my studio window. I had never before worked in so well-lit a room. The inner light of which I dreamed, and which I had found in Vermeer, I captured in my painting, *The Power of Music*★.

On a brief visit to my parents in Vienna, I saw that my father had grown even more old and tired; it was doctor's orders that he should be taken out of the cramped city flat and into the country. My brother Bohuslav had found a convenient little house for sale in a suburb of Vienna. On my return to Dresden, I wrote out a cheque to my brother to cover the purchase price; it amounted to far more than the retainer I was getting from Cassirer. But I waited until the very last moment before asking Cassirer to cover the cheque or suspend my contract. This must have seemed to him as irresponsible as it was shameless and ungrateful, for he had been the first to offer me any financial security. The day of closing the sale drew nearer. My brother sent ever more urgent reminders, and still I did nothing, except, at last, to explain the situation to my friend Dr Neuberger, who himself promptly departed for Berlin to talk to Cassirer. Tragically, he died of a haemorrhage on the way back; I remained in the dark about the outcome of their conversation.

I sat one morning – it was spring – on a bench in the Grosser Garten, trying to pluck up courage to go to the Academy, where I knew my other creditors would be waiting. I was deeply depressed. That uncovered cheque could mean prison. Slowly, a municipal refuse cart approached, drawn by two oxen; horses were scarce in post-war Germany. The sight of the slow, lumbering vehicle, and the meditative gait of the animals, soothed me a little. My curiosity was aroused when the first ox-cart was followed by a second, then a third and a fourth. The great horns made me think of the sacred cows of Isis; all that was lacking was the moon in between. I forgot my worries and gave way to the gambler's instinct – which is entirely in keeping with the irresponsible way I lead my life. When a fifth cart came past, and then a sixth, an inner voice said that if only a seventh were to appear – that is the sacred number – I should be released of all my cares, and all my wishes would come true. A miracle! There indeed was the seventh cart. Just as I started to get up, a girl's hands were laid over my eyes; I heard an unknown, attractive voice inviting itself to lunch with me at my house in the Grosser Garten. I joyfully agreed; but when, after the promised delay, I looked round, the girl had vanished. Still, I went straight to the nearest flower shop where I had credit, ordered some orchids, and proceeded cheerfully to the Academy. In the studio I found not only my creditors but also Paul Cassirer himself awaiting me. 'As the elder, I have made the first move,' he said. He had guaranteed my cheque. The week of real fear was over. 'I'll never forget what you have done for me; but now, please, if you have enough cash on you, settle with my creditors too. They're waiting in the ante-room.' I have never owned a cheque-book since.

In Vienna my parents had already moved into their house. The former owner, a Turk, had planted a mass of sweet-smelling roses, and my mother tended them lovingly. My brother wrote and told me how our father used to enjoy himself on the veranda in a rocking-chair. And now, it seems, the relations who had not shown their faces for years on end, ever since we had become poor, began once more to pay visits, and were greeted somewhat sarcastically by my father: 'So, now that we have a house, we're good enough to visit again. Come in, then, my wife will make sure that you have something to eat for your trouble.'

My Dresden landlord Dr Posse had a housekeeper whom he held in great respect. On Sundays I was invited to lunch with him; the food was still wartime stuff, but it was washed down with red wine and champagne. We had been able to get hold of a few cases of each that had been brought back from France during the war and were now going cheap. At table, Dr Posse never failed to recall that the chairs we sat on were covered with the tanned bottoms of court ladies from the time of Augustus the Strong, and that they must be treated with delicate care. Over coffee he would bring out his visitors' book, kept strictly concealed from his housekeeper, and locked back in the drawer as soon as she came into room. In it I was made to paint comic pornographic pictures, which he painstakingly heightened with gold and silver paint.

To keep my rooms tidy, the housekeeper had found me an old man who in happier days had been a footman in a great house. He was a pietist, and had the disagreeable habit of preaching to me at mealtimes, while letting the thumb of his cotton-gloved hand come perilously close to my cabbage soup. Patiently, I let it all pass without comment.

Dr Posse also employed a pretty young Saxon girl by the name of Hulda. She had imagination, which is why she attracted my attention. Sometimes, when I had visitors, she was lent to me for a few hours. I knew a lot of young women and girls, mostly Russians and Poles who were unable to return home after the war. I used to call Hulda 'Reserl', a common Austrian abbreviation of the name of St Theresa. For reasons which will become apparent, when she served in my rooms she played the part of a lady's maid, for which I provided her with a cap and a batiste apron, together with black silk stockings bought from a reserve soldier who had knocked around Paris for a few years and now kept a black-market store. She changed into this outfit only when she worked for me. As I had an aversion to men – I felt their hands were spotted with blood – she turned many a visitor away from the door with the words: 'The Captain is in bed, thinking.' The girl had a good deal of mother wit, and went through a delicious little act of surprise and fear when she heard the housekeeper calling her back into the other wing of the house; then quickly Reserl would transform herself back into the ordinary housemaid Hulda.

Above all, Reserl helped with the fantasy game I played with my doll. Dr Posse, a lifelong bachelor, had consented to my whimsical idea of having a full-size, lifelike doll constructed. After a lengthy correspondence with a craftswoman we finally reached the point where its arrival was expected any day.

Dr Posse's old father, a retired Prussian general, died upstairs in the house one Sunday without our really noticing. He failed to turn up at Sunday lunch. That evening, Posse came to see me, pale and distraught; his thin neck inside the upright collar seemed longer than ever; in his black necktie he wore a ruby-red stone. He asked me to draw the old man on his deathbed. I had never seen Posse looking so serious. With him I climbed the steps to the attic room where the dead man lay. I was immediately struck by how neatly the old gentleman's clothes were laid over a chair, and his helmet and sabre hung up on the wall. A night-light burned close to the bed in which he reposed, with hands folded – one of the last representatives of the Prussian State which I had once beheld with such awe. A fly circled around his nose, and I found myself expecting him to lift a hand and brush it away. I glanced at Posse, but he was far distant in spirit, as though he, along with the dead man in the shroud, already understood that all is vanity.

Alone, I worked on my drawing far into the night. Afterwards, wanting a bath, I descended the dark stairs into the çellar, where stood a tall water-butt for the use of the whole household. The cast-iron tub had been requisitioned years before by the military authorities. Moonlight shone through the cellar window, and there, to my surprise, like Undine in the story,

Reserl emerged from the water. With a provocative casualness she said that she simply wanted to take my mind off thoughts of death. Though her duty was to act only as lady's maid to my doll, the destined companion of my life, her sound common sense had told her that I would be lacking warmth in my bed. Then her cheerful chatter was interrupted by the housekeeper's cry: 'Hulda!' Hastily she dried herself and got dressed.

I liked the way she blushed so readily; but by now I was preoccupied with anxious thoughts about the arrival of the doll, for which I had bought Parisian clothes and underwear. I wanted to have done with the Alma Mahler business once and for all, and never again to fall victim to Pandora's fatal box, which had already brought me so much suffering. Finally a large packing-case arrived at our little house; inside, protected by a mass of shavings, was the doll.

My aged manservant, hearing of it, was beside himself at the very idea. In addition, he was jealous. He reminded me of a canary I had kept for company in my black-walled studio in Vienna, at the time of my breach with Alma. It had learned to do acrobatics on a string stretched across the room, advancing and retreating at a word of command like one of Frederick the Great's guardsmen. It hated visitors. It would peck at my mouth when I was talking to a lady; and when at night I was not talking to it, it pecked at my closed eyelids. During the war I gave the bird to my mother to take care of, and it grew fat and did not recognize me when I came home. The spectacular arrival of the doll seems to have given the manservant an attack of apoplexy. Reserl finally found him lying motionless in his room, fully clothed. Then he gave notice, and I had to let him go. He was a tragicomic sight as he left the house, his little suitcase in one hand and a feather duster in the other, with which he dusted the banisters as he went.

The packing-case was brought into the house by two men. In a state of feverish anticipation, like Orpheus calling Eurydice back from the Underworld, I freed the effigy of Alma Mahler from its packing. As I lifted it into the light of day, the image of her I had preserved in my memory stirred into life. The light I saw at that moment was without precedent. It was as foreign to the science of optics as it was to the techniques or theories of the Neo-Impressionists. Earlier, when I painted *The Emigrants*, I had argued with God like Job, beseeching him to send me a ray of light in a world devastated by war. Now, the cloth-and-sawdust effigy, in which I vainly sought to trace the features of Alma Mahler, was transfigured in a sudden flash of inspiration into a painting – *The Woman in Blue**. The larva, after its long winter in the cocoon, had emerged as a butterfly.

Theories of art lead nowhere. Imagination is the only guide. Why else has Pygmalion never been forgotten, while the names of statesmen and theorists are scarcely remembered outside the pages of their own memoirs?

Reserl and I called her simply the Silent Woman. Reserl was commissioned to spread rumours about the charms and the mysterious origins of the Silent Woman: for example, that I had hired a horse and carriage to take her out on sunny days, and rented a box at the Opera in order to show her off.

I decided to have a big party, with champagne for all my friends – male and female – and there put an end to my inanimate companion, about whom so many wild stories were circulating in Dresden. I engaged a chamber orchestra from the Opera. The musicians, in formal dress, played in the garden, seated in a Baroque fountain whose waters cooled the warm evening air. We all had a lot to drink. Torches were lit. A Venetian courtesan, famed for her beauty and wearing a very low-necked dress, insisted on seeing the Silent Woman face to face, supposing her to be a rival. She must have felt like a cat trying to catch a butterfly through a window-pane; she simply could not understand. Reserl paraded the doll as if at a fashion show; the courtesan asked whether I slept with the doll, and whether it looked like anyone I had been in love with. In her own bedroom, she said, there hung tapestries of pastoral scenes, and a tiger-skin lay at the foot of her lace-covered bed, to which I was very welcome if I should ever tire of keeping the doll warm. In the course of the party the doll lost its head and was doused in red wine. We were all drunk.

Early the next morning, when the party was almost forgotten, the police appeared at the door, investigating a report that a headless body had been seen in the garden. The postman, of course! Postmen are always the first to spread news of that sort. 'What sort of body?' I asked. By now Dr Posse had been wakened too, and in our dressing-gowns we went down to the garden, where the doll lay, headless and apparently drenched in blood. Though the policemen had to laugh, they still reported me for causing a public nuisance. Thanks to Posse's influence it all passed off smoothly, but the public nuisance still had to be removed. The dustcart came in the grey light of dawn, and carried away the dream of Eurydice's return. The doll was an image of a spent love that no Pygmalion could bring to life.

In Dresden in those days I really could get away with anything.

Travels in Europe

It seemed perfectly clear that I needed a change of scene. One Sunday, at lunch with Dr Posse, as I stared yet one more time at the tapestry of *St Louis at the Head of his Knights Disembarking at Ascalon for the Crusade against the Moors*, I suddenly felt a violent longing for the restfulness of a ship with the regular motion of the waves striking against its sides – a longing for the sea and for the Orient beyond. It was like a child's yearning for a fairy-tale world beyond the mountains. The crusader king had taken ship at Aigues-Mortes. Perhaps the poetic name Aigues-Mortes had something to do with my feeling that Dresden was a dead end, from which I must quickly escape. But why Aigues-Mortes, when the harbour there is all silted up? And why should a crusade have caught my imagination – particularly one against the Moors, who had introduced so much humanist learning into Medieval Europe?

People are surprised today when, instead of giving their professors a hearing, students at European universities shout down the long-suffering academics, who are only there to teach them, after all. And we speak of the Middle Ages as dark because they mounted crusades against the very countries which had saved for the West the treasures of Greek philosophy in translation, fragments rescued by way of the Byzantine Empire, Spain and North Africa. These Islamic countries had been earlier the frontier areas of the Roman Empire, and they bounded the empire of Charles V. Various temporary solutions for the good of mankind had been tried. Many experiments had failed. But never yet had a belief in humanity shown itself to be a fatal error, as it did in the age of rationalism. And now machines are to replace man. Where is mankind headed?

In Dresden the triumph of the victors in the war, like the despair of the vanquished, seemed to be wearing off a little. Political excesses of one kind and another slackened. It went out of fashion to hang about the streets in tattered clothes; Lenin's cloth cap was no longer the symbol of the revolution. Banknotes printed by the State were now worth the same as the autumn leaves that fell from the trees. In the end I had to bring my monthly salary home from the bank in a suitcase; and I developed a sore on my lip, probably from watching the teller wetting his finger as he counted the notes. My *mal du siècle* had reached its peak. My formative years were over; what was this Europe to me?

In my recollections of the First World War, the reader must make allowances for the fact that I now hardly remember those far-off days, that I have never kept a diary, that I preserve no letters, and above all that my memory, always poor, affords no more than a faint echo of the past. I am always more receptive to fresh impressions which still retain the spice of novelty. Merely to have survived those days, and retained a balance, uninfluenced by either the reactionary or radical currents, could easily seduce a man into making himself out a hero. I am in no danger of seeing myself in that light. Rather, I brushed aside what seemed irksome to me, like a tramp driving off flies, and moved on to places where time is not measured by a wrist-watch but by the rising and setting of the sun.

As long as there was still no wall built round Germany, what was to prevent me from going away? Others might have Hegel, Nietzsche and Marx in their heads, and grenades in their hands, but there was nothing to stop me from leaving behind the victors as well as the vanquished. Germany seemed to have been completely written off; even the occupying forces of the Western Powers could no longer find anything to remove from the country. I am not saying that victors and vanquished were equally mad; but I don't deny it, either. Both sides had started out on a crusade for democracy. There has never been a shortage of excuses for war. The dominant idea of democracy is progress, and progress was the faith embraced by a newly bourgeois society in the years of industrialization when modern Germany and the modern world were born together. Ever since the German philosopher Friedrich Hegel enthroned his Time-Spirit, the *Zeitgeist*, in place of the incarnate God of the Middle Ages, people have believed that this *Zeitgeist* is leading mankind progressively from imperfect beginnings to ultimate perfection: a process which makes it possible for mankind to subjugate Nature. People do not realize that they are alienating themselves from Nature itself; one proof of this was the First World War, with its devastation of the countryside and its countless human victims. The *Zeitgist* has time on his side; like the gods of the past, he has all eternity to get things under control – especially in the east, in Russia, where he recently seems to have settled: one five-year plan, another five-year plan, and possibly a few more beyond. Fathered by the age of rationalism, Napoleon led all Europe eastward into the eternal ice.

I doubted whether I had very many five-year periods left to me, for I was already in the middle of my life.

Dear Lord God, I said, if by any chance you are willing to intervene, save me for heaven's sake from an existence prefabricated by the planners of the future, from an historicism in which my thoughts and my subsequent actions would be predetermined, and life would become a refrigerated still-life. Experienced men like Solon, Herodotus, Thucydides, Polybius, Tacitus and Suetonius, the pioneer writers of human history, would have found such an unnatural development of rationalist ideas utterly incomprehensible. They would have held fast to the reasonable principle that when you experiment with two calculable eventualities it is a third, the unforeseen, which decide the issue. Does the reader see why I am against Progress and yet cannot subscribe to the reactionary tendency? Because they are both milking the same cow! I have my own skin to save, and that is my greatest concern.

Perhaps I would have hesitated longer, but at the Academy it was my turn to be Rector. This meant that I definitely had to go, because in that kind of post I could only have brought disaster. I understand nothing of administrative matters.

I had finished my picture *The Power of Music*, in which I tried to achieve an inner, spiritual luminosity, like that of a Gothic window or a Flemish painting, in defiance of the optically orientated theory of the Impressionists and Neo-Impressionists. This, after my long convalescence in a melancholy time, was the fruit of my stay in Dresden. I owed a great deal to a dear friend whom I shall call Indra. She was musically very gifted, and I never tired of hearing her sing me the 'Letter Song' and the chorus of the berry-gatherers from *Eugene Onegin*. Above all, I went to hear Mozart's *The Magic Flute* and *Don Giovanni* at the Opera. I shall never forget Donna Anna, Don Ottavio, Donna Elvira, Leporello, Masetto, Zerlina and the Commendatore, all brought to life in the darkened opera house by the baton of Richard Strauss. Theirs was a transcendental sphere of whispered emotions and passions; of many worlds in infinite space, stars great and small, each alone on its predetermined path, exerting a pull on the others, rousing one moment, bringing tears the next; of nature rediscovered, something only a god could create. Mozart, this purest of all artists, gives us a sensory reflection of events on a higher plane.

A sad event concluded my stay in Dresden: I learned that my father was dying. Never in my life have I thought and acted so fast. I set off for Vienna at once, found doctors, kept my mother and my younger brother out of the way in another part of the house so that they should not witness his death-agony, organized everything for the funeral, rode to the crematorium on a stormy night, sitting beside the coachman on the box, and saw my father consumed in flames. I had come away from Dresden without the slightest idea of how much a death in the family can cost, and I had to run in despair to a rich lady in town, a friend of Alma Mahler's, to ask her for a loan. She never forgave me afterwards for repaying her in cash, instead of in the manner she had expected.

In Dresden I had left a letter with the porter, saying I had been called away on urgent family business. I never went back. Later, I returned to Berlin, where Paul Cassirer asked me what I was going to do next. I answered briefly: 'Travel to the Orient.' Perhaps I was still possessed by schoolboy dreams of adventure on the high seas, of Bedouins, sandstorms, mirages, and dying of thirst in the desert. I stayed as Paul Cassirer's guest in his house in the Victoriastrasse, and he put a Van Gogh, *The Railway Bridge at Arles*, in my bedroom. People are always linking me with Van Gogh, but I like only his early drawings, and those paintings that remind me, in their blackness, of the still-lifes of Velazquez: the ones Van Gogh painted when he was doing mission work among the miners of the Boringe, and in the ensuing years at home in Nuenen, before the blazing sun of the Midi drove him mad and he experimented with the optical theories of the Paris school.

In the 1920s, and later, when I was in America, I carried on a propaganda campaign in favour of a highly original artist, then entirely forgotten in Austria, Anton Romako. I cherish his memory not only because he was a true pioneer of modern painting but also in honour of the Emperor Franz Joseph, who was an enthusiastic collector of Romako's paintings, and who kept him alive, as he did the controversial composer Anton Bruckner, by means of a pension from his privy purse. What potentate in our time has done as much for the sake of culture? Naturally, since I first called attention to him, art critics have considered Romako as an inspiration for my work. Sources in art are as unaccountable as the wind that blows leaves across one's path.

Paul Cassirer renewed my contract as a tribute to the success of an exhibition of my work he had mounted in Berlin in 1918. I had long since ceased to contribute to *Der Sturm*, because I had no taste for artistic groupings of the sort that it was promoting. I left it to others to be influenced by programmes and theories. Those responsible for the new events in art certainly deserved to be taken seriously as pathfinders, but as far as I was concerned they could go ahead and solve their own artistic problems, without me.

My Russian lady friend accompanied me to Switzerland. I stayed at

Blonay, remembering my first visit, when I had painted the Dents du Midi and the portraits of the tubercular aristocrats in the near by clinic. It was there, too, that I had spoken to young Virginia as she lay in the sun on a stone wall above the lake.

At Blonay I painted two views of Lake Geneva; and, after Indra had left for London, where her parents lived, I painted another of Lake Lucerne. Recently, a friend identified the iron balcony in the picture as that of the Hotel National, Lucerne, which still exists.

From Switzerland I went to Venice, where I felt already closer to the Orient. There I made friends with Baron von Hadeln, an art historian and an acquaintance of Dr Posse's. He was the author of a newly published book on the drawings of Tintoretto, who is to me one of the greatest artists. From the balcony of my hotel I painted the Dogana, with the silhouette of the Giudecca, from two different windows, two different angles of vision, so that I doubled the width of my visual field, an experiment I have often repeated since.

With Baron von Hadeln I used to have little trials of strength. To test my endurance he once bent back my index finger so far that it broke. He was very upset; but we were both dead drunk, and anyway even that was better than smashing the mirror-lined wall of the Hotel Danieli with our empty bottles.

From Venice I travelled in the company of an American art dealer, whose wife I admired, to Florence, where his financial backer, an acquaintance of Cassirer's, was staying. In one day, I painted the view over the Arno from the Hotel Excelsior. Elated that the picture had been completed so quickly, we went to the financier's room after dinner and consumed a considerable quantity of alcohol. Suddenly his face went red and blue, and he collapsed on the floor. We massaged him with wet towels until dawn, when he finally came back to life. We were greatly relieved, for his corpse would have been hard to explain to the management. The Americans, having had enough of me, left the next day.

I had no money, or rather just enough to get back to Vienna. There I painted Arnold Schönberg playing chamber music with his pupils, as well as a third portrait of my friend Hermann Schwarzwald, the Austrian states-man.

In Vienna, Jan Sliwinski, another friend of Loos', persuaded me to accom-pany him to Paris, where he kept an attic on the Ile Saint-Louis permanently available as a refuge for homeless friends, political émigrés or anarchists, Poles, Hungarians, Bulgarians, Yugoslavs. People slept on sacks and sat on tea-chests that were bought cheap in the Flea Market. In them you could also store a change of shirt, underwear and a pair of socks. The almost empty loft contained a magnificent organ, on which Sliwinski often improvised for hours. This Polish exile, a fervent patriot, was very musical; before the First World War he had been director of the Hofbibliothek, the Imperial library in Vienna. Later he became director of the Polish national library in Warsaw, and was liquidated by the Russians after the Second World War.

In Paris Sliwinski introduced me to his friend Nancy Cunard, a member of the famous ship-owning family. She was highly gifted, she wrote poems, she was strong-willed, and she had fallen out with her family. Her mother, a very charming woman, several times invited me to visit and poured out her woes to me. Nancy lived with a coal-black Negro, who often beat her at night, so that when she came to be painted in the morning she had more bruises than I could count. But she was quite happy and content to be a pioneer campaigner for the rights of coloured people.

Sliwinski also got me to paint a young Swedish girl who served behind the bar in a little bistro and suffered from tuberculosis. When she failed to show up for several days, Sliwinski and I set out to discover what had become of her. She lay helpless in her bedroom, after a haemorrhage. We carried her down the steep wooden stairs to the street, hailed a taxi, and took her to a little place by the sea where after a while she improved. I painted her there, as well. Time and again Sliwinski somehow found the money to perform such acts of charity.

Soon afterwards I had to go into hospital myself; the probable cause was malnutrition and the cold winter. As I lay there in a fever an old hag of a nurse used to tell me every time another of her patients departed this life. As a finishing touch, Sliwinski and his friend Ferdinand Céline, a slum doctor, put a skeleton into the bed beside me as I slept. Céline was writing a book of which people had high hopes. I bought a copy as soon as it came out. *Voyage au bout de la nuit* is a great work. The skeleton, the ill-tempered nurse, and my own robust constitution made it possible for me to leave the hospital. Only once have I been in another as dirty and bleak, and that was much later, in London.

When, thanks to Cassirer, I was in funds again, I rented an appallingly expensive suite in a first-class hotel. I left it empty for weeks on end, whenever I felt like travelling but not like carting a lot of suitcases and things with me. The suite was useful for another reason, too: since I was now determined never to have a cheque-book again, I kept my money in the pockets of my suits, and in my correspondence and books, until I came back and needed it.

Then I would look through my linen and my love-letters and reap the reward for having so wisely taken thought of the morrow.

A frequent visitor to my elegant rooms was a young poet whose name I have forgotten. He was bound to me by an enthusiastic friendship of the kind young men sometimes feel. He had published a book while still almost a child, which had caused a considerable stir. By the time I next came to Paris he was already dead.

Among the other people I knew were a young Swedish baron and his enchanting wife. He painted pictures of little girls. I always used to bring his wife a bunch of the darkest red roses, and often wondered whether I ought not perhaps to give them to him instead, because I liked him just as much. And then there was my friend the deaf and dumb Hungarian painter Tihanyi, the first Surrealist, whom all the girls loved. But I did not go to the Café du Dôme or the Deux-Magots, where, at that time, sat Ilya Ehrenburg and Ernest Hemingway, writing their novels, surrounded by a flock of admirers. I did not like this genius-market, with its fashionable artists waiting for their American customers. I knew James Joyce slightly through Sliwinski, and loved his Dublin short stories; but I did not care for *Ulysses*, which came upon the literary world like a revelation, and in which the principal role is taken by the bodily functions of a petty bourgeois; it has since been a decisive influence on English and American *belles-lettres*. James Joyce was almost blind. He suffered from a strange condition that caused his eyelashes to grow inwards, which must have caused him great discomfort; he was consequently very bad-tempered. I found his daughter, who sacrificed herself to look after him, much nicer.

Through Sliwinski I had also met the English painter Augustus John. Though his portrait of the German Foreign Minister, Stresemann, is considered his best, I prefer a portrait of his sister Gwen, whom I believed to be a better artist than her brother (he admitted that he thought so too). John fell off drastically in his later years. He was a giant in physique, but he could not hold his liquor, and I often used to have to hold his head over the gutter in the grey light of morning. I painted the Opera from a corner room in a hotel which I think no longer exists, using two windows as usual, so that the streets converging from both sides came into the picture.

To lure me away from Paris, Cassirer sent me a travelling companion, a business associate of his named Jakob Goldschmidt, who took me to Biarritz and Bordeaux. Later we went to Avignon, Aigues-Mortes and the town of the Three Maries, Les Saintes-Maries-de-la-Mer. Two Maries are said to have brought their black servant Sarah, together with the house where she was born, to this place through the clouds from Asia Minor. The Black Madonna of Les Saintes-Maries-de-la-Mer is venerated by gipsies from all over the world, who meet there every year. She reminds the dark-skinned Romanies of their Indian origins. Those of them who escaped extermination during the Second World War are probably the only full-blooded Aryans left.

From the city walls of Aigues-Mortes, the custodian showed me the spot – now in marshy ground from which the sea has receded – where Simon de Montfort herded thousands of Cathars on to ships and had them sunk. The Cathars or Albigensians were a mystical sect hostile to the State and to all authority; even before Savonarola, they had been preaching within the spiritual Orders of Italy against papal rule. To destroy them the Church leant for support upon the strong arm of the State. They originate, perhaps, back in the times when Etruscan culture was rooted out by the patriarchal Romans, to whom the matriarchal system was sinful, although according to another version they derive from Asia Minor, whence they spread, by way of Dalmatia and Italy, to France in the tenth century, and were ultimately wiped out by the Inquisition. A similar sect, the Waldenses, settled in Lyons in the twelfth century, later took refuge from persecution in Languedoc and Dauphiné, and still survive in Piedmont.

In the paintings of Hieronymus Bosch, collected by two religiously inclined Habsburg monarchs, Philip II in Madrid and Rudolf II in Prague, there is more to be learned about the interpretation of mystical doctrines than there is in the writings of the period; this is true even in spite of the obscure symbolism of the pictures. Women always played an important part in medieval mystical sects, from the nun Roswitha von Gandersheim in the tenth century to St Theresa of Avila in the sixteenth, who carried God in her heart at a time when her friend the Grand Inquisitor still believed God to be in Heaven, and the Devil on earth. At the beginning of the eighteenth century there was another female mystic, Madame de Guyon. Possibly, in Christian communities, without formal organization, there survived ideas from the matriarchal age, spiritual currents directed against male supremacy and against authority, both secular and ecclesiastical. Perhaps their origins also lay partly in the social discontents of the Middle Ages. Think of Langland's poem *The Vision of Piers Plowman*, and its German contemporary *Der Ackermann und der Tod* by the Bohemian poet Johannes von Saaz.

When Adam delved, and Eve span,
Who was then the gentleman?

The last historical tracks lead by way of Peter Chelčický, the spiritual Founder of the Moravian Brethren, to Jan Amos Comenius, who taught that sight was the first step to insight. Mothers have always taught their children this way, but male-governed states have never applied it to their citizens. It is to this idea that all my roads have led, as for others all roads lead to patriarchal Rome.

The travelling companion so generously assigned to me by Cassirer took care not only of the travel tickets and hotels, but of painting supplies, and the packing and shipping of completed pictures; otherwise I would never have managed. In Monte Carlo I had to wait for the arrival of my portmanteau, which I had wrongly addressed, no doubt in the unconscious hope of losing it. I always detest carting luggage round, as if it were the burden of the past weighing me down. Goldschmidt could not suppress a smile when I gave my little package of hastily purchased necessities – toothbrush, pyjamas and slippers – to a white-stockinged flunkey, and it was passed from hand to hand, from one storey of the hotel to the next. But in our suite an easel, canvas and painting equipment already stood prepared for me.

I painted the view over Monte Carlo; what else was there to do? To get my companion out of the way I used to send him to the Casino every afternoon. He liked roulette, and always returned from playing with far more money than I had given him at setting out. We were able to pay for most of our very expensive stay in Monte Carlo solely out of his winnings at the Casino. Once I tried playing myself, and of course I lost.

In Madrid I painted the view over the Plaza Neptuno from the Hotel Ritz. In Lisbon I wanted to paint the view over the city from the castle. Just as I had settled down to work on the castle esplanade, rioting broke out, I think that was the last *putsch* in which the army and navy fought it out before Dr Salazar's long period in power brought lasting peace to the country. The commandant of the castle, though very helpful, could only advise me to go back through the battle lines, under safe conduct, into the city; otherwise no one could tell how long I should have to stay up there. I left my canvas, a big one, for another painter to use.

On the open ground below the castle lay the unburied bodies of soldiers in their cotton uniforms, and I was struck by how small they were in death, compared with the Russians I had seen in the war.

Something always delayed the fulfilment of my plan to visit the lands of the Moors. I needed someone to take me in tow; and I was ever eager to see this or that other new country or city, as if the opportunity might never occur again. I was still conscious of a lingering horror at the destruction caused by the war, and, like a historian, I meant to seize my last chance to depict the world as it had been.

In 1925 I went to Holland for the first time. I painted four small pictures in Amsterdam; one showed the draining of a canal. The most important is of the Kloveniersburgval in Amsterdam. At Scheveningen I painted flowers in a window, for relaxation, and also because the fluttering of the curtain in the sea breeze made me think of my impending journey to Africa. The curtain fluttered as if it had been myself, my own existence blown back and forth: but my goal was in sight.

First, however, I made a brief stay in London, and painted Tower Bridge. London should have been protected while there was still time. But the bombs of the Second World War and, still worse, the property speculation that has turned drawing-board architects loose on the most human and the richest in tradition of all European capitals have wrought such havoc that today one can only relapse into a state of Victorian nostalgia.

In November 1925 Paul Cassirer mounted my first big exhibition of travel pictures, thirty-five in all, of which thirty-four were landscapes. I had returned to Vienna for a short time, to visit my mother for Christmas, when I heard of Cassirer's sudden death. He had shot himself on 7 January 1926. I had neglected to go to Berlin at once in answer to his telegram.

At the end of the winter I went to England again, and was as moved to see the white cliffs of Dover as any Englishman returning from the colonies. I travelled with Fritz Wolff-Knize, who, now that in Vienna the Court had abdicated and the nobility had lost its estates, wanted to open a branch of his exclusive men's tailoring business in London, where members of society were still expected to maintain some style in their dress.

On my arrival, I felt that I had to paint a picture of Dover; as soon as he had seen me settled in a hotel with a view of the white cliffs and the town, my friend sent to London for canvas and paints. A day later, when he called for me, the painting was finished.*

During the months I spent in London, I painted eleven pictures in all, mostly views of the Thames. This river has always caught my imagination; it stimulates me, like the patriotic dreams that others have in their warm beds. My Thames! Those were the days when the merchandise of the whole world was still shipped up this river, when London was still a mother-city – as the ancient Greek cities had been – from which a surplus population spread out all over the world. It was the metropolis of world trade, the founder of colonies on all five continents. There the wind did not blow from the Russian steppes, as it did in Vienna, but from all points of the compass at once. I avoided looking into basement windows where the disinherited of the Industrial Revolution, the people of Dickens' novels, still lived. The misery one saw in the streets was enough to wring the heart. But who will presume to blame destiny, when the prospects for everyone appear so horrifying?

I wandered through London on foot, from north to south, from east to west, across the whole patchwork of humanity, and gained an inkling of the immensity of the world. I spent hours walking the streets in a perpetual state of astonishment, as if I had been passing through different countries. Whole districts inhabited only by Italians, French, Germans, Negroes, even Chinese; Jews who had fled from the pogroms; Russians; Bulgarians and other Balkan revolutionaries, who had come to whet their intellectual weapons in the Reading Room of the British Museum.

I tried again and again to capture the Thames in a painting – that artery of life flowing from century to century, the river beside which multitudes gathered to form a community with a style of life all its own, bringing the most diverse races together in a way that can be paralleled only perhaps in the ancient states of Asia, in China, or in the old Danubian monarchy. How small I felt – with my own Austria shrunk to the dimensions of the ancestral lands of the medieval Babenbergs – when I witnessed the royal procession at the opening of Parliament, with its mounted escort, and the magnificent costumes of the knights and dignitaries. Some of the old bridges, including Waterloo Bridge, have since disappeared. London Bridge has been sold to America. Though sadly not one of my London pictures has remained in England, they have all already become historical documents, because the river, as well as the outline of the city and the fortunes of England, has changed unrecognizably. One might feel that life is really no more than a mirage.

> . . . we are such stuff
> As dreams are made on; and our little life
> Is rounded with a sleep . . .

Life is a dream – so said the great Calderón in the one-time world empire of Spain, and so too Ferdinand Raimund in the old Austro-Hungarian monarchy.

My temporary home was in a little house in Ovington Gardens in Kensington, but I painted my pictures in hotels, where I would take a room and lock my work and equipment inside every night when I finished.

I was particularly attached to one painting of a bend in the river, visible from the window of my hotel room, looking down over the Egyptian obelisk known as Cleopatra's Needle. The painting has since disappeared – as has the hotel itself – but may perhaps still be around in France somewhere.

A married couple kept house for me. I was amazed at the quantity of carpets, exotic weaponry, china and bric-à-brac – including, in this case, at least thirty little ivory Indian elephants on the mantelpiece – that the English bourgeoisie in general, and a retired colonial civil servant in particular, liked to accumulate. When I moved in, an inventory was drawn up, and every one of these objects, which were manifestly of no interest to me, had to be signed for. It cost me a lot of money when I left, because some things were missing. The couple who looked after me lived in the basement; the husband, a former sergeant who had been decorated in many wars and in many countries, delighted me by putting a marvellous shine on my shoes with a chicken bone.

I preferred music halls to the opera and the theatre. At one of them the sensation of the moment was Adele Astaire, who so captivated me that I went round to the stage door and waited for her, with my heart pounding. I can never forget her great hit, 'Tea for Two', from *No, No, Nanette*, although I have a bad memory for music. Subsequently she sat for her portrait for nearly a month. She kept on her rehearsal leotard under her dress, and would gambol around with her dog in a constant excess of high spirits, so that I had some trouble getting her to keep still. Her mother, a charming lady called Frau Stern, from a theatrical family in Leopoldstadt in Vienna, often came to the sittings. Unfortunately I never met Adele's brother, Fred Astaire, later a world-famous dancer. Adele Astaire is now married to an Irish peer.*

I also went many times to a suburban theatre to see the old *Beggar's Opera*, with its original text and eighteenth-century street-ballad music: this is the work from which Brecht and Weill were to draw their *Threepenny Opera*.

The director of the London Zoo was then the eminent scientist Julian Huxley, who once wrote about me in a learned paper on the subject of suicide. He granted me permission to paint in the zoo outside normal visiting-hours. At night in the Monkey House, I painted a big, solitary mandrill, who profoundly detested me although I always brought him a banana in order to make myself agreeable. I cannot remember whether it was in London or later in Berlin that I painted the giant-beaked turtles: they are a dying species, not in spite of their protective carapaces but because of them: they are in demand for tourist trinkets.

I arranged in the mornings, before the public was admitted, to set up my easel and other equipment inside the safety barrier surrounding the cage of the tigon. This creature, a gift from an Indian maharajah, was a unique cross between a lion and a tiger. While waiting for the keeper to open, with a chain from outside, the door to the beast's night cage, I would lean drowsily against the massive iron bars. I am always sleepy early in the mornings. But the shock was quite enough to wake me when the giant cat leapt like a flame from the darkness, saw me, and sprang towards the bars as if to tear me apart. According to the keeper, the animal never slept; and it died not long afterwards. One day as I banged on the floor to bring the tigon back from the other end of the cage, where its continual pacing had taken it, I was startled by something touching my shoulder. There stood my old friend Ernst Reinhold, the 'Trance Player'. We had not seen each other for a long time. 'I'd like to give you a piece of advice,' he said. 'If that beast should catch you between the bars with its paw, that'll be the end of you, easel and all.' That gave me pause, and the next day I installed myself outside the safety barrier. I no longer took any pleasure in it, but I did finally finish the painting.*

I was always driven to the zoo by the same young cabby who used to set up my picture, and whatever else I needed, and collect it again when I had finished for the day. His name was Ben Tobert, and he came from the East End. While I was working he waited for me, and passed the time looking at the animals. I liked him, because he used to call me 'rabbi'. After Reinhold's warning I taxed Ben with his failure to warn me of the danger. He proceeded to explain logically that if the big cat attacked and I drew back in fear, then the panther behind me would get me with its claws; if I escaped that, there was a leopard on the right and a black panther on the left. And then there was always the possibility that I might get bitten in the calf by some lady's lapdog. It all depends on chance; Providence governs all. 'But you're a rabbi; you know that better than your pupil does.'

Reinhold had spent years applying himself to the wisdom of India, and had just returned from Ceylon, where he had, with Buddhist monks, been meditating on Gautama's sayings, of which he published the first German translation. One day, we went to the Botanical Gardens at Kew. It was absolutely quiet; hardly a visitor was to be seen. On a bench I saw a governess, of that English type with powerful teeth and cold eyes which had been more than a match for any Victorian child, however obstreperous. In her charge was a half-grown girl with the reddish-blond hair I love so much in Van Dyck's portraits, blue eyes, and a red and white striped dress, bell-shaped, like the gramophone horns of those days. Her little feet, in their short white socks and black patent shoes, danced enchantingly in the red sand on the floor of the palm house, enticing one to approach under the tall palm fronds and between the hanging orchids. My interest was aroused by a low, long Chinese table in the centre, on which was a miniature landscape with rocks and ancient dwarf pine trees. The little girl seemed rather bored, so I lifted her up to show her this landscape. I could feel her heart pounding violently against her ribs, like a landed fish in a basket. I showed her the grotto, and behind it, all in miniature, a waterfall, meadows and hill-pastures, stretching away into the distance. Suddenly the little girl that I thought I was holding in my arms was dancing away in the depths of the landscape like an elf. The child had disappeared. I looked for her, ran round the table, and finally asked Reinhold if he had seen the child or at least the governess. No, he had seen no one; and yet I had noticed him flirting with the governess when we first came in – he was still an old womanizer, for all his Buddhist learning. He maintained that the place had been empty ever since our arrival. I did not want him to call me a liar again; and so I did not describe what I had seen, in broad daylight and in full consciousness, as clearly as a camera could have made it.

During the Second World War my wife and I lived in a top-floor flat in the Mayfair district of London. It was going cheap, because the Mayfairites were mostly in the country, away from the bombing. One day there was a knock on the door; I opened it, and there appeared first a long cigar and then, to my astonishment, my friend Ben, the taxi-driver, now a man of substance, quite the gentleman with a homburg, an umbrella and an off-the-peg city suit. 'How do you come to be doing so well?' 'It's thanks to you, rabbi. I used to watch you when we went round the antique shops, and you got so excited about the beautiful cutlery and plate in the windows. Well, a lot of old silver came on to the market because of the war, and I bought it up. I borrowed money and opened a factory to repair the old silver, melt it down and remake it, and I've sent whole shiploads off to America. I'm a wealthy man. To show my gratitude, I'd like to make you a gift of a racehorse.'

Though touched by his generosity, I could not accept this token of a grateful heart. There was no stable in our house, and one could hardly bring a horse up to the attic in a lift. Nor could I explain to him that, for all the arrogance I often displayed, I was without a bank account and thus had good reason to live in England as modestly and unobtrusively as possible. It is best sometimes to make no explanations even to people who respect you.

On 1 October 1927, during my third stay in Venice, Dr J. H. F. Lütjens arrived to accompany me on my further travels. My painting of the Salute from the Hotel Britannia, done at this time, was later declared to be 'degenerate art', and was presented by Göring to the Regent of Yugoslavia, Prince

Paul. Unfortunately it disappeared in the confusion of the Second World War. I met Prince Paul in exile in London, and after the war he came to see us at Villeneuve, still mourning the loss of this picture.

In the rain, Lütjens and I travelled on the Aosta bus from Venice to Courmayeur, where I painted the Dents des Géants from my balcony, and then we proceeded to Chamonix. Being no mountaineer, I went up in the cable-car every morning at seven to the frontier-post, in order to paint the unearthly glacier on Mont Blanc, in an icy mountain landscape which has remained one of my most powerful experiences of Nature. Perhaps it did not matter, I thought, if the blithe mountaineer met his end in the presence of so much overwhelming beauty. Not that I wished, myself, to be preserved for all eternity in the glacier. Lütjens had taught me how to slide downhill over the scree with the aid of an alpenstock, so fast that I momentarily almost lost consciousness.

At Annecy I painted the blue vista of the lake, and stayed in a hotel built by Napoleon III as a house for his enchanting Spanish wife, Eugénie. Her portrait by Winterhalter hung in the vestibule.

In January 1928 I rejoined Lütjens in Marseilles, where we embarked at last for the sandy deserts of North Africa. The crossing – two nights and a day – was an easy one. I was just out of bed, and had not even shaved, when the ship's bell announced our arrival. My heart stood still: written on a board on the landing-stage, in huge Arabic and Roman characters, was the name Carthage. My dream of the Orient was fulfilled. From here Hannibal had set out on one of the most extraordinary campaigns in history, through Spain and in endless marches over the icefields of the Alps – where I had painted, shivering, so short a time before. In spite of hostile natives and the total absence of lines of supply, he had arrived with his elephants at the gates of Rome, only, in the end, to have his luck desert him.

We met two tall young Moors in white robes. Each held a sprig of jasmine to his nostrils; they walked through the sand with their little fingers entwined. They reminded me of the double portrait I had painted for two lifelong friends, each of whom wanted to have a portrait of the other, one in Hamburg, one in Verona.*

Where the Orient Begins

The West, which expends itself on shaping the future, lay behind me; I had reached the land where time stands still. To forget the westerner in me, I would need only to change my tight clothing for the loose smock worn by the natives. I felt like a man risen from the grave. The very sight of the name Carthage on a street sign stirred me oddly, as if it announced some transformation that had taken place not externally but inside myself, to which I was the only witness.

Lütjens was busy, mistrustfully counting the pieces of luggage, rescuing my easel and paints from the hands of the porters in order to carry them to the hotel himself, and fending off the traders who were offering him a young gazelle, desert lizards, damascened daggers, fake antique vases, and other pressing necessities for a tourist. 'Leave them to it,' I said. 'Haggling began in the Orient, and it'll always be a favourite pastime. Let's not forget that we are on historic soil, the stage of Shakespearian dramas, where the ashes of millennial empires have been swept away as if by a croupier's rake. History was played out here, while the participants thought no more about it than their own place in time allowed. Let's think of Hannibal, Scipio Africanus, Antony and Cleopatra, and old Caesar himself. Or of the founders of the world's religions – they also came from the East. The whole fascination of history lies in those players who know how to hold off the moment when the banker pockets stakes and winnings both, and puts an end to the game. Come, let's go and write postcards while we may.'

In the old city of Tunis, I discovered the roof of a greengrocer's shop, which had a magnificent view of the great mosque and the adjoining square, with its processions of weddings, funerals and circumcisions. Swaying camels and heavy-laden donkeys swung through the dark alleys of the souk beneath me; clouds of flies swarmed around the butchers' shops and sweetmeat stalls. A week later, with the painting almost completed, I fell through the roof of the shop, easel and all; even after lengthy bargaining, I had to pay the proprietor a considerable sum of money for a new roof.

The great sight in the red-light district was a naked blonde woman, excessively stout, whose rolls of fat were held in place by straps of gold. She sat on a high, gilded throne on a podium, and the local men slunk around her like nervous cats. But this was something for a reporter rather than a painter, so I continued along the coast to Gabès, an ancient Roman city, where one could hardly keep one's eyes open because the air was so thick with gypsum dust. It was there that the locally-mined raw material for the beautiful white Tunisian jugs was loaded for shipment.

We proceeded inland to Tozeur, where I made friends with a tribe of Kabyle nomads who were wintering there in tents before herding their flocks, in the New Year, to pastures in the Atlas. They were Berbers, a people whose independence even the French authorities had respected. Often blue-eyed and red-haired, in contrast to the dark-skinned population in whose midst they live, they are perhaps descendants of the Vandals, and of Celts displaced by the Romans from Gaul, who had interbred with the pre-historic peoples of Atlas mountains. The Kabyle sheikh wanted to adopt me into his tribe and make me a present of his young wife, whose portrait I painted together with her younger sister. I rode out to the encampment every morning from the hotel, with Lütjens accompanying me on a donkey. The two of us looked like Don Quixote and Sancho Panza, except that he of course was thin and I not fat. There was a great farewell when I had finished my picture and the nomads struck camp; the herdsmen led the camels, goats and sheep; the sheikh and his retinue rode on horseback; the old women went on foot, humping the tent-poles and cooking utensils on their backs or on their heads; but my girl rode at the rear on one of the finest camels, and struck sparks from the cigarette lighter I had given her as a parting gift. I promised not to forget her as long as the lighter still struck light. That was in February 1928.

After Tozeur came Biskra, where, a week later, my driver, a former Foreign Legionary who was trying his luck as a settler, drove me in a decrepit Citroën out to the Col de Sfa on the edge of the desert. From this vantage-point I painted my friends, whom I could see far away on the plain, moving towards the Atlas, while from all directions other tribes were converging to join them.

Patience is a virtue that painters could well learn from the orientals. Early each morning, as I left my little hotel in Biskra, there was a neatly turbanned old beggar sitting on the steps, who greeted me with a benediction; when I returned at dusk he greeted me again. Quite likely he had sat there all day in the blazing sun, without getting bored. He passed his time in waiting.

I always took bundles of old newspapers with me when I went out to paint. By burning them I made a wall of smoke around me to keep out the murderous mosquitoes which not only flew into my eyes but also stuck to the wet paint on my canvas. I often used to send Lütjens out into the desert for a few hours; a sportsman and an athlete, he could get some exercise while I fought my battle with the Lord of the Flies. I always wondered at his ability to find his way back at dusk to my isolated spot in the sand, although meanwhile the earth had swung in its orbit around the sun.

Driven by curiosity to venture forth myself, I came across the *wadi* or dry river-bed where the solitary German traveller Isabella von Eberhardt had been drowned when a sudden cloudburst turned the ground where she was sleeping into a torrent. The Berbers revered her as a 'marabout' or sage.

In the southernmost oasis, in the little village of Témacin, I met one of the White Fathers, the missionaries who played such an important part in the colonization of North Africa. This monk had built himself a cell in the desert, like an Early Christian anchorite, and was passing his last years trying to decipher ancient potsherds and Phoenician inscriptions which he had unearthed.With his permission I painted a picture, unfortunately lost during the Second World War, called *El Kantara*. He introduced me to the powerful marabout of Témacin, who lived in a sizeable palace and traced his ancestry back to Ayesha, the last wife of the Prophet Mohammed. Ayesha had fought heroically alongside her sons to win the independence of the Berber people – perhaps the last act of resistance by a matriarchal culture in historic times. The Shiite Muslims claim to descend from Ayesha's son Ali.

The marabout was a holy man with miraculous powers of healing; he needed only to lay his hands on the sick person. Pilgrims flocked to him from all over North Africa to be cured. He was engaged in building a mosque whose progress one could follow day by day. The building site resembled an Egyptian frieze; chains of local people, mostly women, trudged through the sand, each one with a basket of lime or mortar on his head. Inside the great dome, the architect squatted high on a palmwood scaffolding.With a large knife he drew incisions on the vaulting, free-hand and without preliminary sketches, wherever panes of coloured glass were to be inserted for allowing sunlight in to illuminate the interior. The patterns were marvellous, like an oriental carpet. I climbed up to where he sat, and he showed me the implements – a knife, a lath and a length of ordinary string – with which he had measured out the columns and the vault. Seeing him at work up there, I was reminded of Michelangelo, painting the ceiling of the Sistine Chapel by the light of an oil-lamp. The architect was a grey-bearded old man with a furrowed face, a broken nose and gleaming eyes.

One day, accompanied by the White Father, the marabout himself came to see how the work was progressing. I felt possessed by a wish to paint this powerful personality, a prince of the desert. The White Father conveyed my desire to him, and there ensued a long and animated debate, because of course the Koran forbids the depiction of the human form. The marabout was amenable to argument, however, and the two spiritual authorities, despite their different beliefs, agreed in the end that, since a representation painted on canvas casts no shadow, it is not like a graven image of stone or metal that might be worshipped by idolaters. Learning prevailed over religious prejudice, and I was invited to stay in the marabout's palace as a guest in order to paint his portrait.

The annual fast of Ramadan was in progress, and daily the Berber prince's complexion grew paler, and his temper shorter and shorter. During the thirty days of Ramadan a Muslim may not eat or drink until he can see a piece of thread by the light of the first star of the evening.

The marabout was expecting a visit from the French military commander of the area, who had asked for an audience. Although there were splendid Arab chargers in the stables, the prince insisted on going out to meet the general in a huge, newly acquired Cadillac. Passing through the narrow village street this vehicle brought down the wall of a house, showering the marabout with lime. I happened to be watching from a street-corner, and saw the sheikh's massive hand reach forward and tumble the Negro driver from his seat. A moment later, attendants brought up a fiery black stallion whose hoofs struck sparks from the cobble-stones. In an instant the prince was in the saddle and greeting the Frenchman, who had come, accompanied by the White Father, to enquire about the progress of the new mosque. At this same period a French consortium was engaged in setting up a bank at Témacin. Expert French personnel were at work on it with modern cranes and other building machinery; I learned later that the mosque was ready on schedule, but the bank was never completed.

During Ramadan, I had to be careful, for I had seen the sheikh fly into sudden violent rages. In the courtyard strolled one of his uncles who had a habit of blazing away with an ancient blunderbuss at anything that moved; and I did sometimes sorely need a breath of air after my work. The food was equally disquieting. The unleavened bread contained grubs, and the eggs smelt rotten. I lost weight. I worked nevertheless with great intensity because

I had so many interesting conversations with my sitter. He was much grieved, he told me, that his only child, a little girl – in contrast to the normal Muslim practice he had only one wife – was suffering from trachoma. This eye disease, which ends in blindness, is common in eastern countries because of the flies. The Témacin medicine man was powerless to help. I persuaded my host to send the child, before it was too late, to see an eye specialist I knew in Constantine. He was able to cure her, and the marabout was very grateful for my advice.

On the day following the end of Ramadan – my picture finished, I was preparing to depart – my friend entertained me to a magnificent feast. Servants in white stockings presented the successive courses on dishes of Sèvres porcelain; the table was adorned with costly silver, glass and flowers; and round it sat the menfolk of the sheikh's huge family. Glittering crystal chandeliers illuminated the scene, and everyone addressed himself assiduously to the food. The host offered me the choicest morsel, the eye of a roast sheep, in his great bluish fingers. I was given wine; the others made do with orange-juice. After the meal the marabout withdrew with me to the Arab-style salon, where we were served excellent coffee. We had become fond of one another, and it was hard for us to say goodbye. I pressed him to agree that we should meet again in Paris. This remarkable man, whom half Africa vener-ated as a saint, took on an expression of ineffable mildness, like an ancient Buddha, and told me that he lived like a bird in a golden cage; he could not permit himself to leave.

I returned to Tozeur, and there had an unpleasant brush with two hefty fellows I met on an evening stroll. I was interested in the ancient method of regulating irrigation in the palm-groves, whereby each cultivator drew a certain amount of water from the irrigation channels for a fixed length of time. Surely this rule dates from antiquity; as long as it is honoured there will still be oases in North Africa. The two men had followed me, probably assuming I was one of those foreigners who shared the inclinations of the famous French writer who lived in Old Biskra. As darkness fell, they became more insistent, and it was no easy matter to ward off their impor-tunities, for if I rebuffed them outright they might simply toss me into one of the muddy watercourses on which the livelihood of the village depended. Luckily Lütjens came to my rescue at the last moment; never had I been so glad to see him.

On a hair-raising journey from Touggourt south to Ghadames, we were forced to take refuge from a sandstorm in the lee of one of those strange, tall, conical rock formations which are often capped by a mass of precariously balanced stone. Washed out by cloudbursts, blasted smooth by sandstorms, they look like fossil coral crags on the bed of the sea, wrought into fantastic shapes by the currents. It is hard to believe that North Africa was once the granary of Imperial Rome, and the Sahara a hunting-ground where lions and elephants were trapped for the gladiatorial combats. While he waited for the storm to abate, I began to pick at the crumbled stone lying about us. I found trilobites and parts of oyster-shells which must once have been as big as cart-wheels; but what astonished me most was a fragment of a bone fish-hook, delicately worked, reminiscent of the La Tène period. I had found three similar fragments a little while before, when my brother and I were digging in our garden in Vienna. These finds reaffirmed that the Mediterranean sea once covered both these sites, and that prehistoric lake-settlements had existed along its shores. Everything from the edge of the Sahara to the Vienna Basin must once have been covered by water, which had receded, perhaps because of a gigantic natural catastrophe, and thus caused the destruction of fish and other marine animals.

On the rest of my journey I frequently found similar remains in the desert sand. In one of the biggest Berlin daily papers, belonging to the Ullstein brothers, I later published an article saying that south of the Atlas, along the Algerian and Libyan portions of the Sahara, there were probably oil deposits, just as there were in the Vienna Basin where trial borings had begun some time previously. Exploitation would not require a very large capital expenditure, I thought, because in contrast to the petroleum of North America – where the configuration of the earth's crust is different – the Sahara oil was comparatively close to the surface and more recent in origin. The Ullsteins invited a distinguished oil expert, whose name I think was Figner, to debate with me, and proposed that I should go with him to Baku, where he had a research centre and a fleet of boats, to learn the fundamentals of oil prospecting. Unfortunately other things intervened. Time, however, has borne out my prediction of the richness of the North African oil deposits.

Near the Libyan border, some scarcely-clad natives came out of their caves in a ravine and addressed us in a few words of German, which they had learned in Cologne while serving with the French army during the Allied occupation after 1918. What was that slogan – 'A war to end all wars'? These people certainly didn't look as if they would live to see a second world war.

More than a year later, on another trip to North Africa, I passed through Gabès to catch the ferry for Djerba, a little island in the Mediterranean, off Medenin; in Roman times it was linked to the mainland by a bridge which can still be clearly seen through the blue waters.

I had heard that on Djerba there was a Jewish community dating from before the Diaspora, with an ancient synagogue in the Jewish quarter – and with the most beautiful girls. This captured my imagination; and, indeed, when I arrived I saw by the fountain in the market square, where the women came to fetch water, a maiden of such loveliness that I resolved at once to paint her as the Madonna in remembrance of Titian's *Assumption* in Venice. Never have I been so set on anything; I sought out her father, who was the mayor of the Jewish community. He received me cordially and I was invited to meet the girl on a particular day in his house. I sent at once to Tunis for a large canvas. With beating heart I saw the girl, like the Bride in the Song of Songs, in voluminous trousers of coloured silk and a short embroidered jacket that left her little breasts free, sitting with legs crossed on the divan in the reception room of the house. Sisters and aunts chattered excitedly, straightening the girl's hair and the folds of her garments. The girl said nothing, but she looked so lovely that it was only with some effort that I mastered my feelings sufficiently to get the charcoal outline down on canvas.

The girl was not used to putting her beauty on display or to being the object of public admiration, and she averted her face. 'Oh, look at me, don't turn your eyes away,' I begged – and all was lost. Though I knew a bit of Arabic in those days, I didn't know that to mention the eyes is extremely unlucky, because it attracts the evil eye. The girl fainted and was taken away by the women. After a long wait I realized that I would not be able to continue. I came back the next day. No luck. She did not reappear. This went on for a whole week.

Her father told me that she was tired, and had gone to Tunis. Since I could not remain on Djerba indefinitely, I went to Tunis myself, to have a serious word with the father of the young man to whom she was betrothed. The father was a rich grain merchant, with a large shop in the souks of Tunis. Being rather more a man of the world, he was flattered that I wanted to paint a picture of his future daughter-in-law and show it in a great museum in Europe or even in America. He expressed regret that the bride's family, although orthodox Jews, were still as full of superstitious prejudice as the half-savage Arabs; but there was not much he could do for me. Back on Djerba the girl remained in concealment, although I knocked at the mayor's door every day. The village children, who had previously been so friendly, now became hostile and threw stones at my car. The adults avoided me, and I could get no information about the girl from them. But the Arab postman advised me to see the local magician, who would perhaps be able to help. News in a village travels fast.

The magician lived in a corrugated-iron hut outside the village, in the desert, behind a cactus hedge where refuse was dumped, at the back of beyond. His customers used to come after dark, mostly childless women wanting a fertility charm. I had hired a deaf and dumb black chauffeur, who knew the local roads. I could see that he understood what I wanted, by his gesture of cupping his hands to his chest to signify that a woman was involved. At midnight we went. The medicine man sat on a low stool; his previous customer was a woman to whom he had given a magic spell written on a lizard-skin. Now, sliding a string of moonstones through his fingers, he patiently heard me out, although he already knew what I wanted as well as the postman did.

'I can help you, but you must answer for the consequences. Give me your handkerchief.' He spat in it and rolled it up. 'Take this to the girl's house on the night of the next full moon, and throw it down in the sand in front of the door. She will appear. Be careful not to speak to her. Get her into the car at once and drive away.' On the night of the full moon, I went as instructed to the house of the mayor; the desert foxes were crying in the distance, and it was icy cold. My driver was muffled up to the eyes in his burnous; I was shivering too, but mainly with excitement. In that part of the world the temperature drops very sharply at night, although the days are searingly hot.

When we came to the courtyard wall with its great wooden gates, I threw the crumpled handkerchief down in the sand as I had been instructed. Slowly, and without the touch of a human hand, the gates opened. In the forecourt of the windowless house – Arab houses have no windows on the outside, only round the inner courtyard – there appeared, draped in white, the longed-for maiden. What had I not done just for the chance to see her again! I had bribed an old hag in the hotel to put magic herbs into the food of the mayor's household; and I had bribed the pilot of a private plane belonging to Baron d'Erlanger, who had a lot of property in Carthage, to help me abduct the girl. Now she stood before me with her eyes closed, as if blind, and sighed. How I had waited for this moment! How many feverish, near-sleepless nights had I spent! But could I really carry off a woman who had no will of her own, who was under the hypnotic influence of a medicine man? 'Go back to your father.' At my words she awoke from her sleep, turned away and went back into the house.

My friend Albert Ehrenstein, whom in the autumn of 1929 I had invited to be my travelling-companion, had to summon all his patience when we reached Cairo; his dearest wish was to tread once more on the soil of the land of his fathers. First, however, he had to accompany me every morning to the Pyramids of Gizeh, where, in the blazing heat, I was painting the Sphinx, who crouched there in the desert like Lot's wife. I felt my self-assurance somewhat diminished in the presence of the Sphinx and the Pyramids, for they seemed incomprehensible to the human intellect. What could one say of them except perhaps the famous words Napoleon is supposed to have spoken to his grenadiers: 'Soldiers, from these pyramids forty centuries look down on you.' While painting at Gizeh, I was frequently forced to ward off the sexual advances of young boys and girls, all under age, who offered themselves in return for *baksheesh*. They spent their days pursuing tourists whom their fathers guided around the Pyramids or took for awkward camel rides.

At the hotel, Ehrenstein used to amuse himself by putting out breakfast scraps on the window-sill for the vultures, as at home one feeds pigeons. As soon as we arrived he had at once tracked down a Viennese acquaintance, an oculist; he was always bothered about his health. Trachoma is a scourge in Egypt. The god Baal is the Lord of the Flies, and a plague of flies is still regarded as an unavoidable natural (or supernatural) phenomenon. It is distressing to an outsider to see so many children on the streets who have lost their sight because they tired of warding off the flies. This eye-specialist often invited us to his house, where he also had a clinic. He occasionally showed us with pride his day's handiwork: a tall beer-glass full of dead human eyes, extracted from his patients, who could often be heard, through his padded doors, groaning or crying out with pain.

Ehrenstein also knew a German who lived like a native in the old part of Cairo, in an Arab house full of antiques in which he sometimes traded. There I met the beautiful Princess Eloui, who was living in exile in Cairo after the murder of her young husband, the heir to the Moroccan throne. This young lady afterwards set out to show me the city, better than any guide could have done. She took me up the Nile valley, between steep reddish rocks, to a Coptic monastery where the abbot received her with great respect. As a special compliment to her, he had a magnificent hawk perched on his glove. In her company I admired the sun as it sank, a glowing ball, behind the Pyramids in the desert.

I was often invited to her villa, where I was amazed to find a green lawn; usually only the English can manage such a feat in an arid climate. The drawing-room contained great copper bowls full of fragrant Maréchal Niel roses, which have been my favourites ever since. She lay expectantly on the divan in a Venetian silk dress; I wanted to paint her just like that. She promised to spend a night with me at the columns of Memnon in the desert, as she had done with a famous French poet, because, at night, the columns begin to speak with human voices and predict the future. That she had spent a night there with another man made me jealous; I declined her invitation, said good-bye and left Egypt the next day. To my regret I learned much later that my supposed rival was not attracted to women, but had initiated my princess into the use of narcotics, of which she later died, still young, in a Paris clinic.

Finally I took my friend Ehrenstein to Israel, then still called Palestine, where a British army of occupation was doing its best to keep the Jews and Arabs from each other's throats. I painted Jerusalem from the Jewish ceme-tery, located on a hill with a good view over Zion and its ancient walls. The centre of the city is the El Aqsa mosque, which, to Muslims, is the next holiest place in the world after Mecca. The Holy Sepulchre could not be seen amid the sea of roofs. Nor did I feel any desire to visit it, because at Easter there were always scuffles among the various Christian sects, each of which claimed precedence. In the Jewish cemetery, where I was painting, there were no gravestones; in the adjoining Turkish one there were carved stone turbans to mark the graves of males. As an unbeliever I was not permitted to paint in the Turkish cemetery, though cows grazed there freely. In those days unbelievers were not allowed into the great mosque either.

I left my friend behind in Palestine and went on alone to Athens. But I was too profoundly moved by what I saw at the Acropolis to be able to paint there. And so I went on to Constantinople, in haste to see it before modern civilization, under the regime of Kemal Pasha, could race ahead and put an end to all the romance of the Orient. An end to the veiled women, an end to the baggy trousers which the men (carrying immense loads on their heads, up and down the many flights of steps) were still wearing instead of tight-fitting European cast-offs, an end to the colourful sailing-boats at the Golden Horn and the wooden houses of the old Turkish quarter, soon to be destroyed in a fire. The picture I painted came into the possession of a Jewish indus-trialist, who left it behind in Moravská-Ostrava in Czechoslovakia when he was forced to escape to Canada; it was taken over by the State as national property, and now adorns the office of a party official.

At Christmas 1929, while I was still in Constantinople, I received a tele-gram from a young Swedish woman to whom I was greatly attached, asking me to join her at once. She came originally from Finland, and her mother had been a lady-in-waiting at the Russian Imperial court. I called her Snow-Fragrance. Her telegram had stirred up strong emotions, and I set out immed-iately, taking the seaplane from Terapia on the Bosphorus – the only air service that then existed – to Geneva. The whole story of this adventure can be found in my book *A Sea Ringed With Visions.*

A year later I followed her to Paris. There, after my dear friend Jules Pascin's tragic suicide, I had taken over his house, the Villa des Camélias, where I had often spent nights drinking with him and his odd friends. It was a very cold winter. There was no furniture except a camp-bed, reached by a flight of bare wooden steps from the studio. The water pipes had frozen and burst, and the studio floor and the steps were covered with ice. In the depth of night I slipped – the electric light had been cut off for non-payment – and fell to the studio floor, where I lay until morning with both ankles sprained. Fortunately one of my friends then showed up, an avant-garde Bulgarian painter, who always prudently carried with him a paper bag full of onions and other provisions. In my suitcase he found some drawings which he was able to sell straight away to a rich acquaintance of his; with the proceeds he bought aspirin and a bottle of brandy, which roused me back to life. By evening I not only had some money in my pocket, but could force my swollen feet painfully into my shoes.

The young lady was expecting me to take her out to dinner. When she called at the house, and I told her about my accident, I saw a great tear roll down her cheek. I carefully noted the spot where it fell, and cut out a little piece of the wood from the floorboards as a memento for which, when my tenancy ended in the spring, Pascin's widow made me pay dearly.

From Paris I went to Berlin, where Cassirer's heirs had successfully presented a large exhibition of my North African and Turkish pictures. The firm of Cassirer had a rival in Paul Flechtheim, editor of the magazine *Der Querschnitt* and owner of a gallery, specializing in the work of the French Fauves and their German disciples. I was now labelled as a *Mitropamaler,* a Cook's Tours painter, and this epithet stuck to me for a long time. The German press was interested in 'progressive' ideas, and considered Paris the centre of the world. I survived it. But soon the worldwide financial crisis left me stranded again.

I met a rich Dutchman, a homosexual, who invited me to his estate at Rapallo. I painted a large portrait of his pregnant wife, and then one of him as Bacchus. Still I could not persuade him to part with the money for a ticket to Vienna. When one of my friends advanced the fare home, enabling me at last to depart, I boxed the Dutchman's ears, the only time in my life I have come to blows with anyone. Much later he sold the two paintings to American collections for a very good price.

While at Rapallo I once more met Dorothy Thompson, the great American journalist, who tried to persuade me to go to America. She arranged a job for me as professor of art at an exclusive college for girls in California; however, I let the chance slip, because the renewed danger of war made me reluctant to go too far from my family. Dorothy Thompson also gave me a copy of the *Frankfurter Zeitung* for 8 June 1933, in which my letter about the doyen of German painters, Max Liebermann, had been published in full.

The Editor,
Frankfurter Zeitung,
Frankfurt am Main.   Paris, May 1933

Sir – 'It was a Liebermann who drove the English off the Continent,' – so said a proud kinsman of Max Liebermann's once at a reception given by the future Kaiser Friedrich when he was Crown Prince. This earlier Liebermann was said to have introduced into Germany a new kind of loom, capable of producing dress-fabrics that previously had to be imported from England.

The Old Master, Max Liebermann, whose native wit has made him an institution in Berlin life, has followed his ancestor's example by throwing open a window in his chosen profession, at a time when painting in German studios, with a few shining exceptions, was in a pretty poor state. This began around the 1880s, when Max Liebermann got off the train at the Lehrter Bahnhof, with his paintings done in bright light and in the fresh air, and banded together with Leistikow to found the Berlin Secession. His Kaiser, Wilhelm II, did not apparently think very much of this particular innovation on the part of the Liebermann family; he dismissed Liebermann's achievements as 'gutter art'. He had more feeling for sculpture than for painting.

Max Liebermann has always been stubborn. Romantic, but stubborn. After this setback he continued on his own way; he did not move over to join the Court and history painters who vary their approach to suit their patron's taste. In an age when, as a result of rapid material progress, there was rather a tendency to ostentation, and one heard the view that to possess even a fake Florentine madonna was an essential part of *le bon ton*, Max Liebermann announced, in a celebrated remark, that he preferred a well-painted carrot. An intelligent and responsible artist must inevitably win success by virtue of his professional superiority: these must have been his reflections. Nor can we blame the artist for thinking so. We know that he will outstrip his age in his pursuit of the goddess of truth, and that in his compelling need to grasp his own identity and find his place in the scheme of things, he will inevitably see himself as a little Zeus. This is not surprising, considering that the great Zeus himself is said to have embraced a cloud instead of a goddess.

It is understandable, especially now that the State and the leaders of the community in Germany, and the nation as a whole, have more important things to occupy them, that the individual artist no longer arouses public interest; but for me it is a comradely duty to give my testimony on behalf of Liebermann.

Max Liebermann recently announced his resignation from the Prussian Academy of Arts, after the Aryan Rule had been applied there. He was president of the Academy for many years. The Berlin Secession, which has also incorporated the Aryan Rule in its statutes, will in future be without one of its founder members and former presidents.

I have observed with profound sorrow, a sorrow which increases as I become more remote from Germany and from the events of the present time, that among his fellow artists, men who have followed him all their lives, none has felt – or rather stepped forward to express – regret that this old man of eighty-six, as he passes beyond all artistic associations and their interests, may now do so with a bitter reflection on human insufficiency.

My own life is only half lived, my work is not yet finished, and what I have achieved is problematical. Misunderstood, hounded and hungry – that has been my life since my eighteenth year. A thorny path, like that of most artists. And therefore I may be permitted to speak on behalf of Max Liebermann, whose life's work is done, in the name of his friends and colleagues, the artists of Germany. I know that for me there is no courage involved in taking Max Liebermann's part and saying this: if his decision is now irrevocable, then the parting must take place in friendship, lest a tragic misunderstanding ensue, which can only create discord between teacher and pupils, and damage the building of a new art in the new Germany.

We all know that Max Liebermann was a leader who led us into freedom, into light, into the German forest and the German fields. And we also know that, however great our involvement with a national identity, the root which draws nourishment and strength from eternal human values must not be allowed to wither, but must continue to govern our growth and give us our crown of leaves. Let us not forget that all Fatherlands are rooted in the lap of Mother Earth. Not pyres but beacons of joy should be kindled in honour of the divine mother, to whom the ear of grain, the vine and the rose are consecrated.

Oskar Kokoschka

Dr Heinrich Simon, the publisher of the *Frankfurter Zeitung*, told me later in London that, after the publication of this letter, Government pressure on the paper steadily increased.

Prague

At the beginning of 1934, while in Budapest to give a lecture, I heard from Hungarian friends of an impending putsch in Vienna. I hurried back. My mother and my younger brother still lived in our little house in Vienna. Though a long way from the city centre, the Parliament and the Government offices, where demonstrations were likely to take place, they were close to the workers' housing estates which had just been built on the outskirts, through the efforts of Adolf Loos. The buildings were acknowledged, at home and abroad, to be models of their kind.

Dollfuss, then Chancellor of Austria, had sadly underestimated the danger presented by certain adherents of the Pan-German party. These were largely people impoverished by the loss of their property in the former Crown Lands – estates, and above all factories. They hoped to recover their position of power if Austria were annexed to the Reich. Their political conflict with the Labour Party had led them to form a right-wing private army on the German pattern, led by Prince Starhemberg. In reply the workers armed and dug themselves in within the perimeter of the housing estates, which then the bourgeoisie regarded as Communist armed camps. There were demonstrations and bloodshed, and Dollfuss called in artillery. The like had not been seen in Vienna since 1848.

From our house, looking out over Vienna, we could see buildings burning, and hear the thunder of guns. My poor unworldly mother was at the open window day and night, in despair at the thought that people could be shooting at one another in our own city. She refused to eat or drink, and fell into a sharp decline. Once more I shielded my brother from the sight of death; and I kept the news from my sister Bertha, who lived in Prague and was herself ill, until after the funeral.

Bertha needed an operation, and her husband had gone to pieces ever since the collapse of the Monarchy. He was out of work, and they were living in emergency accommodations. I went to Prague, paid for my sister's operation, and bought a piece of land, where they both began, in the depths of winter, to dig out the foundations for a house. They were to live there for years, in tolerable peace and comfort. My brother-in-law obtained a legal job in the Czech War Ministry, and busied himself with his various collections, brought back from an earlier trip round the world with the Imperial Royal Navy, and above all with his collection of old Bohemian glassware, an interest which I had stimulated. My sister wrote poetry and tended her garden. Their happiness was among the many things I owed to a good friend in Prague, the art dealer Dr Hugo Feigl, who always stood by me.

The *via dolorosa* had begun for millions of innocent human beings. I still find it hard to comprehend the sudden spiritual paralysis that gripped first Germany, then Austria and later all of Europe. That people in Austria started to wear white stockings, or a cock's feather in the hatband, or a swastika on the left arm I could understand; but it remains incomprehensible to me that people fell for the propaganda, the ideological advertising pumped out by the official information media, which stifled free opinion.

All new systems today find their purposes well served by the technological infrastructure of modern civilization, which is able to channel its human material through the labour market and to keep check on it by means of identity cards, party cards, time-cards, and allocations of food and living-space. Now not only a fascist regime but *any* modern political system is in a position to exert a similar effect on the human psyche, restricting the individual freedom we thought had been finally secured. Hence, I suspect, this same 'technostructure' is the reason why modern man looks into the future as fatalistically as a rabbit stares at the cobra which has hypnotized it. The evolution of modern science and technology, promoted by contemporary social systems, has led to those hideous catastrophes we call world wars. It is not enough to single out this or that leader – Hitler or Stalin – or this or that nation, as a scapegoat to bear our sins away. This has served too long as a convenient excuse for the rhetoric of democracy; it certainly does not help the millions who lost their lives, their homelands, their property. I suspect rather that the technostructure of Progress and Enlightenment is itself to blame for the catastrophe: the machine has escaped from our control.

We see the machine today as a sort of human double, preventing us from being what we once were, the measure of all things. We have lapsed into dependency on the machine and its products. One has only to think of the war production with which many States buttress their whole economy in a total denial of rational social existence. Science and technology, like the priestly religion of ancient Egypt, have taught us to believe only in the future – an endless series of five-year plans, offering a utopian prospect. The Egyptians put into the grave with a dead man a number of surrogates, the so-called *ushebti* (also erroneously called *shawabti*), whose duty it was in the next world to work in his stead, draining marshes, watering the soil, carting stones, and also bearing blows and other punishments on his behalf for every act of clumsiness or neglect. Now we ourselves have become, so to speak, surrogates for the machine, mere numbers, or figures like those glazed clay dolls, *ushebti*, on which the name of our vanished personality is written – all that remains of us in a depersonalized world.

The technostructure of our civilization limits our individual expressive possibilities. There no longer seems to be anything incomplete, incomprehensible or infinite about us. Cerebral anatomy already teaches us to conceive of human consciousness as a controllable function. Only the machine becomes ever more complicated, more incomprehensible, and more incalculable in its possibilities. The computer takes over thinking from us. It all verges on magic, in the face of which we remain paralysed, robbed of autonomy, while the earth is laid waste, the rivers, lakes, seas, and the atmosphere itself are polluted, the human race breeds at a pathological rate, and the machine goes on overproducing. World crisis becomes a permanent state of affairs, and East and West alike look calmly on as the Unknown God passes sentence on humanity. It is just as if we were already in the next world, and not in this one for which we are responsible.

Why have the psychoanalysts – who have sprung up in thousands in the United States since Sigmund Freud made his attempt to interpret society's waking dream – concerned themselves almost exclusively with the problem of sex? Why not with the human psyche in general? Why have the scientists and technologists not kept their eyes open? Why did a humanist of the stature of Albert Einstein send his famous letter of 2 March 1939 to President Roosevelt, urging him to initiate the experiments necessary for the production of an atom bomb? In Germany, scientists more far-sighted than Einstein had given up this line of experimentation, telling the Führer that it was too time-consuming, in order to prevent Hitler from getting his hands on such dangerous toys. President Roosevelt's successor, Mr Truman, in the course of a war that once more was to end all wars, carried the experiment to its logical conclusion – Hiroshima. This was inevitable.

Clearly, the consciousness of individual responsibility has gradually diminished in the course of 'Progress'; human existence has become the mechanized production process itself; our acts are becoming meaningless. One cannot with impunity locate consciousness in a section of the cerebral cortex. Consciousness is identical with the sum of the perceptions received through the gates of our senses. If a truly alert consciousness were to hold our attitudes, our behaviour, and our reactions up before us as in a mirror, we would realize, in the west as in the east, that we are crippled beings living in a madhouse. One symptom of our spiritual sickness is the fear of life, the *Lebensangst*, from which modern society in general suffers, and for which no cure is possible without the right diagnosis.

'I am going to Russia,' cried my old friend Albert Ehrenstein, who was a Jew and an optimist. He had read in a newspaper that Jews had been given a special national status there. When he and I arrived outside the door of the Russian Embassy in Vienna, and saw the barbed wire and the guards with fixed bayonets, I thought to myself: No use believing anything you read in the papers. Ehrenstein had obtained the necessary cards, exit visas and passes for me as well. But when I saw more uniformed men in the doorway, I pressed my friend's hand and wished him a good journey. He was lucky enough to come back after a few months, safe and well, but bitterly disappointed.

What kept me in Prague for nearly four years? For one thing, I had to learn to stand on my own feet once more. For another, I was penniless again. I did not believe in Destiny, nor did I feel any inner call or sense of mission, however much I might have needed such a feeling. When people write their memoirs they often claim that their actions followed from some sort of mystical intuition, but I tend to think that such things are tricks played by the imagination. I know that, after my years of good living in the Orient, I felt the danger of getting rusty and the need to get myself back into working order. Periodically one's tools need sharpening.

The Ministry of Education in Vienna had offered me the post of director of the Kunstgewerbeschule, where I had been a student and had once been banned from teaching; but I made my acceptance contingent on the simultaneous introduction, in the whole of the truncated national territory of Austria, of a general educational reform in the spirit of Jan Amos Comenius. How little prospect there was of that, I knew only too well. In Austria, hoping for a magic solution to the problem of unemployment, people had already adjusted to the idea of Anschluss. Nobody grasped that the economic miracle in neighbouring Germany was entirely due to Hitler's preparations for war.

Shortly before the Anschluss my old friend Carl Moll put on a big exhibition of my work in the Österreichisches Museum für Kunst und Industrie; it was a kind of swansong, with the intention of rehabilitating me in Vienna. I wrote an urgent letter to the Chancellor, Dr Schuschnigg, asking him not to return the pictures lent from German collections, because I had already heard from German friends that the Gestapo was planning an exhibition of 'degenerate art' in which my life's work would be exposed to the derision of the mob, and probably destroyed. But in Vienna they stood by the letter of the law and punctiliously sent the pictures back. In 1937 the Nazi exhibition took place in Munich, moving after the Anschluss to Vienna, the capital of what was now called Ostmark. I responded with a poster in the streets of Prague, urging that the Basque children, victims of the Fascist attacks on Guernica, should be given a home in Bohemia, and at the same time warning of a future attack on Czechoslovakia, represented in the background of my picture of Hradčany Castle in flames. My posters were torn down by the Prague police, in order to avoid unwanted diplomatic complications, but overnight some young people stuck them up again. From Breslau the German radio threatened me: 'When we get to Prague, you'll be strung up from the nearest lamp post!'

But I am running ahead of myself; all this happened only in 1938, the year of the Munich agreement, when out of fear of the German dictator the protectors of the Czechoslovakian republic deserted the cause of their people. At that time the well-equipped Czech army would still have been strong enough, with the help of the Allies, to hold the upstart in check. Its only function thenceforward was to keep order inside the country itself.

I had arrived in Prague in the late summer of 1934, and taken to wandering round the city to become familiar with it. In the market – unlike Vienna's, it was laden with meat, fruit and vegetables – I bought a load of stinging-nettles, well known as a remedy for rheumatism, from which I had been suffering ever since Paris. Early each morning I would lay them out on the floor and roll in them, naked, until I was covered with nettle-rash. After two weeks I no longer felt the irritation, and the nettles had no more effect. But I was cured.

I liked being in Prague. The city had once more become a cosmopolitan centre, as it had been after the Thirty Years War. Here, for the last time, all Europe could meet. By comparison with modern cities, their uniform sky-scrapers and their concrete proletarian barracks, Prague had remained the creation of a cultivated society – or had become so again. There, in the Middle Ages, in the Renaissance, and again in the age of the Baroque, the architects, sculptors, painters, goldsmiths and woodcarvers of all the nations of Europe – Italians, Frenchmen, Flemings, Germans, Tyrolese – had vied with the native Bohemian artists in creating churches, palaces, and town houses, as if to warn future generations against discord and to prove what nations can achieve, in harmony and in the work of skilled hands, if only they behave like human beings. Today this precious jewel on the Vltava is falling into decay, partly from neglect, partly from sheer poverty. The present Czechoslovakian republic is a tributary state; its production – purely industrial in nature, as the age demands – must be sent abroad. Culture has become a forbidden luxury.

In the four years between 1934 and the autumn of 1938, I painted sixteen landscapes, mostly in Prague, utilizing a number of viewpoints within sight of the Vltava. This river fascinated me as the Thames did. I enjoyed painting the city, not to represent its topography, nor to capture momentary sensations in the Impressionist manner, but because cities today are built upon sand, and their inhabitants neither preserve the past nor count on the future, which they tend on the contrary to fear. When, with Olda Palkovská, I left Prague for ever in October 1938, I felt as if the red sunset reflected on the river were signalling Europe's final hour; in London I painted Prague again from memory, and called the painting *Nostalgia*.

In Czechoslovakia there lived five nationalities: the majority people, the Czechs, who might be anything from janitor to government official; the Moravians, who had once possessed a great kingdom reaching to the North Sea and a culture of their own, and who now worked in agriculture or industry on which the country lived; the Slovaks, who were mainly day-labourers; the Germans, whose traditional crafts were dying out and who were becoming, as a result, politically conscious; and finally the Jews. The Jews of Prague were a strange sort of people – mystics who interpreted the Kabbala and believed in the Golem. Modern Austrian literature was the exclusive creation of Jews from Prague and Brno who had been brought up in Austria-Hungary in the humane and enlightened tradition of Joseph II. Today in Czechoslovakia the Jews have been exterminated. They faithfully hung on to the Czech ship of state as if it had been Noah's ark, but the ship was not seaworthy.

During the years I spent in Czechoslovakia these five nationalities lived there side by side and did not interfere with one another. They may not always have understood each other, or spoken the same language; but a bird in a tree does not understand a squirrel, nor does the squirrel understand the mouse at the foot of the tree, yet they all rest content with their lot and accept the proffered chance of staying alive. Perhaps they are even useful to each other, like the bee who carries pollen from flower to flower and thus fertilizes the plants.

One day I received a visitor, Dr. K. B. Palkovsky, who knew my work through Cassirer, and who invited me to call at his house. He subsequently helped me a good deal both in Prague and London. I did four little etchings for a stage play he had written; unfortunately only a few proofs were taken. On one of my visits to Palkovsky's I met his daughter Olda. We became friends. She was studying law and preparing for her doctorate, though she would have liked to become an art historian. She often called for me at my studio, and we would walk through the old gardens and parks to her parents' house, on the heights behind the Hradčany. On the way we bought roasted chestnuts from an old street-seller and I told her stories, which I later wrote down; but she was to maintain, long afterwards, that at first hearing she did not understand them. I have never lost my Viennese dialect, whereas at school she had learned the precise old High German of Prague. Still, we understood each other very well.

We went to the theatre, although I have never mastered the Czech language. There were two theatres we particularly loved: one with a musical revue, written and performed by two clowns such as I have never seen since, Voskovec and Werich; the other, an avant-garde theatre which made a great impression on me because the actor-director Emil František Burian had devised a modern system of staging that really succeeded, instead of remaining a mere aspiration. I knew the play *Spring Awakening*, by Wedekind, very well, and so the performance was a real experience for me even though I did not understand a word.

I wonder, have I ever really believed in humanism, enlightenment, free thought? My favourite opera, *The Magic Flute*, reflects the conflict between dark magical powers and the bright light of consciousness. A little while ago, when my wife was in Prague – I never go back there – she made a discovery. For a time I had had my studio in a tower adjoining a house by the river. Revisiting the house she found a bricked-up spiral stairway which had once served to connect the studio with the rooms below. At one time apparently my studio was accessible only through this secret entrance, a variant of the English priest-holes of the Reformation period. The studio was probably in the past a meeting-place for the banned Freemasons' lodges, a supposition reinforced by the fact that there are still acacia trees (the acacia is a Masonic symbol) growing on the quay beneath.

My father had a ring which, because he was in debt, he sold to his brother. The ring bore a Masonic sign, which my father used often to show me proudly when I was a child. He had inherited it, as the eldest son, from his father which means that my grandfather was probably a Freemason. Hence, it is even possible that he attended secret meetings in the very same room in which I worked for a short time in the 1930s. Rooms have a history of their own, and they preserve and pass on something intangible – if Progress does not too rapidly sweep them away.

Early in my stay in Prague, as I have said, I made the acquaintance of Dr Hugo Feigl, a small-time art dealer, who accompanied me for days on end, as I wandered about the city looking for places to paint from. When I located a house, garden or even a flat from which I thought there might be a good view he persuaded the owners to allow me to paint there; and it was he who found buyers for the resulting pictures. I needed money, and times were hard. Feigl was one of those dealers who have a sense of mission and are not only in pursuit of money. Neither for nor against the modern, he believed in the eternal nature of art. Luckily he escaped just before the German troops marched in. He fled to New York, where the all-powerful local art-dealers ignored him, as a wren might be ignored by vultures and hawks.

Feigl put me in touch with the President of Czechoslovakia, Tomás G. Masaryk, and persuaded him to have me paint his portrait. Though invited to be Masaryk's guest at his summer residence, I preferred to remain in town. I was collected every morning by his official car with the registration number I, at the sight of which the sentries at his gate sprang to attention. I had never met a Head of State before; and here was one who owed his place not to the mystery of God's grace but to the rhetoric of democracy, who might be a human being, and not a Nietzschean superman. Masaryk wore neither crown nor sceptre, nor yet a Jacobin cap; he did not sit on a throne, but looked rather like a senior civil servant under the old Monarchy: a gentleman with a slim silhouette, and an aristocratic bearing, although he is said to have been the son of a coachman on a country estate. A fortunate combination of circumstances had enabled him in his youth to go to university in Vienna, where his ability had later won him a professorial chair; he had then become a celebrated parliamentarian, acquiring an international reputation through his courageous interference in political trials. His people had deputed him to sign the Czechoslovakian declaration of independence in Washington, and he came home as first President of his country. Once, in private conversation, he told me that if he had had his way the Habsburg monarchy would not have been dismembered, but rather transformed into a federal association of nationalities.

Masaryk's daughter instructed me to be very careful because the great man was rather frail; he had recently suffered a slight stroke. For his portrait, he wanted to pose astride the arm of a chair, because he looked well in riding-breeches and boots. I dissuaded him, realizing that to hold such a pose daily for several weeks would have been too much of a strain. While I worked I was in the habit of drinking strong black coffee, which he was not allowed to have. Once he asked if he could have a cup too, without his daughter knowing. I poured one out, and as he drank he laughed so much at his own naughtiness that I wagged my finger at him: 'Mr President, you look like a mischievous boy who has stolen an apple.'

During the three or four weeks I worked on his portrait, we became friends and talked a lot about the educational ideas of Comenius. He agreed with me that the educational system run by the State is wholly one-sided and misconceived, a second-hand education, all from books and hearsay, instead of from looking facts in the face and from experience. It does not turn young people into human beings but into material for the labour market and the barracks. But Masaryk could, I told him, with his authority as Head of State, reform education, and put into practice those methods for which Comenius fought so hard. And this is why, on Masaryk's left, I painted Jan Amos Comenius, pointing to a chart showing the organs of the five senses, the sources of awareness, the gates of perception of the human experience.

Masaryk used to enjoy tracing the etymology of his own language. In an old dictionary he found that my name, which in other Slavic languages has the meanings of 'cat', 'cockerel', etc., stands in Czech for the plant called shepherd's purse, a well-known weed. This gave pleasure to us both, for the proverb says that 'ill weeds grow apace'. Later I heard that when there were differences of opinion in conversations with his family and friends, he would sometimes declare, 'If only Kokoschka were here, he'd agree with me.'

During one of our last meetings, Masaryk said to me, in a troubled tone: 'If the Czechoslovakian republic is allowed to reach its twentieth anniversary in reasonable peace, then there is some hope that it will survive.' The year was 1936; just eighteen years had passed. In the twentieth year after the founding of the state, German troops marched into the Sudetenland and, a few months later, into Prague. Masaryk himself did not live to see the collapse of his house of cards. His idea of a humanistic state, like the educational ideas of Comenius, was fated to remain utopian.

Even before the annexation of Austria, which cost me my citizenship, Masaryk had offered me a Czech passport. After his death I took up the offer; you can't exist anywhere today without a rubber stamp on a piece of paper. After I fled to London, this document saved me from being interned.

Unfortunately Dr Eduard Beneš, who was elected President by the National Assembly after Masaryk's retirement, made a serious mistake. He had been elected by the almost unanimous votes of all four nationalities within the republic. I myself saw the special trains that brought the German-speaking citizens from the frontier areas to vote in the National Assembly in Prague. There had been wholly erroneous fears that they would switch their votes to the pro-Nazi Henlein party. Beneš gave them pretty poor thanks for it. One of his first political acts after the Second World War was the expropriation and expulsion of nearly a third of the population of his country. The Gestapo had been there before him, virtually exterminating the adherents of the Social Democratic Party of the old Monarchy, most of whom lived in the frontier areas.

I never trusted Beneš. I was introduced to him at a reception in London during the war. He had a trick I saw through. Because he was a small man, he used to crane his neck to listen in such a way that any taller person who was introduced to him had to bow all the deeper. When my turn came to be presented, I played a trick of my own on him. Bowing deeply, I reached into my pocket and pulled something out, looking round furtively to see if I was being observed – just as I had seen vendors of pornographic postcards do in the streets of Paris. 'Mr President,' I whispered, 'if the secret policemen here knew what I have in my pocket, then not only I but you too would be in trouble.' The President was irritated, because what I showed him was the book *The Net of Faith*, which was forbidden reading in the Czech army. Its author, Petr Chelčicky, is a religious thinker I very much admire. Chelčicky, in contrast to Hus, the fighter, denied the state's claim to authority and power, preached against capital punishment, oath-taking and military service, and promulgated the pure doctrine of Christian charity. In fact, even Masaryk, though an impassioned believer in Comenius, had his reservations about Chelčicky.

I heard the news of Masaryk's death in Moravská-Ostrava, south of Prague, where I had been invited to paint a view of the town. I met there Ernst Korner, a friend of my youth, whose brother, the wealthy Professor Emil Korner, commissioned me to paint a self-portrait for him, a picture that became well known as the *Self-portrait of a Degenerate Artist*.

This was the summer of 1937, when the notorious exhibition of 'degenerate art' took place in Munich. I had the honour of being represented by a number of pictures. The Gestapo had already confiscated my paintings from museums and private collections all over Germany and the occupied territories, and these were in imminent danger of being destroyed. Thanks to a

Prague Jew, Masaryk's portrait reached New York. It was finally acquired by the Carnegie Institute in Pittsburgh, where it still hangs today.

The Institute's president, Homer Saint-Gaudens, came specially to Prague to present me with that year's Carnegie Award. But upon his arrival he received a telegram from Pittsburgh saying that it was impossible to give the prize to a German, political conditions being what they were at the time. The forcible incorporation of Austria into the Reich had already been accepted in America as a legal fact, another example of the notorious naivety of the Americans. I could have done with that prize. Mr Saint-Gaudens was an honest man, and he was highly embarrassed. He arranged to get me a job teaching art at one of the major American universities, having seen with his own eyes how precarious my situation in Prague was. Under the circumstances, I had already signed the contract, when suddenly I thought of my sister in Prague and my brother in Vienna, and began to feel that America was too far away. I have never liked the idea of being an émigré, but since my youth I had been accustomed, whenever I grew tired of a place, to moving on to somewhere else where I could live. The only problem now was where to go.

The cosmopolitan society of Prague was rapidly dissolving into thin air. I seemed the only person without a plan. I simply could not decide. Many went to France, but I had only bad memories of Paris, and was distrustful of the French authorities. One episode exemplifies those many occasions in my life when I have been right more through my 'sixth sense' than through reason. In my Dresden days I had drawn two lithographs of my friend Walter Hasenclever for the Paul Cassirer publishing house. As usual, I had given one copy of each to the director of the firm, Dr Walter Feilchenfeldt; they were often inscribed with comical or whimsical remarks. As it happened, much later Feilchenfeldt smuggled his son and his property from Berlin to Holland, where that truly courageous man Dr Lütjens concealed the Jewish child from the Gestapo. In 1947, when we saw the Feilchenfeldts again in Zurich, the remnants of the collection had just arrived from Holland. We looked through the many proof impressions that had survived and found, to our astonishment, these words that I had written on the big lithograph of Hasenclever: 'Dear Feilchen, don't go to Paris. W. H. went there and that was the end of him.' What I had ironically predicted in the 1920s had come tragically true in 1940. The Vichy regime had many opponents of the Nazis, especially Jews, in its internment camps, and after the fall of Paris it began turning them over to the Gestapo. Hasenclever killed himself in the camp at Les Milles in 1940.

Now that the guarantors of Czechoslovakian independence, led by England and France, had refused to make good their word, it was impossible for me to remain in Prague. Since the infamous Munich agreement it had become increasingly difficult to leave the country. By the end of 1938 only people on official business were permitted to travel. I had hesitated long enough; now I decided to make for England. Olda Palkovská realized that I could not stay. For days on end she stood in queues, waiting to buy air tickets which could still be purchased with Czech money. It galled me that the government, apparently intent on keeping the national wealth intact for the invaders, whose armies were poised to strike, allowed us to take out no more than ten English pounds each. But there was no point in arguing.

We still did not know whether we would be allowed to land in London, because the Immigration Officers had complete discretion over admissions. In the English papers there were fresh stories every day about refugees who had been refused.

One Friday Olda returned with surprising news. There were two seats left on a plane to London the next morning, and she had booked them without waiting to ask me. It was a good thing she did; otherwise, I would most probably not be alive today. That evening we went to a well-known coffee-house frequented mostly by foreign journalists, the remnant of cosmopolitan Prague. Naturally we were worried that we might not be admitted into England. Olda had immediately sent a telegram to Jan Masaryk, the Czech Ambassador in London, whom we had known in Prague some years before, to tell him we were coming. But it was a weekend, and no self-respecting Englishman – let alone a diplomat – will let himself be seen in Town at the weekend. A Canadian journalist I knew by sight came to our table. Over a schnaps we explained our situation, and he put our minds at rest. 'You're arriving in London tomorrow afternoon. I'm catching an earlier plane, and I'll take up your case right away with Lord Cecil.' This was the Lord Cecil who had been a very important diplomat at the League of Nations, and had won the Nobel Peace Prize in 1937. 'He'll call the Home Office, and everything will work out.' And it did.

We were allowed only hand luggage, but we did manage to take with us a little picture that is now in the National Gallery of Scotland in Edinburgh. It went as excess baggage, and cost a good part of our ten pounds.

The flight was really very pleasant; sunlit landscapes passed beneath us like photographs in a holiday brochure. It was still daylight when we arrived in London, where the Immigration Officer flicked through our papers, looked at our faces and into his book, and said, 'All right.'

The Years in England

Soon after we arrived I left my card on John Rothenstein, the Director of the Tate Gallery, who telephoned the same day and invited me to see him for tea. Perhaps I had been counting too much on getting dinner; I was very hungry. But we had to be content with sandwiches. Olda and I concealed our smiles when the Director, in his charming way, asked me at once, 'What beautiful things have you brought over from Prague? Our modern collection would very much like to possess a picture by you, if you will present it to us; we do feel the lack of a work by such an important representative of modern art.' Later the Czech Government in exile presented one of my paintings to the Tate.

One of my earliest friends in England was Edward Beddington-Behrens. He liked my work and once persuaded his acquaintance Mr Dreyfus to commission from me a portrait of the Russian Ambassador, Ivan Maisky, which I have mentioned earlier.

Before long I was able to make a living. My first commission came from a young English friend, Michael Croft (the future Lord Croft), who asked me to paint portraits of himself and his sister. He was also the first Englishman to understand me properly; I was still relatively unknown in England, although I was already over fifty and had achieved an international reputation before being pilloried on the Continent as a degenerate artist.

Shortly after our arrival, I had received a hundred-pound note as a loan from our friend Professor Korner. Compared with any of today's banknotes, this was the most elegant form of money since gold went out of circulation. In its paper, type, drawing, layout, it was a masterpiece of craftsmanship, comparable to showpieces of the applied arts such as the Chippendale furniture and Lalique vases in the Victoria and Albert Museum. It was a wrench to part with it, but it was all the money we had at the time.

We stayed at first, by necessity, in a cheap boarding-house full of immigrants of all colours. Then we moved to Polperro, on the south-west coast,

12. *OK as a dragoon*

13. *OK on the Isonzo Front, 1916*

14. *Daisy Spies sitting for OK*

15. *Lithograph of Olda by OK*

16. OK in London, 1942

17. OK in Hyde Park, 1962

18. OK in the library at Villeneuve

19. *OK at work*

20. OK with Olda in their garden at Villeneuve

because it was cheaper there than in crowded London, and because we could breathe the pure sea air. We lived in a block-house on a cliff towering over the sea. Unfortunately, for security reasons, painting in the open air was soon forbidden; instead, I took to sketching on the beach with coloured pencils.

A shy young man, an industrial draughtsman named Phillip Moysey, often came to watch me draw. He asked to become my pupil. To test his serious-ness, I laid down the following stipulations, to be fulfilled before I would take him on: first that he should in my presence throw his paint-box, brushes, eraser, and ruler into the sea; and next that he should watch, as I did, the crabs running in the sand, the seagulls flying, the scudding clouds, and the fish in the sea, until he thought he could reproduce his impressions with coloured pencils on paper. He was rather taken aback by this, because he was poor; but he followed me, and we are still friends. For the last thirty years he has been living in a gipsy caravan which he bought cheap and decorated in gay colours; he eventually added a horse. He does splendid nature paintings which no modern art-dealer will buy, for nature is out of fashion. Perhaps he will be discovered when he is dead.

In front of our house at Polperro I painted a large foul-smelling crab some-one had given me. Another picture, called *Private Property*, shows a cat stand-ing guard over some dead fish, and in the background an old lady with a parasol and a little bag, going for her constitutional along the beach. I was astonished at the sheer phlegm of the English, who remained heedless of the war, while on the Continent people were letting the Führer drive them over the edge of the abyss like panic-stricken sheep.

France capitulated, and there were no more onions to be had, for they came of course from Brittany. That was something to worry about! The coast was declared a Protected Area, and foreigners were forced to move inland. A few days earlier Michael Croft had paid us a visit. He was already in uniform. We sat on the grassy cliff top, just after hearing the news of the fall of France, which seemed so near that we almost felt we could see it. With con-viction our young friend said:'We can't lose the war. That's impossible.' To the majority of Englishmen, who have often lost battles but never a war, it was inconceivable that they might lose this war that they had declared to protect Poland. Meanwhile, pleasure-boats rescued from Dunkirk what was left of the British army.

We returned to London, this time to an elegant if rather dilapidated house that had been left empty on account of the war. It belonged to a lady who had moved to the country, the friend of a friend of ours, Lady Drogheda.

In September 1940 the bombing of central London began in earnest. A bomb went off near by, tearing a great hole in the road, and shattering the big window in the room overlooking the garden, where I did my flower-painting. Because I needed light, we could not board up the window, though in winter it was freezing indoors, and fuel for heating was scarce. Fortunately we had a bathroom in which the hot water still worked. Its walls had been decorated with lifesize photographs of film stars: Marlene Dietrich, showing her legs, Greta Garbo, the enigma, Lilian Gish, whom I specially loved, and Mae West with her lavish bosom. Years later, at a champagne reception in New York to celebrate the opening of a retrospective exhibition of my pictures, Marlene Dietrich showed me her legs in the flesh. But then, in London, the photographs were peeling from the steam of the bathroom, and the ladies bowed their heads in greeting when you opened the door.

Every night, air-raid or no air-raid, Olda would go to bed after her bath and read a book. She was untroubled by what happened in the sky; you can't get worked up every day of your life. I too refused to spend the night in an air-raid shelter, where one could only get rheumatism or worse.

At Christmas we heard that a local pub still had some stocks of French wine. We had just started home with our priceless booty – the sirens had sounded the All Clear – when a brilliant burst of magnesium flares overhead momentarily lit up the area, disclosing the wall of a graveyard disused since the eighteenth century. These flares were to show the bomber crews their targets. We fled round a corner, and lost both each other and the wine-bottles in the ensuing pitch-darkness. We found one another again when our eyes readjusted to the blackout, but we did not find the bottles until the next morning, just in time for Christmas Eve. The street was littered with disinterred skulls and bones; their souls, I hope, had long found eternal repose in Heaven.

We often visited some émigré friends who served by day in the British Home Guard, and entertained at home in the evenings with chamber music. Their music room was hung with enormous pictures by minor masters. One night I sat on a sofa beneath one of these great daubs, depicting Luther at the Diet of Worms speaking the celebrated words: 'Here I stand, I can do no other!' The massive wooden frame, weighing several hundredweight, shook every time a bomb went off. Olda, who sat opposite, watched me and thought: 'If the house shakes any worse, that picture will fall on him and break his neck.' Quietly, to avoid disturbing the music, she crept over and tried to get me to move. I was just protesting that I could hear quite well where I was, when abruptly a girl burst in with the cry: 'London's on fire!' It was a clear summer night. The Germans had dropped incendiary bombs on the City. St Paul's Cathedral had not been hit, but the whole area round it, the City of London, the heart of world commerce, with all its offices and law-chambers, was in flames. From the roof of that house in Hampstead we watched London burn as Nero had once watched Rome. It was said that no one was killed in the raid; even the cats followed their instinct and escaped over the many-gabled roofs of the business houses.

The next morning, a Monday, we had to go to the City to see our lawyer about passport problems. Without thinking, we took the Tube, and came to the surface in the midst of an inferno. Iron railings were glowing red, trade signs were falling from the gateways, façades had burst open, there were ambulances and casualty stations with uniformed girls handing out cups of tea, and fire-hoses blocked our path. The girls chattered gaily to the firemen, although they had all been working through the night. The wall of a building collapsed before our eyes. The whole district was filled with smoke and flames. We gave up our errand and turned back in a mood of exhilaration such as is possible, in the face of disaster, only in England.

The giant captive barrage balloons, which were much mocked when they first went up, saved London from destruction. The new invention of radar played its part as well, making low-level approaches by the Luftwaffe too costly, so that the decisive air battles were fought not over London but over the coast. That is what one heard, anyway; I understand nothing of military matters.

In the worst days of the war, music and the theatre played a major part in maintaining morale. I have the feeling that there has never been so much good acting or music-making since. London was full of theatres and small concert halls. The huge Albert Hall was too dangerous, but it remained, together with the Albert Memorial, intact for posterity. During performances, two little lamps, one red, one green, lit up to signal the Alert and the All Clear. People could, if they wanted, go down into the air-raid shelter; but I can hardly remember anyone actually leaving. Tickets, though not expensive, could be obtained only by queueing up six weeks in advance; there were none for sale on the night of a performance. It was a major disaster if you then forgot to go.

We saw an unforgettable *Peer Gynt* at the New Theatre, featuring Laurence Olivier as the mysterious button-moulder and Ralph Richardson as Peer Gynt, with his vision of carrying his dying mother up to heaven; there was a wonderful Solveig, singing her eternal love-song from the depths of the forest. It made us forget how small the stage was. We also saw Donald Wolfit as King Lear, a Rembrandtesque vision.

The National Gallery – its valuable pictures removed to the country – presented lunchtime chamber concerts every day, for which the admission charge was one shilling. The idea had come from the pianist Myra Hess; she had in mind the young office-workers who would rather go without lunch than miss the chance of hearing a classical concert. Together with Lady Clark, the wife of Sir Kenneth Clark, Director of the National Gallery, I opened in the Cooling Galleries in January 1943 an exhibition of drawings and paintings by refugee children under the title 'The War as Seen by Children'. In my opening speech I said: 'The astonishing spirit of solidarity among children derives from their love of creation, which is common to children the world over, before they are spoiled by education. An uncreative child is the exception. Unfortunately the creative grown-up is also an exception.'

I had been elected honorary president of the Freier Deutscher Kulturbund, the Free German League of Culture, which in keeping with the times was, as people said in London, 'very left', and in whose periodicals and books I tried to lay a few humanistic cuckoo-eggs. I believed that freedom cannot be grasped in terms of theory; freedom is an individual matter and depends on the capacity to think in a truly unfettered and unprejudiced way.

In 1941 Olda and I were married at a registry office in an air-raid shelter. A friend from Polperro days, the German sculptor Uli Nimptsch, whom our friend Lady Drogheda had rescued from internment, was a witness. It was no time for celebrations; that night we went to the cinema.

During this period I painted a series of 'political' pictures, not out of any political commitment, but with the intention of opening others' eyes to the way I saw the war. *The Red Egg* was painted between 1939 and 1941. In it, a roast chicken prepared for eating – Czechoslovakia – flies away and drops a red egg on the plate. In the background Prague burns; round the table sit Mussolini and Hitler with a soldier's helmet made of paper; under the table is a cat with a Napoleonic hat and cockade, and behind, its tail curled into a pound sign, the British lion on a pedestal with the inscription IN PACE MUNICH. The picture was prophetic, in its way. In 1942 I painted a second picture, *Alice in Wonderland,* about the Anschluss, and shortly afterwards, *The Lorelei.* In this painting Britannia no longer rules the waves; inaction has lasted too long; an octopus swims away with a trident, the emblem of marine power. Queen Victoria, who built up the British fleet into a dominant position, rides on a shark and stuffs white, brown and black sailors into its mouth. Only the frog on her hand refuses to accept the same fate: it represents Ireland, where there are no reptiles except frogs. Another picture is called *Marianne-Maquis*. Marianne, the personification of France, has not been able to hide herself behind the Maginot Line; now she sits in a café, where she draws back her little skirt for fear of a rat; around her, coffee-sipping field-marshals do nothing but look on.

The last of these pictures, *What We Are Fighting For*, painted in 1943, was the one I meant most seriously. A bishop is blessing the troops, and with his free hand is dropping a penny into the Red Cross collecting-box; an endless procession of prisoners file along with hands raised; in a rickshaw pulled by Gandhi sit the Governor of the Bank of England, Montague Norman, the President of the Reichsbank, Hjalmar Schacht, and a Marshal of France; in the foreground lies a starving mother holding an emaciated child who is play-ing with a rat. The prospering American munitions industry appears as a globe-like monster with two levers for arms, one pulling out a blue rabbit, signifying peace, as an emblem of hope for the future, while the other crams human bones into the armaments machine which turns them into cartridges. In the right foreground stands a bust of Voltaire with the inscription CAN-DIDE, i.e., 'the best of all possible worlds'.

One visitor who saw the finished picture remarked on its sadness, despite the presence of so much yellow. 'Yellow should be a happy colour; the sun is yellow,' he said. But for me yellow has an effect similar to that of white; it is like the dead moon, in opposition to red, the colour of life. For the Chinese, yellow represents death. Black, the colour of mourning, I consider no colour at all: it does not exist in life. Colours always have values to me, like warnings or traffic signs; but this has never consciously influenced my painting, nor has it anything to do with colour symbolism. It is simply that I conceive of life and death in terms of colour. When that visitor, who was no art expert, appeared to be so downcast by my picture, I felt that I had been understood.

Let me say once more that I did not paint these pictures because I felt a political involvement of any specific kind. I was staying in England only in order to see war this time from the other side of the barricades. People are all the same.

Unlike George Grosz, who painted his whores and his fat, lustful bour-geois in Berlin in time of peace, and in a spirit of criticism and hatred, I raised my voice in London in wartime because the time and the circumstances made it imperative to become human once again. In the same year it was painted, the picture *What We Are Fighting For* was shown under a temporary roof in the bombed-out John Lewis department store on Oxford Street. A number of artists had been invited to contribute pictures on this theme of what we should be fighting for. My paintings attracted little notice, because they contained no promise of an idyllic peace. Yet I marvelled that in the middle of a war for survival no one bit my head off. That was only possible in England; there I could hope to carry on my life, not as a tolerated refugee, but as a free human being. A daring hope, when in other countries it was even forbidden to perform Beethoven's symphonies!

I was moved to a public protest by reports of the saturation bombing of German cities – Dresden above all, the old city I knew so well, which had no strategic significance, and was full of hundreds of thousands of refugees who had fled from the Russians. In England one was free to make such protests. Still, I was afraid that after the frightful tragedy of this war, after the constant bombing raids on English cities, the English people too might fall prey to panic and chauvinism. It is easy for a deliberate hate campaign to warp the character of a nation, however exceptional it may be. Meanwhile, the debris and the ruins were cleared up after every air raid, and life went on as before.

My friend Edward Beddington-Behrens arranged for me to have a room to paint in on the top floor of an office block in Mayfair. It was not far from Marble Arch, where orators of various persuasions and races stood on little podiums every Sunday, haranguing groups of hearers. Many people went there purely for entertainment. In this room I painted a portrait of my dear friend Lady Kathleen Drogheda. In her youth she had been one of the first women pilots in England and had made sensational journeys to the Orient, including China, and had been a star of high society. She was no longer very rich, and I painted her for nothing. Though she had the air of a great lady of the old school, she was actually the daughter of a Scottish minister. In spite of her age, she turned up bright and early for the sittings, after having already cleaned her little flat; she washed the stairs herself, with her arthritic hands, because, as she said, the housemaids were all working in factories.

I had arranged the pose and the composition of the portrait, after a moment's reflection, on the assumption that my sitter would fall asleep after half an hour. And so she did, every time. But once, on a Sunday morning, one of the enormous new V-2 bombs exploded directly opposite my studio, in Hyde Park, where a little later hundreds of people would be gathering to listen to the orators at Speakers' Corner. A single Methodist preacher had set up his pitch rather early; nothing more was ever seen of him.

The explosion shattered windows for a mile around, including those of our house. Only my attic ones remained whole. Kathleen woke up. 'What's happened? A bomb?' I soothed her: 'Someone's merely slammed a door!' I went peacefully on with my work. When I showed the old lady out after the sitting, she saw what had happened, and for long afterwards took great pleasure in telling her friends how brave she had been. The portrait, after her death, went to a faithful friend of hers, an Albanian diplomat.

In summer we occasionally accepted an invitation to stay with friends in Scotland, where I did watercolours of the fish, pheasant and partridge that they caught. We also gathered flowers from a neighbouring estate; they were withering on the stem for want of someone to pick them. The game provided a chance to eat fresh meat; but I made do with the abundant eggs and vegetables. When I paint I identify with my subjects; how then could I eat them afterwards?

One day on a walk, we rescued a mother ewe. The pitiful bleating of its lamb attracted our attention to a ditch, where the ewe had fallen in and could not get out unaided. Its thick fleece had become waterlogged, and it took so much effort to extricate the struggling animal that it was surprising I didn't pull my arms out of joint. I liked drawing sheep, and it upset me to see, on the moor, the skeletons and eyeless skulls of those animals which had perished in the severe winter of the previous year. I also loved to draw the bison-like, long-haired, terribly small Highland cattle; they looked pleasantly less dangerous than the bulls in a Spanish ring.

We knew two eccentric Englishmen, both keen shots, who lived an isolated life with a pack of lazy gundogs, in a once fine house that lay deep in a boggy wood, overgrown with mouldering creepers. There were so many dogs lolling about on the sofas and chairs that one had trouble finding a place to sit down. Pheasant being out of season, rabbits were the only game; what the dogs left over, the men ate. Once, out of boredom, they began firing at their own reflections in the ceiling-high mirrors. We called on them no more after that.

The bleak Scottish moorland is a human creation. In the early nineteenth century the local lairds evicted their tenants in order to get a higher rent from Englishmen shooting grouse. All landscapes are given their shape by man; without a human vision no one can know what the world really is.

Just to get out of London during the last few weeks of the war, we visited Scotland again. I viewed the approach of VE Day, and its attendant orgies, with some trepidation. The Allies' ultimatum called for unconditional surrender. This made me fear a moral catastrophe worse than world war, not only for England or for Europe, but for the whole world: an ultimate catastrophe. As had happened in the past, the victors might give free rein to their primitive impulses and thus perpetuate the very barbarities that this war had been fought against. Fortunately, lunatic ideas of vengeance such as the Morgenthau Plan were soon abandoned, thanks to the lesson of the First World War, and to a timely application of English pragmatism.

At the end of the war I got to know the highly intelligent English publisher Victor Gollancz. Although a Jew, he took a courageous stand in favour of a rational peace settlement, and was much insulted by the chauvinists for so doing. At his house I met a German doctor from Hamburg, called Enoch, who had been developing, somewhere near London, a new serum rather like penicillin, which was later to save the lives of thousands of men suffering from gangrene. At that time I myself was undergoing a nasty and spreading case of furunculosis. Hitherto Dr Enoch had tried out his remedy only on horses, but I had faith in him, and straight away offered myself as a human guinea-pig. In my general state of depression – a result of the increasing misery of life in wartime – I could no longer endure a physical condition as psychologically lowering as this one. The result seemed miraculous; Enoch's serum helped me after a single injection. I asked him, in vain, to give me more, for I have seldom experienced such euphoria as followed this treatment.

To the great dismay of world industry – which was still running in top gear with armament production – the Reich capitulated, and Hitler killed himself in his bunker. In the ruins of Berlin rats devoured the unburied corpses.

Roosevelt and Stalin had carved out their respective spheres of influence in Europe. Churchill had been overruled, because his country was exhausted, and de Gaulle had been ignored. And so the Russian empire had won the war. Half Germany, the former Crown Lands of Austria, Hungary, and the whole of the Balkans as far as Greece now belonged to the Red Tsar who had a free hand to organize, liquidate, decimate, dispossess and evacuate the peoples under his control. In this manner the principle of self-determination promised at Yalta was interpreted in practice. Later, as I have already said, President Beneš, under Communist control, dispossessed and expelled a third of the population of Bohemia because they spoke German.

In the winter of 1945, I put up a poster in the Underground railway stations, where more people would see it than if it appeared in a newspaper. Christ bends down from the cross to a group of imploring children. The inscription runs as follows: IN MEMORY OF THE CHILDREN OF EUROPE WHO HAVE TO DIE OF COLD AND HUNGER THIS XMAS. Olda and I used sometimes to watch the people who stopped in front of it. Some seemed puzzled to find that it was not an advertisement for a charity of some sort. Some scrawled comments on it. The poster was distributed internationally; a special edition was printed for South America with a Spanish inscription. It was also illegally reproduced behind the Iron Curtain, and even today I am sometimes given copies printed there. I differed from the writers of Communist propaganda by addressing myself not to the masses with an ideology, but simply to the human conscience. I was a kind of one-man underground movement.

Before leaving England, I wrote a lengthy essay, 'A Petition from a Foreign Artist to the Righteous People of Great Britain for a Secure and Present Peace', which was eventually published there in the book *Kokoschka, Life and Work*, by Edith Hoffman in 1947. English readers, who had their own worries, took little notice of it, and it has never appeared in Germany.

Through all the long years of war I had not dared to correspond either with my sister in Prague or with my brother in Vienna. They must not know where I lived; one had heard of the tortures the Gestapo used to extract information. After the war I travelled to Prague on my Czech passport, now once more valid in Czechoslovakia, to see my sister. She was disturbed by the mounting wave of chauvinism in the country, and had begun to suffer from anaemia, for which, when it is the consequence of anxiety and depression, there is no cure. She was frightened of becoming unfit for work and perhaps even being sent to an old people's home. I could do little. Letters to an acquaintance who was a former Czech Ambassador in Vienna, asking for an exit visa for my sister, remained unanswered. My sister's house, garden and collections were confiscated as national property after her death. A party-line writer lives there now.

I returned to London and applied for a British passport, because I could see no future for me in Austria. It was now occupied by the Russians, Americans, British and French, all four of whom had helped, in their various ways, to liberate this vestige of the old Monarchy. With my new passport I was free once more to travel where I wanted – first to Vienna to find my brother. In hiding for a time under Hitler, he had come through safely. Our house had been requisitioned, and he had lived as a labourer with a wife and child – he had meanwhile got married – in a little shed in our garden, to which he returned every night, often after wandering for hours in the midst of the bombing. Later I was able to get the house back for my brother; it had fallen into disrepair and been used as a storage depot. His son, in spite of all the hardships of his childhood, shows promise of becoming an outstanding surgeon.

That first visit to Vienna almost cost me my life. Through Cook's in

London I had collected my tickets and all the papers necessary for travel during the state of emergency that still existed in 'liberated' Austria. But during a blizzard at night, in a wilderness somewhere beyond Linz, Russian soldiers stopped the train, and with fixed bayonets directed all the passengers holding British passports to get out. Carrying a heavy package of medicines, food and so on, I was forced to scramble up a steep slope, and fast, or risk ending up with a bayonet in my back. Resistance would simply have led to my arrest. I stood in the freezing cold, trying to decipher official forms printed in English, which the soldier in charge could not have read even if they had been in Russian. I was shivering and helpless. And then the engine driver recognized my name. He was a Viennese converted to Communism while a prisoner of war, and could make himself understood in Russian. He hid me for the time being in his coal tender. The other passengers were made to wait for a train that did not touch the Russian zone; my train went on.

And so I arrived at the Westbahnhof in Vienna, once so beautiful; of all its Art Nouveau splendours only an iron skeleton remained. St Stephen's Cathedral was half burnt, half reduced to rubble; its medieval roof had gone. I located my brother and his family; he had been ordered to clean out barrack latrines, as punishment for not revealing my address, and had finally been a conscript in the home guard. But he and his fellows had no desire to fight for the Germans, or for the Russians, either. Afterwards the Russian troops – Kalmuks and Tartars, savage peoples who had been let loose in their zone of Vienna like an army in the Thirty Years War – are said to have run wild, murdering and raping. That was the peace for which millions of soldiers of all races had trustingly laid down their lives in the course of nearly six years.

I met the mayor of Vienna, Theodor Körner, who later became President of Austria. His nickname was 'The Red General', because as a Socialist he opposed all wars. In the Bukovina during the First World War, he had held out against the Russian avalanche with a tiny band of men in the depths of winter. The Russians respected him. He did everything in his power for the thousands of refugees from Bohemia and Hungary, requisitioning beds and setting them up in the City Hall, and distributing bread and soup to the hungry out of the scanty stocks that were left. In the ornate Victorian–Gothic council chamber, we cooked ourselves American canned lentils on an iron slow-combustion stove. Later, in 1949, I painted a portrait of Körner. In human terms we got on very well, but I do not know whether he had much feeling for art. When I had seen to my brother's welfare, I went back to London.

In Basle in 1947, for the first time since before the war, there was a major exhibition of my pictures, many of which I had thought destroyed by the

Nazis. I was very proud of that exhibition, which brought my work, much of it forgotten, back to the public domain. The Hitler regime had not, after all, destroyed most of my pictures, but had sold them abroad for foreign currency.

That spring in Basle I met an old Swiss friend, Dr Gubler, who had first attached himself to me when he was a young student of theology in Dresden. Knowing that I had hardly any money, he advised me to go at once to Sierre, in the canton of Valais, where he had a good friend, a rich patron of music, who during the war had supported musicians fleeing from the Nazis. 'He will get you to paint his portrait.' I took Gubler's advice.

One May day about noon, I arrived at the railway station at Sierre. I had left my wife in Basle, to spare travelling expenses should the enterprise be un-successful. The heat was electric; buds on the chestnut trees were swelling almost visibly. Werner Reinhart was waiting, a tall, rather diffident elderly gentleman, who greeted me with great courtesy as his guest, and took me to the Hôtel Bellevue, which had formerly been a large and splendid town house. To me, something of the great merchant princes of fifteenth-century Germany clung to Reinhart. I knew that he still carried on a trade in spices, tea and cotton with India, where he had plantations. He seemed distressed by the heat, and I suggested that he rest on the divan while I waited for my luggage to be brought up. Out of the corner of my eye I observed his power-ful chest rise and fall. The porter brought my bags, I unpacked, we exchanged a few polite generalities.

Time passed, and I became rather impatient. When would he speak of the portrait which was the reason for my visit? Studying him, I decided that he would do very well as a subject. His remoteness tempted me to try out my skill at handling people. Was he hesitant, or mistrustful, or merely sly? I must find the right can-opener, I thought irritably to myself; I had not come for an idle chat. But he had still not got round to the subject of the portrait – had not even hinted at it – when he rose to leave. Taking my courage in both hands, I made a frontal assault.

'I believe you invited me here to paint your portrait, Herr Reinhart. Now I suggest we make what the English call a gentleman's agreement. I will paint you, but if you don't like the result you don't have to buy it. In return, however, you must promise to sit for me as long as I consider necessary.' I was taking a big risk because I badly needed money. And then I saw in his eyes a split-second movement, like a lizard darting under a stone. I had touched a living nerve in this impassive man: the courage and daring which had once been the soul of the merchant venturer whose wagons, escorted by armed mercenaries, had passed through the gates of this very house and out over the Alps to Italy and the Orient.

We shook hands on the deal, and got down to business, arranging the time and place of the sittings. He invited me to send for my wife at once. Since I don't like painting in the room where I sleep, he suggested the chapel of the former mansion, which now stood empty and could be used as a studio. However, a corpse had been lying in state there a little time before, and the smell of withered wreaths and the spirit of the dead man were repugnant to me; Reinhart probably felt the same.

Finally he showed me into a large corner room with an old coffered ceiling. In the compartments of the ceiling, painted ornamental motifs alternated with family portrait-medallions. The room was empty, and the shutters were closed; brilliant shafts of sunlight fell through the cracks on to the parquet floor. Reinhart led me to the middle of the room. I scanned the ceiling. One of the portraits, a Renaissance merchant prince in black, stared back at me as if suddenly aware of the presence of an intruder. I looked away, under the spell of his searching gaze; then, in the darkened room, although there was no mirror to explain the illusion, I saw my own *Doppelgänger* standing before me. He stood out quite clearly against the narrow beam of light on the parquet, in a posture entirely characteristic of me, arms akimbo, head held high – as I stand when aware I am being watched. I am over-sensitive to light, I thought: first the dazzling sunlight and then the zebra stripes made by the light on the floor. It must be a hallucination.

At that moment Reinhart's housekeeper opened the door, uttered a soft cry and closed it again. I forgot about the reflection of a fevered brain; Reinhart had noticed nothing and not even heard the cry.

He had a new idea. Perhaps we would be freer from disturbance if the picture could be painted on the terrace under the chestnut trees at his summer residence not far from the town. There we would be in the fresh air, and feel more at ease than in a confined space; in addition, a background of greenery would provide a better contrast for my sitter, who normally wore grey. At his country house, the Château Muzot, I sat Reinhart in a shaded garden chair under one of the large trees. My easel was set up in an instant, and I started to paint on the same day. The Château Muzot is in fact a single tower. On the ground floor there is a flat for the housekeeper with a rather more spacious dining-room and kitchen adjoining. In the upper storey there is a little suite of rooms where Rilke spent the last years of his life as Reinhart's guest, and finished the *Duino Elegies*. The housekeeper, Frieda Baumgartner, had come to the house as a young girl, and had looked after Rilke

THE YEARS IN ENGLAND 173

during his illness; that had virtually been her life. Frieda later told my wife that on the day of my arrival she had had a great fright; looking into the room with the coffered ceiling, she too had seen me together with my *Doppelgänger*.

For whole months, I worked on the portrait. When, eventually, it was almost finished – and a good likeness, too – Reinhart kept saying: 'Why don't you stop now? What more does it need?' I answered: 'No, it's not finished. Lightning hasn't struck yet.'

He was startled by this, and asked his housekeeper: 'Frieda, what does he mean by that? Surely not that my house is going to be struck by lightning?' She said calmly, 'Don't you understand Herr Kokoschka? He just hasn't finished with you yet, that's all.'

Several times Reinhart had to leave on trips; once, I think, he flew to India in order to see to his plantations there. But I held him to his agreement, and as a gentleman he kept his word.

It was now October, and getting cold. Reinhart lay swathed in blankets, so that I could hardly see his face. The leaves of the great chestnut tree began to fall. He set a limit of three days more. The first day passed, then the second, and I still had not finished the picture. On the third day I would have to stop work. And then I observed a sudden involuntary movement of the man in the garden chair, as he threw off the blankets. It was the same gesture I had noticed at our first meeting, when he had so ponderously stretched himself on the divan in my hotel room. He was a heavy man and breathed in great heaving movements, so that his powerful rib-cage worked like a bellows. He was actually a very good amateur clarinettist. But this movement also reminded me of an earlier movement I had seen in the eye that looked out from that granite-hard face. I had an inspiration, and called out to him: 'Didn't you tell me that you went to the British Museum in London when you were a young man? Do you remember? And you stood for a long time looking at an Assyrian relief. There is a lion on it, transfixed by a spear. You still have a cast of it hanging in your bedroom, don't you?'

His face was transfigured: it had come to life. Hesitantly he answered: 'Yes, that's right. What I have is not a cast of the original, but a large photograph that I had taken specially by the Museum. How did you know about it?'

Actually I had just imagined it, but now I had the look I wanted, the flash of lightning, the significant experience. The portrait was finished in a few minutes.

Reinhart was always rather shy of this portrait; he often surreptitiously visited my dealer's to have a look at it, and sent his friends to see it; but he did not buy it. He too stood by his rights under the agreement. His family, however, later acquired the painting, and after his death it was presented to the museum of art in Winterthur.

For me the purchase had long since ceased to be a financial necessity. During Reinhart's periodic absences I had painted a landscape at Montana-Vermala, which was bought by the Kunsthaus in Zürich, and other landscapes at Sion and Zermatt.

The School of Seeing, and the Power of Music

A little while ago someone sent me a photograph taken one May day in 1955 when I spoke to hundreds of schoolchildren in the large open space fronting the Vienna Secession building. The occasion was my first exhibition in Vienna since the Second World War. I stood on a wobbly metal table which my brother had to hold steady – such was the enthusiasm of my audience – to prevent it from being pushed over.

I like talking to young people: so much so that I had the idea of founding, in Salzburg, where I had painted in 1950, a 'School of Seeing'. It was not to be a school in the usual sense of the word – under State supervision and with a curriculum weighed down with sterile routine – but a school in which, in Austria, where I had previously been so much misunderstood, I would be able to educate young people to *see*.

Art cannot be taught in a school, least of all an annual summer school. It would take generations, as in the Middle Ages or the Renaissance, to educate people in seeing. The State bureaucracy, which is invariably responsible for art education in our day, has no idea that seeing in itself is a decisive human experience, capable of being absorbed only if the individual is either prepared for it, thanks to tradition, or gifted enough to grasp it immediately. This immediate talent is one of the gifts which distinguishes human beings from the animals. The child tries to make for itself a picture of its surroundings. After its first haphazard attempts to draw its mother or father, it tries to make a picture of itself. A leaf blown aloft by the wind, the solitariness of a stone kicked out of our path, or an empty water-glass left standing on a table, any of these can momentarily alert us to the nature of the basic experience – awareness of our own existence – to which art alone gives form. Like our existence, art itself has become alien to us; but we can still see.

With the help of that indomitable art dealer Friedrich Welz, and with the sympathetic understanding of the then provincial governor, Dr Josef Klaus, I succeeded in getting the Salzburg city council to place at my disposal a part of the great fortress of Hohensalzburg which stood half empty. The school furniture – tables, benches, and beds for the dormitories – was provided by Welz; I have absolutely no idea where he got it all from. In the summer of 1953 I opened my international School of Seeing, with twenty-four students. In my prospectus I made no promise of turning them into artists, but only of opening their eyes to what art is for. They were to try to depict, in a primitive fashion, what in the short time available they had learned, with my help, to see.

I did not permit the use of oils; they take too long, often they get painted over, and meanwhile the initial vision is lost. I encouraged the students to paint from models in motion, and to use watercolours, which allow no correction or overpainting. Drawing from a model, motionless for hours, would have been a waste of time for young people, themselves so mobile. The very transitoriness of visual experience constituted the heart of my teaching. It was this to which students must learn to respond and give form. But if drawing is an act of abstraction, it can only be successful as the result of intensive observation and experience: hence Raphael could make an unforgettable drawing of Leda and the Swan, now owned by the Queen of England. And so, not with words, but through practical example, I tried to educate these young people to discover their own sense of sight, atrophied by a second-hand education in an ordinary school. I spared my students what I had gone through, drawing lifesize nudes from the back row of a class, where they appeared no larger than dwarfs. Posing became a positive pleasure to our models, as I showed them how, for example, a girl combs her hair, or reads a love-letter that she has been hiding, or laughs at a bird pecking at the window, or bites with relish at a cherry, or feels grief because she is alone; or how a man gets angry during an argument, or picks up a stone, or, finally, to revert to the antique, sits down to extract a thorn from his heel. There are thousands of possible ways of arousing surprise and getting students to see. Anyone can learn, just as I had learned through the educational method of Jan Amos Comenius in his *Orbis pictus*. The results may not yet be art, but then art can scarcely be achieved today even by the man who feels himself to be an artist.

Every piece of work done by every student received my personal attention and criticism. Piles of torn-up sheets of paper, which I had decided were valueless, lay at my students' feet every evening when I made my last round from room to room, from floor to floor, visiting each individual.

In the years that followed, my School of Seeing became known all over the world, and the numbers of students steadily increased. In one room there

were Germans, in the next Italians, in a third English, Dutch, and others. I
had to engage assistants, people I had trained myself within the school. And
still the students streamed in, from the Argentine, the USA, Canada, Egypt,
Turkey, and all the countries of Europe – even from France, although there
had actually been a warning issued at the Ecole des Beaux-Arts in Paris
against my 'erroneous method'. Students of mine are now teaching at universities and art schools everywhere. One of them is even teaching Eskimos; I
hope they enjoy it, and don't start imitating modern art for the export
market.

By the eleventh summer, the enrolment had grown too big for me; I
could no longer bear the physical strain of my teaching method. I left, and
my School of Seeing was transformed into a State-run academy, where, I
hear, instruction is now given in the execution of so-called non-objective art.
I shall take the liberty of printing here one of the many letters that I still
receive, even after so many years, from all over the world.

Dear Master, Dear OK!
Please forgive me for calling you that. But, to introduce myself briefly,
I am one of your many hundreds of female students. I attended your
Salzburg school for three summers. Three lessons for my whole lifetime.

I am writing simply to thank you a thousand times for all that you so
unselfishly gave us during those summers. At the academy in Vienna I
studied music as well as painting. My present immediate boss is Carl
Orff, at whose institute here in Salzburg I am teaching.

This evening, with my friends, the talk was all of you and of Orff.
I can very easily imagine that you and he would get on well together.
After tonight's conversation I picked up, for the first time in years, my
signed copy of your book. Inside I found the newspaper article 'To the
Apostles of Art all over the World'. I remember every sentence. It was a
hot day, at the end of the 1961 course. It was absolutely quiet when you
were speaking. I believe that Seemann had tears in his eyes, and Ruth was
there and all the others. . . .

And now I sit here and read all you said about experience and about
looking, about inner peace and about life, which is as brief as a mayfly's.

It is because it all seemed – and was – so free, and yet such a serious
message from you to us all, that I am venturing to write this letter to you.
Just as spontaneously, and perhaps even rashly. But I must tell you, dear
OK, just once, although it was ten years ago, that everything still holds
true for me. It was not transitory; for a short time you really 'educated'

us. (For a very long time, as far as I am concerned.) You have become my mentor in life. That is what I would like to thank you for now, after so many years. I can still see; I am still able to experience the world, in the way I think you meant. I hope for my sake that I remember it often; and I hope you remember, too, that when you spoke to us you were not talking into thin air but saying something that will always remain valid.

Yours, Felicitas

Baroque was essentially a popular art that had spanned continents in bringing people closer together. Its end was sealed by the official academies late in the eighteenth century. The earliest academies of art under state patronage were founded by the mediocre painter Raphael Mengs. Born on the borders of Bohemia and Saxony, he was a court painter in both Saxony and Spain while still a young man, the author of books on art, such as *Schönheit und Geschmack* (*Beauty and Taste*), and a very influential person in the new society that was coming into being. In Madrid he displaced his great rival, the old Baroque painter Tiepolo. As a theorist and believer in the Goddess of Reason, he introduced logic into the visual arts. A fly might be able to cling to a ceiling, but in Mengs's opinion such objects as ships, obelisks and palaces had no business being painted on the inside of a cupola. This was his great innovation: painting must be satisfied with representation on a two-dimensional surface, and a canvas, like any other surface, has only two dimensions. He declared that the representation of three-dimensional space was contrary to the teachings of reason. The French Revolution was just around the corner. A new age had dawned whose effects were visible in art as everywhere else. Mengs's rationalism is still operative in the teaching of art in the academies: painting must be decorative and not three-dimensional.

One day the German Minister of Economic Affairs, Ludwig Erhard, came to visit the summer school. He climbed the stairs from one floor to another, and in each room stopped to watch me teaching. He understood at once that my aim was not the mass-production of artists. Rather, in the enthusiasm and devotion of my students, who worked to the point of exhaustion, the father of the so-called Economic Miracle found a confirmation for his belief that only an example of total dedication could restore lost human dignity.

Erhard turned beggars into human beings in Germany. I respected him, and in 1959 I painted his portrait. I can still vividly see in my mind's eye that massive figure, who looked unwieldly, but was quicker than I to pick up a fallen paintbrush from the floor. 'I am no Titian, Minister,' I said apologetically. 'And I am no Charles V,' he answered promptly. As we talked, he wondered out loud whether the German people would survive its sudden windfall of good fortune without losing its historical perspective. I hoped that through his influence my idea of 'education in seeing' might take root in Germany where, for long and bloody years, the image of a truly human existence had been utterly obliterated.

My summer schools in Salzburg began, conveniently, about a fortnight before the Salzburg Festival, so that we had the opportunity of attending Wilhelm Furtwängler's rehearsals. We had met him some years before in Rome, where we had also heard him conducting Beethoven's Pastoral on a stormy night. During the concert, the lights failed suddenly, and we could barely discern Furtwängler's magic wand in the Calibanic darkness, until the light returned and brought with it the liberating rain. We felt as though we had been present at the creation of the world.

Furtwängler was born in the same year I was. We were fortunate enough to see him often at our home in Switzerland, to which we moved in 1953; he had settled with his family at Clarens, on Lake Geneva, some years before. Furtwängler was present, silently watching, while I painted the *Thermopylae* triptych*. He had retained from his youth a profound feeling for Greece, fostered by his mentor, the archaeologist Ludwig Curtius, and by his own father, the famous archaeologist Adolf Furtwängler, whose grave is in Athens. On a later visit to Greece with Elisabeth Furtwängler, we found the gravestone, surmounted by a sphinx. It had been damaged by bullets during the political troubles when the Communist ELAS had taken up positions in the cemetery.

As I sketched in the figure of the traitor Ephialtes, in the central panel of *Thermopylae,* Furtwängler broke his long silence. He spoke with great effort, as if, like Demosthenes once by the stormy sea, his mouth were full of pebbles. His words, direct from the heart, became progressively clearer and more coherent. It was as though he himself had been one of those who died for the freedom of the human spirit at Thermopylae.

On the same occasion, Furtwängler invited me to design a production of *The Magic Flute* which he was to conduct in Salzburg the following summer. We discussed the commission with the chief scene-painter, Gustav Vargo, a dedicated craftsman. It presented something of a problem: the performances were to take place in the Felsenreitschule, on an open stage without a curtain, where the many short scenes of the opera would normally require a single static set, and this I did not want. Instead of following the usual practice of having one set until the interval, and then another until the end – an arrangement as boring to the audience as to me – I wanted to try something unusual.

I had an idea. We would interpret the moods of the various scenes by changes of colour in the lighting; in addition, through the use of coloured projections on the flats, the stage as a whole would become deep, high, low, narrow or elongated as the action required, without the necessity of shifting scenery. This was a novel tactic by comparison with the conventional operatic lighting scheme, with its single spot picking out the star singer. My only fear was that, with all the tourist hotels, beer-halls and cafés in Salzburg, the local power supply might not be able to provide all the current I would need.

In autumn 1954 I had my designs ready to show to Furtwängler; he studied them very closely and gave his approval. Sadly, however, he died on 30 November of that year. I have kept the bare canvas on which I was going to paint his portrait. The sittings had been postponed again and again because of his health. Under Georg Solti, in the summer of 1955, *The Magic Flute* was performed in accordance with my lighting scheme. I had been given an unusually free hand by the director, Herbert Graf, to employ special colour effects on the chorus and in crowd movements as well, to enhance the overall visual impact.

Furtwängler possessed the great gift of arousing through music the spiritual nature within one. In my youth I remember hearing Gustav Mahler, whose electric power fused the whole orchestra into a single organism. Generally, I have had closer relationships with contemporary musicians than with painters or writers. Trakl, Ehrenstein and Kraus were the exceptions. I felt no bond with Rilke, for example, though he wrote a poem about my lamb still-life, nor with Hofmannsthal, whose approaches I rebuffed (I regret having done so, now that I know something about the tragedy of his life), nor with Thomas Mann, whose manuscript of the Joseph legend I refused to illustrate. Gerhart Hauptmann also failed to make an impression on me when we met at Rapallo; his young wife, with a leopardskin draped over her bare back, had led me to the coffee table where he was holding court in a green tail-coat, like Goethe's.

Lest my readers accuse me of name-dropping, let me say that I have had a long life and made many journeys; naturally I have met great numbers of people. Even in my early days comparatively few made a lasting impression upon me. Many are wholly forgotten. But the importance of those I remember is the same whether they have gone down in history or faded into oblivion.

I have always found friends among musicians. From the early days there were Alexander von Zemlinsky, whose sister Mathilde married Arnold Schönberg, and Rudolf Kolisch, of the famous Kolisch Quartet, who impressed me enormously by relearning to play the violin left-handed on account of a war wound. His sister Gertrud became Schönberg's second wife, after Mathilde Zemlinsky's death. Schönberg himself I painted in 1924. He was a gifted 'cellist, and in the evenings used to play chamber music with his pupils, who worshipped him. The uproar that his concerts – arranged by Loos – caused in Vienna at that time was incomprehensible to me. His twelve-tone system is only one of the many possible ones (think of the music of the Indians and Chinese), and Greek music is partly based on five-tone systems, as Egon Wellesz showed me. In that period I painted him too. In his *Well-Tempered Clavier* Johann Sebastian Bach clearly foreshadows, on a tonal basis, the later emancipation of the semitones in the scale, which manifests itself so conspicuously in *Tristan*. So it has been explained to me; I'm only a layman.

In England, much later, my wife read in the programme for a performance of Schönberg's early monodrama *Die glückliche Hand* at Covent Garden that, when it was proposed to film the piece, the composer had wanted me to design the principal scenes 'with apparitions of colour and form'. In its article on him, the *Encyclopaedia Britannica* allies Schönberg's experimental period after the First World War with my own. It was during the Second World War that Schönberg, from America, last wrote to me. He was teaching music at a girl's college and was very depressed. Why should he teach his students how to compose a mass or an oratorio, when soon afterwards he would meet them in the street wheeling a baby and find that they had totally forgotten about music? To me, Schönberg was one of the last remaining links with classical music, late Schubert, Bruckner and Beethoven. I felt the same way about Anton von Webern, the most gifted of his many pupils, whom I had also painted in the old days in Vienna. Webern was shot at Mittersill in Austria by a cook in the American army of occupation, when he stepped outside his front door one evening to smoke a cigarette. In London I heard his last work, the Cantata, Opus 31, which strengthened my belief that he was a more gifted composer than Schönberg. Berg was another who trod his own path. His music for *Wozzeck* fulfilled the demands of Büchner's stringent text. I was present at its premier performance at the Berlin Opera, on 14 December 1925, under Erich Kleiber.

When I was still in Dresden, I remember getting a letter from the youthful Hindemith, asking permission to set my play *Mörder, Hoffnung der Frauen* to music. Dr Posse read the letter out to me one Sunday after lunch, while we were both rather tipsy, and said: 'Let him go ahead and compose!' In a drunken moment I wrote these same words on Hindemith's letter and sent it back to him. He must have taken it amiss; although we were close neighbours for years in Switzerland, I never met him, nor have I ever heard his setting of my work. However, I did attend the première in Kassel of Ernst Křenek's opera based on my play *Orpheus und Eurydike*. I am still not sure that my plays really benefit from being set to music.

I have known many violinists, pianists and conductors. There was Bronislav Hubermann, for example, who played magnificently in rehearsal but in public suffered so badly from nerves that he often left the orchestra completely behind. I shall not name contemporary artists here, except to offer them my thanks for all they have given. I will however make an exception for Pablo Casals, whom I painted in 1954, when he was giving master classes at Sion near where we live. Casals asked if he might practise while I was painting; I answered that I could not paint him unless he did. He played the same passages of Schumann's Cello Concerto over and over again. He was a small, stocky man, and he was virtually invisible most of the time behind his large instrument. He practised those difficult passages for weeks on end. I painted the first picture in one morning; I still have it. The second took me until Casals left Sion. When he got a phrase right, and I succeeded perhaps in catching at the same instant a flash of his little, dark, screwed-up eyes – he pressed his lips together so that they looked bloodless, like those of a turtle – he would raise his bow excitedly and say, 'C'est beau, n'est-ce pas?' I held dirty paintbrushes in both hands, so we would rub noses, as Eskimos do when they greet one another.

I was introduced to Toscanini by Eleonore von Mendelsohn (whose brother, Francesco, was the cellist), but I could not paint him. He made me think of a cat on a frosty night; in place of a heart, I thought, he must have had a metronome.

I love chamber music, and above all the late quartets of Beethoven: the one with the *Grosse Fuge*, and the other which he wrote in a spirit of humility after his recovery from an illness; in it there is a passage in which for a number of bars one's heart seems about to stand still.

Five years after the Salzburg production of *The Magic Flute*, I did sets and costumes for three plays by Ferdinand Raimund at the Burgtheater in Vienna. I also painted a drop curtain showing Raimund's apotheosis: he was being remembered on the occasion of the 170th anniversary of his birth. The three plays were *Moisassurs Zauberfluch, Die unheilbringende Krone* and *Die gefesselte Phantasie*.

This was theatre as Shakespeare had written it, but as no one wrote it after the passing of Raimund – or of Nestroy, his mocking *alter ego*. Both were great actors as well as playwrights; they had the theatre in their blood. For one last time, in Raimund's plays, everything returns to life that had appealed to my youthful imagination: the Baroque world I had seen in palaces, churches and waking dreams, the world of gods, genii and daemons. Here spirits stand equal to bourgeois philistines; while nobles in their mansions appear no more solid than the gods. Theatrical perspectives ample enough to portray the universe, to hold up a mirror to the whole panorama of existence, are necessities when one is young and poor. One might still then feel a thrill of terror at the marble representation of Cerberus, though one was already no longer afraid of the poor old devil himself, for even the young have tasted the fruits of the enlightenment.

When I was a child, a marionette theatre given me by my father represented the whole beauty of existence as far as I was concerned; it was surely responsible for my passion for the theatre. The suburban parkland in which I might have played was already falling into neglect; building-plots were being staked out, country houses converted into hotels. The ruined castles where we went on school outings were no longer deserted: a disabled veteran collected fees at the entrance and sold picture-postcards.

It was only in the theatre of Ferdinand Raimund and Johann Nestroy, the two last great poets of the Monarchy, that the social order, once accepted as divinely ordained, had not yet yielded to the *Zeitgeist*. These two, poets of humorous fairyland as well as of bitter farce, peopled the already magical world of the Baroque with figures of their own imagining, tragicomic characters who aspire to ever-greater heights, reaching even to the spirit kingdom. Vienna today sees no more in their plays than a satire on the bourgeoisie.

But in my childhood everyone was 'Herr Baron', or at least 'Your honour' to the doorman who opened the carriage door; and there were still horse-drawn carriages in those days. The shabbier the present day became, the more threadbare the frock-coat, and the less gloss remained on the top hat which gentlemen still knew how to doff in a graceful curve. Goethe and Schiller, after the French Revolution, established the classical theatre in place of the popular play; but in the plays of Raimund and Nestroy the Viennese theatrical tradition enjoyed a further brief spell of independent life. While fairies and spirits walked arm in arm with the newly rich bourgeois, the Viennese Hanswurst, the clown whose tradition goes back to ancient Greek and Roman comedy, and who can never feel at home in the prosaic present – but who still gets his ration of hard knocks – escorted the audience, and society itself, with his impudent, consoling, ironic patter, between the false

Corinthian columns and through the papiermâché gates, into the heavenly kingdom. And so the bourgeoisie found death easier to take. In Karl Kraus's drama *Die letzten Tage der Menschheit*, the Viennese, and not only they, were finally forced to take their death seriously.

My designs for Raimund's plays were not particularly well received in Vienna, and the performances have never been repeated; nor has the Burgtheater preserved any of the sets or costumes. The *Zeitgeist* is not defied with impunity.

New Friends

As I have already said, we spent the first years of the war in London, in a small and somewhat dilapidated house, whose owner felt unsafe there, and let us have it virtually for nothing. Bombs fell near our house; one tore up the street, and the entrails of the Underground – railway tracks, cables, wires and pipes – glowed red. The explosion also broke our windows, and fragments of glass crunched underfoot. One was used to that.

But it was spring! Many former pacifists, whom I knew well, were now devoting themselves, on land, in the air and on the sea, to the task of winning the Battle of Britain. This will not be the last war, I said to myself, and leaving the depiction of bomb damage – houses with their façades ripped away, brutally revealing the intimacy of bedrooms inside – to the official war artists who were better qualified for the task, I began to paint flowers – in water-colour. The so-called non-objective painters already considered this to be an occupation exclusively reserved for elderly spinsters; but then what else was I to do? I would, anyway, have had to prove my artistic ability by submitting all my war work to a censor who undoubtedly knew much more about strategy than about painting. Meanwhile I must at all costs keep my eye and hand in – especially when, in the first sunshine after the thaw, snowdrops, crocuses, bluebells, daffodils and tulips came into flower. If only we would open our eyes, every day could be a new experience.

After the war people sought once more to round out their world by setting forth like Columbus to discover new lands, and to see if, indeed, all human beings, friend and foe alike, are everywhere the same. Tourism sprang up. Whoever could escaped from an everyday existence which threatened to become routine once more; people had lost faith in their own lives. Even I, who had fewer years to spare than most, flew to America five times. Sea-trips were too slow: who knew how long the peace would last? Anyway, on a ship, one would have met the same people every day, as at a week-end party; and I was too full of curiosity.

On my last visit to America, in 1966, I finally managed to paint New York. I tried to catch the essence of this city, impossible to photograph, because it constantly changes as you look at it. Skyscrapers shoot up; slums and garbage heaps disappear and reappear; the city has no face of its own, only a dynamism.

I have been to Greece five times, too. For all of us, Hellas is an ideal, like the Garden of Eden. Why? Perhaps because there man came closest to realizing his true nature. Rome, and the whole of Europe until the eighteenth century, lived on the heritage of ancient Greece, building their civilizations on its foundation, while they themselves progressively became less and less truly human.

An abyss has opened up between the ancient Greeks and the modern world. Modern governments – in Germany, and sadly, in England and France as well – are gradually abolishing the study of classical languages, as irrelevant to society's needs, but also because such study stands in contradiction to the spirit of the age, which is entirely dominated by the exact sciences, and would burden the young with useless ballast. No one fears that one day, without ballast, the young might drift weightless and defenceless, at the mercy of the nihilistic current. Even the Catholic Church has now given up, in its sacrament of divine love, the ancient language which once united all nations.

The ancient world differed from the modern in its approach to competition: it was formerly a rivalry between individuals and between peoples under the sign of Eros. To the men of antiquity, Eros meant the culmination of the ego – whether in victory or in defeat; and, in accordance with the Delphic maxim 'Know thyself', this culmination made possible the full unfolding of the genius of the individual or of society as a whole.

The people who lived in Greece before our Christian era have become incomprehensible to us. They did not shut their eyes in panic, but met reality through their senses – the only way it can be empirically experienced. The ancient Greek, alone, said to himself: It is impossible to run away from an existence that one does in the last resort have to live. The oriental peoples found a way out in fatalistic religions; we have similarly taken refuge in the determinism of technology, itself rapidly turning into a metaphysic. But the Greeks took a critical look at fatalism; they made images of their gods which, unlike all others, corresponded with human experience and with a human criterion of what they could and should be like. They rested content with what really is, and did not believe in a world beyond.

We learn from Plato's *Symposium* that Eros is not a god whose home is in another world, not a son of God who has become man, not a god of love, not

the inaccessible Beloved, but the Lover. Eros, as the child of Wealth and
Poverty, is always accompanied by Want; and he always pursues the beautiful, like the inspired, clear-sighted creative artist. And so he stands, as a seeker
after truth, between the divine – gods who have no need of wisdom, because
they are all-wise – and the human, which is eternally unknowing. Diotima,
the wise woman of Mantinaia, answered her pupil Socrates, when he asked
what was the value of Eros for mankind: 'Eros enters the human soul together
with the longing for beauty.' 'If beauty and goodness are mine, I shall be
happy,' answered Socrates, whom the prophetess had thereby initiated into
philosophic thought. Socrates could not simultaneously unite beautiful and
ugly, mortal and immortal, real and abstract, in his thought. He was not a
Sophist, seeking, in conformity with public opinion, to embrace a shadow.
Socrates was a humanist, conscious of his own unique sense of being; and
democracy condemned him to death. He might have run away, but he voluntarily chose the cup of hemlock, as Jesus did the Cross.

The revolt of the young, in east and west, is a disturbing symptom; and
like all extremes, this rebellion against society has unpleasant emotional over-
tones. But it is important not to miss one thing it is saying: youth is rebelling
against the determinism of democracy as we know it. The young, at least,
frankly admit that they do not know what democracy really is. Our misunderstanding of 'democracy' blurs our vision of society, lulls us all into a
dream, and constitutes a threat, to the young above all, as a drug might do.
The laughter of Aristophanes warned the democracy of Athens, even under
the glorious rule of Pericles, against forgetting the mission of the Greek
people: 'to be, in the true sense of the words, in love with life'.

Perhaps I am setting my readers' teeth on edge by this attempt to bring
words like 'beauty', 'goodness', and 'happiness' back into fashion. We are
unhappy, because we do not dare to be happy. But the Beautiful, the Good,
the Happy, retain their meaning, just as one retains one's name even in old
age, although the body shrivels and one's needs, hopes and perceptions
change. Our decadent age should seek to preserve the heritage of Greece for
posterity, however uncertain and unknown that posterity may be. Even if *we*
no longer know how to live, we do have a responsibility for the young.

And now I dare to pronounce a word that is more or less taboo at the
present time, but which is potentially the most productive and the most
dangerous of all as far as our time is concerned: the word 'soul'. Soul is a
wonderfully flexible phenomenon; it cannot be interpreted as a purely functional faculty, even by mistrustful psychoanalysts. The ancient Greeks erected
temples to the deified personifications of humanity, the children of their

souls, as other peoples do to an Unknown God. Nowadays, instead, we erect
cenotaphs to the Unknown Soldier, and pay him official honours, without
even asking what or who it is that we worship.

In Bonn, in the winter of 1955–56, I painted a portrait of the then President
of the Federal Republic, Theodor Heuss. Until the death of his teacher, the
pastor and Socialist politician Friedrich Naumann, who led the movement
in Germany known as the Innere Mission, Heuss had been his collaborator;
and until Hitler came Heuss was the editor of Naumann's magazine *Die
Hilfe*. Heuss had been one of the last liberals to retain his individuality, holding out against German group-thinking and group demands, and against the
German conviction of racial superiority. Even in his high office, he remained
true to himself.

The half century of German history which followed Bismarck's dismissal
and which witnessed the tragic end of the First World War under Wilhelm II,
the Weimar Republic and Hitler's Caesarism, led the world to judge that the
Germans were a politically immature people. But one is led to ask whether
other nations would have behaved differently in the age of mass society,
itself the consequence of the uncontrollable development of technology.
Although the eyes of the world no longer seem to rest on the pages of the
Bible, but rather on those of *Das Kapital,* I still do not believe that materialism can be accepted as the sole key to a valid conception of the future.
Eros was buried by St Peter and St Paul, along with the paganism of the
ancient world. Now Marx and Engels, in the world of democracy, threaten
the ego with the same fate! In order to balance the accounts and to see what
had become of the German people, I was eager to set eyes on Heuss, a democratic Head of State, the first in Germany since Hitler. And so I had agreed to
paint him.

In the window, behind the curtain of the President's study, we had set a
bottle of kirsch to cool; whenever there was a visitor, we hastened to close
the curtain. We had forgotten that the patrolling sentry must have seen us at
our childish trick and drawn his own conclusions. Heuss laughed. As a
Swabian, he had a sense of humour, and he knew something about *Gemüt-
lichkeit*; on election tours he had no inhibitions about emptying a tankard of
wine in front of a crowd, without any fear of losing face. His memoirs of his
youth are a minor literary masterpiece; he was conscious of his literary fore-
bears in an age when the bourgeoisie in Germany had not yet gone wholly to
ruin. Between the Protestant Bible of bourgeois tradition and *Das Kapital*
which points to an unimaginable future, a political vacuum had appeared.

Well might Germany be thankful that an honest and courageous man had
been found who could still act in this difficult transitional time. And Heuss
was courageous; I know from experience.

At Delphi – the navel of the ancient world, where once the Pythoness gave
her oracle, and the whole world came to hear – I was painting a landscape:
a view far out over the olive groves which stretch down to the sea. There I
received word from Professor Kunze, director of the excavations at
Olympia, to come at once; President Heuss was expected, and on his visit
would be shown things not normally open to the public. The hotel at Olympia was full, so we stayed in the rather primitive archaeologists' rest-house.
Then, on our way to the excavations, we were stopped by the security
police because the President had arrived before us. Catching the Greek
major by the sleeve, I persuaded him, very much against his will, to take me
to President Heuss, whom I could see in the distance waving to us. The
major was relieved; I was not an assassin after all.

Back at Delphi, the next day, Heuss decided that he wanted to escape his
watchdogs and spend an informal evening with us and Frau Furtwängler at
Arachova, a little village perched in the mountains above Delphi. During
the German occupation nearly forty hostages are said to have been shot there.
Heuss and I were driven up in his car, with the German presidential standard
fluttering from its radiator. We arrived in the village early in the evening at
the time when virtually the whole population was gathered in the square to
enjoy the evening breeze. Our car was quickly surrounded, and the chauffeur
forced to stop. Retsina flowed from goatskin bottles, and we were constrained
to drink to everyone in turn, so that no one should feel slighted. Frau
Furtwängler, Olda, and Heuss's private secretary soon arrived to join us. In
a trice tables were set up; but the ladies did not like the strongly resinated
wine as much as Heuss and I did. That night Heuss was hailed, in the legen-
dary home of old Pan, as a solid drinker. My wife told him that, on her walks,
she had found the local people either strongly pro-German or strongly anti-
German. A female goatherd who spoke hardly two or three words of
German, had called back her fierce sheep dogs and shown pleasure at
meeting 'alleman, alleman'. Perhaps, in her isolated farmhouse, she had once
given her heart to a German soldier. Another time, however, an old shepherd suspiciously asked the two women, 'You English?' When Frau Furtwängler answered in German, he turned away as though he had not seen
her.

On our return to Delphi, we found the Greek general in charge of the visit
waiting for us in the hotel foyer with his staff. He was understandably indig-

nant at our unofficial escapade. Poor man, I felt for him; but it had all turned out well, and Heuss had greatly enjoyed himself.

In December 1963, Ezra Pound came to Villeneuve to sit for a drawing. I had met T. S. Eliot in London years before, and James Joyce even earlier in Paris. Pound had strongly championed them both, but I had never met him. I was familiar with his work, which revolves around the question of whether, for the individual, life is worth living – a question that at the present time does not seem to deserve an answer, though in Pound's work there still merge all the traditional currents of civilized awareness. One thing I was especially curious to discuss with Pound was James Joyce's transformation from the poet of the early Dublin days to the author of *Ulysses* and *Finnegan's Wake*, in which, in an age when the language of poetry was impoverished, he pioneered the literary use of clinical vocabulary. This appealed to his successors, who could apparently not get their fill of descriptions of bodily functions, or of the mechanics of sexual life. They clearly want to prove just how bestial we are today. Joyce had been by this time dead for more than two decades. He was well known to have been a sick, choleric man, one who could never have castigated, as Aristophanes did, with bitter, tragicomic irony the decline from humanism to materialism – a decline which broad-minded politicians, high ecclesiastics, scientists, members of the avant-garde and social planners are helping on its way because their right hand doesn't know what their left hand is doing. Perhaps Joyce's ghost was there to witness the Spirit of Melancholy sitting outside a Paris avant-garde theatre the night when, in front of an élite audience, an actress urinated on the open stage.

The systematic degradation of human life is a kind of escapism, as it was in those periods of the Middle Ages when the end of the world was expected. Perhaps technological progress is moving too fast for rational consciousness to keep up with it. Such literature reveals the panic of modern man.

I was prepared, in the presence of Pound, whom I revere as a poet, to cast ashes on my grey hairs, but definitely not to rend my garments. In spite of everything, I consider our age to be, not sterile, but an age of biological maturation, in which, perhaps, we must learn all over again to be human.

For Pound's sake I had at one time added my signature to a plea for clemency sent by his American admirers to the Administration in Washington. Mistaking the true nature of technology, which he saw as no more than a secondary phenomenon, he had attacked the imperialistic capitalism of America, and had laid himself wide open by broadcasting on the radio of

Fascist Italy. After the war, refusing to run away, he was arrested as a traitor and put on show in a cage in a camp near Pisa. A black soldier made him a desk out of a packing-case, and at this he wrote his *Pisan Cantos*. A bare electric lamp burned day and night above his head. His crime, like that of Socrates, consisted in failing to conform to the official view of what democracy is. He faced the electric chair. The plea for clemency was successful. Pound was shut up in an American madhouse for so long that he forgot how to speak.

While I was drawing him, he opened his mouth only once, to say 'Thank you' for a cup of tea. Otherwise he remained silent for the whole four or five hours, looking intently at a Greek sketch-book of mine. His eyes flashed when he drew out the sheet which shows an Attic tombstone carved with an ageing, bearded wrestler; he returned to it again and again. The wrestler resembled him. The drawing I was doing came out well, too. I could see this from his smile, but it had not been easy to stay in contact with one who did nothing but brood. I had talked to him for hours on end, in vain; his lips remained closed. When he left, and the lady who was escorting him suggested bringing him back the next day, I made an excuse. I was too exhausted to repeat the experiment. The word is the poet's very essence. Pound's silence was his only remaining defence against society. No psychiatrist could do anything for him, I thought, and I washed my hands of him, like Pilate – I am not responsible for the antics of modern democracy. The collective conscience of humanity had passed judgment on Hitler's crimes in one of the bloodiest wars in the history of the world, a war in which not only those who believed in him, but also millions of innocent human beings, were – and are still being – destroyed.

A German magazine invited me to paint a portrait of Konrad Adenauer for his ninetieth birthday. The picture was intended for the Bundestag in Bonn, and I was to receive a big fee, which I donated to a home for destitute children at Bad Godesberg; there were still too many such children in Germany. I did not want to paint Adenauer in Bonn, where I had already painted Heuss; and he had more important things to do than spend three or four weeks in my house at Villeneuve – the minimum time I normally need for a picture.

And so it was not until the spring of 1966 that I got round to meeting him, at Cadenabbia, where he usually spent his holidays. Italian security men opened the gates of his villa. We drove up a steep, heavily-wooded road, and there, in the thin spring rain, stood the aged ex-Chancellor, waiting for us.

Hat in hand, he opened the car door for my wife, and complimented her on negotiating the steep bends without having to reverse.

Immediately we set about choosing the best room to work in. Only the dining-room had large windows, and Adenauer decided at once to have it cleared, although he entertained guests every day. A temporary dining-table was arranged in the drawing-room, and the local carpenter was commissioned to make a rostrum, which was ready the next day.

The next morning, when in the bright sunlight I started on the first sitting, Adenauer had, as his secretary told me, already spent two hours working on his memoirs, either dictating, which he mostly did standing up, or leafing through reference books from the shelves. I had a comfortable armchair placed on the rostrum, so that he should not overtire himself. To stand and pose for two or three hours every day – and he was, after all, over ninety – would be too much for him, I thought. He rebuked me with a grin; after all, he said, I did not sit down to paint, and we both belonged to a generation that does not age. I preferred, myself, to paint him standing up, as he had been when he welcomed us, for that was how I had instantly imprinted his image on my mind.

Luck was with me from the very first sketch. His tall figure was without a trace of heroics; the arms hung loosely by the sides of the thin body; the bony hands were expectantly pressed together; I was close – I am shortsighted – to his hard, bony head. The light of the morning sun fell on his open face, with its deep furrows, and on the penetrating, inquisitive eyes. He remarked on the way I gave every touch of colour its own definite form, as if it had a special function in the whole, like notes in music. Colours, I told him, are like the facets that a diamond-cutter cuts out of the crystal. In my mind's eye they were all already there on the canvas. To me, I said, painting is more than a matter of putting colours down one on top of the other: it is a process of formal creation, absorbing me wholly. He understood this, and told me about his collection of medieval paintings, which was one of his main relaxations from the exertions of political life. We were friends from the start. We did not talk, however, about the time when he was arrested by the Gestapo and faced possible execution; or about the other time, after the war, when he was mayor of Cologne, and was arrested once more, because he refused to accept the abasement of his people as a necessary part of the democratic mission of the victors. We did not talk about it, because I myself had lived through the Third Reich and the ensuing peace and safety in England, while this man had preferred to stay and wait for the worst, as though unwilling to escape his destiny.

While I was painting, I thought of how much Adenauer's mission resembled Bismarck's, who had set out, a hundred years before, to achieve the
unification of all the Germans in one State. By comparison, Adenauer had
come into a bitter heritage. His task was like that of Moses: to lead a humili-
ated, defeated, impoverished nation, in a country which had been partitioned
and plundered by its enemies. Unlike Moses, he could not look forward, in
his old age, to a new and guiltless generation. Have his supporters, and his
opponents, whose understanding of the idea of democracy still seems to be
rooted in a mechanistic and illusory idea of Progress, ever really understood
this?

Some politicians want to reform mankind; others want to reform the
conditions in which mankind lives. Ever since the French Revolution people
have, with near-religious devotion and self-sacrifice, believed in the nation
state, and in this respect Bismarck's programme was the child of its age.
Adenauer's task was to make the German people, after a catastrophic bout of
insanity, conscious once more of its lost human identity. Nationalism everywhere had been dehumanized. But the democracy offered by the Allies to
the Germans after the great brain-washing of the defeat was no more
promising. Adenauer saw no safeguard for the future in the mere fact that
everyone in Germany, whatever his previous opinions, had changed into a
democrat overnight, as one changes one's shirt, just because the authorities
had told him to. The habit of obedience had taken root in Germany in the
Wilhelmine period; and Hitler after all had come to power as a result of a
democratic general election. The Morgenthau plan, which rational people on
the Allied side rejected, had proved that for a moment even the democratic
victors contemplated extirpating a whole nation, like rabbits, just in order to
remove an industrial rival from the path. All this had melted away like a
nightmare in the face of reality, and affluence, soon followed by superfluity,
had already begun to produce something like a guilty conscience. To Adenauer, Erhard's affluent society was less like a necessary miracle than like the
mess of pottage for which Esau sold his birthright.

The Allies saw no farther than their noses. They did not exactly lack
tolerance, but the feeling of guilt for the mass murder of the Jews affected
Adenauer alone. Talking about Israel, I told him how I had once invited my
good friend, the poet Albert Ehrenstein, to visit Palestine with me, and how,
with every port of call that brought us closer, we marvelled at the Providence
which had led the Chosen People to the very edge of the oil deposits
over which the Great Powers fought their world wars. It reminded me of the
circus clown who acts as the front legs of the camel and gets kicked by his

partner every time he falls out of step. Adenauer's son, the Monsignor, laughed at my naivety, but his father rebuked him, saying that I was one of the few people with whom he could talk politics.

As far as I could make out, Adenauer had two ideas. He wanted to rehabilitate his own people morally. The Germans had to pay reparations to the victors whether they wanted to or not; but he wanted them also to make some amends, voluntarily, to the survivors of the Jewish communities which had been almost wiped out all over Europe by Nazi antisemitism; and he set himself to work for this goal. The Jews had been badly let down by the Great Powers during the rise of Hitler, and in France they had even been deported. In Palestine the Jews launched a State to which they could flee in their need, for the Christians, Catholic and Protestant alike, had forgotten that Christ was a Jew, just as the Communists have forgotten that Karl Marx was one. Adenauer visited Israel during the time I knew him. He was glad that the Jews, who had at first looked askance at him as a German, recognized the genuineness of his attempt to make amends, although – or perhaps because – every one of them knew that murder can neither be avenged according to the principle 'an eye for an eye, a tooth for a tooth' nor paid for with blood money. But at least a German had started a dialogue with the Jews.

His second preoccupation was to try, through his friendship with the otherwise unapproachable de Gaulle, to end the hundreds of years of fraternal strife between Frenchmen and Germans, who had been fighting and laying waste to each other's territories since the age of Louis XIV. Once, at the collapse of the Roman Empire, both peoples had shared the mission of setting up a civilizing bulwark, the Carolingian Empire, against the migrations from the east, in order to save Europe. Like Adenauer, de Gaulle had a feeling of historic destiny. He had found a way, admittedly under duress, to end the conflict in South-east Asia and to avoid a civil war in France by withdrawing from its colonies in Africa. But Germany's post-war recovery had made France envious, and England too, which had won the war, but nearly gone bankrupt as a result. In his drily humorous way, Adenauer said that he worried about France because de Gaulle was getting old.

On a flight from London to Vienna shortly after the end of the war, my plane was forced to make an emergency stop at Frankfurt. Taking the opportunity of this delay, I left the burnt-out airport buildings for a walk through the ruins of the city; to my astonishment, I witnessed people crawling out of holes in the ruins where they had presumably spent the night. The men clean-shaven, the women with lunch-bags, they set off to work with a will.

Later on, under Erhard, in the affluent Welfare State, skyscrapers sprouted up, airlines burgeoned, neon lights lit up the streets. Traffic – including many luxury cars – choked the cities; ladies wore mink coats. There was cause enough to envy the Germans. How could Adenauer deflect de Gaulle's Joan-of-Arc complex into fruitful channels?

Adenauer could not reconcile himself to a democracy capable of saying yes and no at the same time, a democracy which wanted to live in two worlds at once, combining luxury with a bad conscience. Society must try to acknowledge its collective guilt and make amends. That is the test of an ethically sound democracy.

We usually took a break for a quarter of an hour and strolled in front of the house, while I smoked a cigarette – which I would not allow myself to do in his presence indoors, although he protested that I should – and Adenauer drinking a cup of broth. Looking in at my painting through the open French window, I had the feeling that it would not produce the right effect from a distance, when it was hung in a large room. He had already taken a liking to the picture, and had misgivings when I wanted to alter it. He was amazed when I managed to repaint it in a quarter of an hour, but I explained to him that there was nothing marvellous in that, because the picture had already been complete in my imagination. Adenauer had always followed my work with great understanding; he was a particularly kind and co-operative sitter.

At the end I told him a little story: Olda and I were once guests in the house of an elderly lady in London; the conversation turned to Gandhi, who had come to London, in 1931, after being imprisoned several times, and had been honourably received as a delegate to the second Round Table Conference on India. He had come off the ship, clad only in a loincloth, and leading a goat; he lived on its milk, and on vegetables. The lady was deeply shocked that such an uncouth visitor should be thought fit to lead a country – how could he, when he did not wear trousers in front of the King? Gently I turned her round to look at the wall, on which hung a painting of Christ on the Cross. She never invited us to her house again. We all put on our prejudices with our clothes – and this applies equally to nationalism and democracy.

When the moment came to sign the portrait, I raised my glass of whisky to drink to Adenauer. 'What about me?' he demanded. My wife poured him some whisky too, and he, who was accustomed only to his native Rhenish wine, embraced me and kissed me, to my embarrassment, on both cheeks, unperturbed by the photographers who had been besieging the villa in vain for weeks.

I met Adenauer once more, among his family in his house at Rhöndorf, where he tried to teach me to play bowls. Exactly one year to the day after I had finished the picture, this man, to whom I had come so close in friendship, died.

The Inner Light

Summing up the last twenty years or so of my restless life, I find that visual experience is all that remains to reconcile me to this 'best of all possible worlds', as the great mocker called it. As a creative artist, I have not been in the least concerned with discovering the regulatory principles of the universe, those principles in which the exact sciences, physics and chemistry, nowadays take so burning an interest. Unfortunately, life is too short; there is not time enough for anything, not even for wonder. The invisible belongs to the province of metaphysics; it is not the task of visual art to make visible what does not exist. However, I claim no right to make a definitive pronouncement: I am not the *Zeitgeist*, to whom Hegel ascribed a divine omniscience.

I have seen first the Habsburg Empire and then the British Empire fall apart; the rest of the world, in terms of civilization, has descended towards chaos. I am no reformer, yet I dislike remaining passive while an uncontrollable mechanized production process attempts to mould me into its own prefabricated creature. I am not a follower of fashion; I ignored the artistic modes of my own day, such as Analytical Cubism, at a time when everyone wanted to paint Cézannian dissections of guitars. All that is past. Today it merely reminds me of the obnoxious guitar-strumming of the Wandervogel movement during the Jugendstil years. That too was a form of escapism, like that of the present transistor-toting hippies whose dope ampoules foul the ruins of the Acropolis.

I took advantage of the interlude of peace to do some travelling, in order to see for myself those monuments of ancient culture, and those works of art of the heroic ages of society, which have escaped the attention of vandals, politicians, generals and planners. I did not travel with the romantic idea of shedding tears over the past. What is gone is gone. But I do not share the disillusionment of my contemporaries – especially the artists – who subscribe to the fashionable idea that existence is in itself absurd. I do not make

collages out of the detritus of industrial life – although this no doubt provides
a very appropriate reflection of our age. I am more like the Romans, saving
their household gods from a burning house – or, rather, like the ant whose
nest has been disturbed by a vandal with a stick, and who digs her grubs out
of the debris to carry them to safety: I am unwilling to forget my own
spiritual ancestors. I have not made a break with the past, for without it there
can be no future. Neither Neo-Platonic idealism, in search of the principles
which regulate the universe, nor the metaphysic of mechanization, would
suffice to bring me into harmony with a world which countless men of my
own kind – by which I mean the artists of the past – have discovered with
their own eyes. For me, European civilization has not lost its meaning. There
is still some hope in the records that artists have left us; even in time of
drought, organic sediment permeates the arid soil. One wakes up in the
morning, opens one's eyes, and is conscious of belonging to the pattern of
mankind.

At all costs we must not lose heart. The main task before us today is to
distinguish between reason and mere function, which leads to inhumanity.
I cannot accept the modern deification of the machine. I see the machine as
no more than a parody of the Mephistophelian attempt – a mechanical sub-
stitute for the alchemist's dream of a homunculus from a test-tube. Nor can I
respect the technology of the future – even in metaphysical guise – as the
proper end to which we are led by Progress, any more that I can respect the
new homunculus promised by modern biology. Progress may delude us for a
while, as long as we continue to credit it with a magical significance, like the
men of the Stone Age with their idols. The motor car, which replaces on
today's macadamized roads the mule of bygone days, is something I cannot
with the best will in the world gaze upon as if it were a miracle. In any case,
the traffic hardly leaves one time to gaze at all.

The Enlightenment planned a philosophical experiment: human reason
was to be freed of irrational ideas. The Industrial Revolution subsequently
reformed the social environment so radically that the gods themselves
abdicated. The behaviour of the laboratory rat, lured to its food through an
ingeniously planned maze by taking advantage of its innate impulse to run to
safety, recalls modern man's escape from the world into his scientifically
planned living space, with his precisely calculated calories, his precise number
of cubic feet, his precise work-norm – an existence which is slowly turning
him into a caged animal.

The art of today overlooks this reality. Since the Baroque, visual art has
had more and more to do with theoretical principles and logic, and less and

less to do with the vision of life. An impoverishment of human creative power was already apparent in neoclassical historicism, as well as in the sentimental nostalgia of the age of the French Revolution. Historicism was followed by Impressionism, with its attempt to subject the faculty of seeing to scientific analysis. And today Progress lands us with the formlessness of so-called non-objective art. Is this not a proof of the failure of the progressive experiment, which had as its goal the awakening of the human ego? Since the art of every period is its true reflection, one should not blame the artists of our time for their lack of talent, but heed the warning that lies hidden beneath: that humanity's instinct for artistic creation is threatening to disappear. Art never lies!

Naturally, man in a rationalist age will no longer see madonnas floating in the skies, or meet a Venus on earth. But no amount of pondering on non-objective art, however ambitious, will help us perceive the world through our senses, nor will any torrent of books about contemporary art manage to prove the existence of something that does not exist. Though reality reveals itself differently to every new generation, the essence of art has always been the communication of human experience. The modern artist cannot exempt himself from this rule. Persuasion, logic or metaphysics cannot argue away the risk that is inherent in existence. Rhetoric leads only to semantic gymnastics. In contradistinction to philosophers, scientists and technologists, the creative artist's task is to safeguard his own realm from the perils of nothingness. The ancient Greeks symbolized this formless menace in the terrible figure of the Gorgon. The art of our day has so far created no modern counterpart.

Eloquence can persuade one to believe in what is not real, nor even possible. Hitler's followers believed that the Thousand-Year Reich, with its concentration camps, was Socialism; similarly the Communists believe that a prison behind the Iron Curtain, with its barbed wire, machine-gun towers and walls that are death to approach, is democracy. It is rather thought-control.

The warning that art gives us is an obvious one. I rather doubt whether Stone Age man would have had the leisure to read books on art appreciation, but he did need art in order to survive – even though it reflected his existence only in the mirror of magic.

Let us look for example at Venice, where motor traffic is banned and where hordes of tourists pack the museums, not in order to see the pictures but in order to be educated by listening to the explanations of the bawling guides. I wanted to look again, after an interval of many years, at a painting by

Titian, perhaps his last; I had to fight hard for a point of vantage, stop my ears, and possess my soul in patience, until the tour groups had finally gone off to lunch. The secret of this strange work cannot be grasped all at once. At first glance one sees no more than a religious subject dating from the period when the Pantocrator of Byzantine Christianity had given place to the suffering Son of Man who sacrificed himself for the sins of mankind. As a subject, this is irrelevant to us. People today lack sufficient heart to identify with the Passion of another human being.

The Madonna is holding her son's body in her lap. My eyes run over the area surrounding the central group: in the left foreground an agitated female figure steps forward; on the right, in front of a stone archway, a flying angel holds a torch, while below him kneels a half-naked old man. On the step in the centre foreground, within the onlooker's reach, lies a slip of paper bearing Titian's signature. So much for the inventory of the picture. The keynote is set by the motionless, limp figure of the Son of Man in the lap of the blue-clad Mother of God, placed centrally in the depths of a grotto. But what a blue that is! I had to look closely several times, because within that carefully calculated perspectival space I had the impression of a movement: the central group seemed to be retreating into the distance before my very eyes. The explanation must presumably lie in Titian's use of colour. He knew better how to exploit the optical effect on the retina of apparent movement than we do today after all our scientific experiments. Is it then the extraordinary effect of the Madonna's blue robe? No, there is more to it than that. What is involved here is neither kineticism nor optical experiment, but a statement in visual terms, such as no theory can explain. The creation of a distinct plane in which to set apart the mother and her dead son is an expression of grief at the annihilation of the human spirit as it had been known since antiquity. To rationalist beholders this painting will hold no message or warning; for they live in a world whose reality consists exclusively of measurable, countable facts, which can be photographed or otherwise mechanically reproduced.

My friend Benno Geiger, the discoverer of the macabre work of the Baroque painter Magnasco, once invited us to the weekly banquet that he and some of his friends used to hold in a former abbey. It was pouring with rain. Out of the darkness of the night we entered a hall with a smoke-blackened, heavy, panelled ceiling, lit by flickering candles; a great refectory table stood in the middle. The light barely enabled one to discern strings of onions, garlic and salami hanging from the cornice. Round the long, massive table sat the dinner guests; as far as one could make out, they were mostly bearded old men with bald pates. From great copper cauldrons the host ladled out enormous lobsters, crabs, fish, oysters and other sea beasts, all dripping with tomato sauce. With greedy, bony fingers the old men tore at the food, and the table was soon covered with shells and bones. An old witch with a cat on her shoulder went round with a great demijohn and poured blood-red wine into the cups of the revellers. One could almost believe that the scene had been created by Magnasco himself, the painter of hermits and stormy landscapes. Outside, a violent thunderstorm raged. For a few hours I forgot the admonition of the Titian painting. People will feast and drink in Venice as long as the world goes on.

There is no sense in criticizing the *Zeitgeist* because one dislikes such things as the current wave of pornography in the visual arts. Gluttony and porno-graphy are merely symptoms of social disintegration, an after-effect of the shock that came in Victorian times when mankind's evolutionary descent was first proclaimed. The shock has thrown society off-balance, destroyed its psychic equilibrium, and called moral and ethical values in question for all time to come.

Voltaire could still end his novel *Candide* – which depicts man's beastliness in a different sense – with the well-meant advice that we should enjoy the pleasures of life, and plant our cabbages in peace. It was a more humanistic conclusion than Swift's ironic proposal in a pamphlet in 1728, during a famine in Dublin, that the superfluous children should be served up as food.

The *Zeitgeist* may express itself in a political demonstration, or in the long-ing for a new religion, or in the appearance of an orgiastic, nihilistic mysti-cism; but I think of the simple farm-girl who is already carrying out artificial insemination mechanically, and wonder about her feelings. What has become of the Bull of Zeus, in the heat of his blood, who has been put out of work by the march of progress? How are we to understand animals, in this age of machines? We know as little of them as we do of ourselves; at the most we may have sniggered at monkeys in a cage. And pornography leads no further than does the modern anti-art movement. It is nonsense to ignore the signi-ficance of contemporary art, as expressed in Dada and all the ensuing anarchy, nihilism, absurdity. In times of revolution even those who destroy works of art do so with a revolutionary aim. The anarchists, in their attempt to break through the barrier of being, came to grief only when they dealt with art, which demands that form be created with open eyes. The Greeks tells us that Icarus wanted to fly to the sun; it dazzled him, and he singed his wings. Today's art is a kind of seismograph, warning that the uncontrollable productive capacity of mechanical civilization might one day spring open like Pandora's box.

The profoundly thought-out writings of a Kandinsky or a Klee seduce people into a discontent with the *Zeitgeist*, which leads them to abandon the human image to technological inventions such as photography, cinema, television and so on. The mere enumeration of features in a human face – two eyes, two ears, a nose and a mouth – could satisfy only those who did not want to look any further. But the artist's mission is not to compromise; it is to show society, which has today increased out of all proportion, the right path, and to ask, *quo vadis*? I am certainly the last person, at my great age, to make a compromise with progress. I would feel like someone on a scenic railway at a fair, who holds on tight to his seat to prevent an accident that he feels is coming. Can the artistic avant-garde still have a guilty conscience, when ideas like that of the Fall of Man are outdated? Personality, individuality, are words that lost their meaning. In their place is a vacuum.

Isn't it curious that in Titian's *Pietà*, perhaps the last great work of the Renaissance, the decomposition of the human body could still be represented with the traditional means of artistic expression? We eagerly pursue the traces of primitive cultures, we imitate idols and Negro masks, and yet when we look back at the Stone Age we find that man has always concerned himself with the secret of his life. Why else would he have been at such pains, wherever he has lived, to make from the hardest stone, with the most primitive tools, an image of the so-called Fertility Goddess, in which I can see, despite all the theological commentaries, no more nor less than a human sublimation of the irresponsible sexual impulse?

Matriarchy and the fire at the hearth led to the socialization of the original horde. To give up cannibalism must have cost more in terms of individual self-mastery that we today can well imagine. But in the age of the great climatic changes which engendered the shift from a vegetable to an animal diet, one could not go on eating one's neighbour even though the art of making fire had given rise to that other important art – that of cooking. Women were the earliest potters, and they have contributed more to the shaping of our existence than can be repaid by granting them the vote.

Nor was it mere playfulness that led the male creators of the cave paintings to show the hunter creeping up on the game, himself disguised as an animal. This was not *l'art pour l'art*, no mere instinctive love of decoration, but rather the magic of representative art, which became to those cannibals an event, or as we might say today, a Happening. In that moment of significant experience they were roused from their waking dream, to wonder whether they were men or beasts. They did away with the social convention summed up in the words, 'You eat me, and I'll eat you.' To capture this humanizing vision in a picture was something that Stone Age art was still capable of doing. Time and again, in the most varied epochs, human society has succeeded in making from the most disparate forms a humanistic picture of life without any need to escape from reality.

In Venice in 1948, I once more painted the Santa Maria della Salute, to replace an earlier attempt that had been lost. That same year the picture was shown in a special exhibition of my work at the Biennale. I looked very carefully at the Biennale, one of the oldest of those international exhibitions of contemporary art that are becoming so fashionable. An initial brief inspection gave one the instinctive feeling that the end of art was at hand. It was like the premonition of a road accident. American, Italian and German artists, as well as the French, had already gone part way over into automation, montage, cybernetics, photographs and electronic noise – as if they could no longer see what is the real, central issue: the human image. In sculpture there were mobiles, moved by a draught of air; in former times the Chinese hung Aeolian harps in the trees, which the wind not only set in motion but moved to music as well. Meanwhile, modern music has abandoned the rules of sensory perception embodied in the traditional patterns of notes of distinguishable pitch, and now lives by theories derived from mathematics.

At the Biennale I met Giorgio Morandi, who painted only still-lifes of glasses, vases, pots and bottles. Even the sight of a child's face perturbed him so much that he could not paint it. As early as 1922 I nominated him for the First Prize at the Biennale; he received it a quarter of a century later, when such a distinction no longer meant anything to him. He endowed the objects in his still-lifes with an entirely individual significance, worlds removed from the functional existence of the same objects in daily use. His little paintings have a radiant power which reminds me of Vermeer; the inner light inspired Morandi and brought his simple objects alive, with a life which belongs otherwise only to the noblest handiwork of the Japanese craftsmen.

Why does a Greek temple grow so unexpectedly out of empty space, like a natural configuration, a tree or a plant? Accustomed as we are to the concept of centralized perspective, we cannot grasp the secret of a harmony which nevertheless manifests itself to any unprejudiced beholder. We must try, at least, to follow with our sense of touch, feeling with our hands and imagining that they have raised aloft the columns and built the steps which diminish into the distance, where the eyes, guided by the light of Greece, can follow their movements in the atmosphere.

This dynamic quality is already absent from Roman architecture; Roman classicism is directed at colossal effects, like a theatre façade. Classicism belongs to a planned society in which the individual is no longer active but a mere onlooker. Rome shares with modern drawing-board architecture the principle of centralized perspective, as if the architect did not have two eyes in his head like a normal person but only a Kodak lens.

Ancient Greece is bathed in light. One feels the difference when one comes there from Egypt, for instance, where the sculptures serve primarily as structural elements of architecture, and the power of the sun's glare defines the stone masses as two surfaces: a reflecting surface and a spatially indeterminate zone of shadow. In Egyptian temples the transition was first made from primitive man's simple hole in the ground to a space with an articulated form; but they are dwellings for the dead. A Pharaoh stands or sits against the temple wall; his architectural function is to support the superstructure which contains the labyrinthine resting-place of the dead. For thousands of years, the same stereotyped poses are repeated: standing, with one leg forward, or seated, to balance the structural mass. The gods of Egypt had no more concern for the human image in its corporeal reality than had the Pharaoh who is buried within, a god-king, half-way between animal-spirit and human being.

The Greeks knew Egypt. It was a Greek sculptor who ventured on the first step towards bringing the idol to life. He observed that the twist of the pelvis was decisive, if the arms were to be brought into play. The arm, the hand, make motion possible. Action is truly human. The stone comes to life. And so the stereotyped block of a Pharaoh or an animal-headed god gives place miraculously to the Greek *kouros*, the runner, the victor in the Olympic Games, who had earned a commemorative statue. Man awoke as if from a nightmare. For too long there had been no human beings, in a true sense, only classes: soldiers, workers, and a sacerdotal bureaucracy which had created symbols of authoritarian power like the idols of the leader, the soldier and the working man we see today in certain countries; but no individuals. There were none, either, in the great ancient empires of Asia. The decisive step towards human individuality, with which European history begins, was taken by an artist belonging to a small nation on the Balkan peninsula.

Who the Greeks were then is hard to discover. They were an event unique in human history. You must first be drunk with the radiance of the sky – as at Delphi, where light from snow-capped Parnassus streams over still-standing columns and endless olive-groves to caress the wine-dark sea; you must first have absorbed the Greek landscape, in order to comprehend the miracle of Greek art. And then you understand, as if you were returning home: the story of Pygmalion, the sculptor of Cyprus whose prayer was answered by Aphrodite, causing life, a being, to spring out of the cold marble under his hands, *is our own story*. It is impossible to estimate how much the Greeks have contributed, by virtue of the luminosity of their skies, to the discovery of the human image as it is understood in Europe. There is an immense difference between knowing light only as the difference between night and day – because it makes objects appear and its absence makes them disappear – and experiencing the light of the human spirit, the inner light. It was this inner light, ultimately a product of the sky of Greece, which inspired the first Greek artist of all to express in living form the laws of nascent movement, of structure and of dynamics. This is seeing with the spirit. The stone lives; the marble loses its rigidity and comes to life.

In the art of Attica and the Islands there ensued one discovery after another; the light of Greece is incompatible with spiritual stagnation. The perception of the fleeting moment, the consciousness of transitoriness, becomes the essential, underlying motive force of the individual's existence. *Panta rhei* – universal flux – vanquishes time. There are in the museum at Delphi votive offerings made by the Siphnians 2,500 years ago, preserved almost intact in spite of earthquakes and vandalism. The individual panels of the frieze are about thirty inches high and as many wide, but hardly more than four inches deep. The mental dullness typical of modern times, in contrast to the alert imagination of the ancients, makes it hard for us to grasp how an artist can transform a marble slab into a succession of planes, as if the marble were a book. The frieze represents the battles between the Titans and the Gods. An inner light streams over the whole clearly defined motion of countless bodies; even the halting movements of the dying possess a sensuous reality which was only to reappear two thousand years later, in the Michelangelo figures in the Medici Chapel in Florence.

One cannot see everything at once. When I went to the Medici Chapel I contented myself with studying the carving known as *Day*, a massive male figure high on a pedestal, his back turned to the viewer. Infused by inner light, Michelangelo's *Day*, like Titian's *Pietà* in the Accademia of Venice, or like the later works of Beethoven, pulls aside a veil from our eyes, confronting us with the central issue of art – the eternal problem of giving form to existence.

None of the artists of Egypt, of Asia, or of the South American or African cultures, has been inspired by light in the same way; and they have created nothing to match this. Anatomically the figure of *Day* could perhaps not exist in life; perhaps it could not even stand up; but its function is not merely to pose on a dais in front of the artist. *Day* stretches from the hips just as the dawn light emerges from the night. Segments of the lifeless mass of stone roll across his back. Spatial depths like those on the Siphian frieze open up and split the stone. I could not help but weep, in spite of the tourists and their astonished guide, who all fell silent. My wife gave me a good scolding for making an exhibition of myself.

On the way to Florence from Venice we narrowly escaped being struck by a landslide; a mass of stones and earth slid down the slope on to the road just behind our car, jarred perhaps by the vibrations of passing traffic. With Michelangelo, what moves the mass of stone is not a material cause; it is his spirit. Where a tourist is reminded only of the debris of a landslide, dead material, which might have cost him his life, a genius has given the experience of resurrection to the beholder who opens his eyes.

This can be observed particularly in the *Captives* by Michelangelo in the Accademia in Florence. These figures are said, erroneously in my view, to be unfinished works, fragments. The caressing light, as if from a Delphic sky, falls on the belly and the loins, the most significant parts of a body raising itself. The sight of them takes the breath away. At other points the bare rock is left intact. The action of this light of the mind must be experienced in Michelangelo as if seen for the first time by a new-born child, emerging from darkness into light, overwhelmed by the impact of reality.

More and more young people – disproportionately many in relation to the population – are thronging into the activity of making art. The stimuli provided by modern mechanical inventions, and by the natural sciences, are so tempting that many people inevitably want to try their hand at artistic experiments with them. But it is an experience of a different order when, through titanic struggle, a man of genius lays bare the eternal process of becoming human, as in the *Pietà*, where the Son of God, a lifeless corpse in the blue lap of his mother, is transported for ever into this transitory world – or as in the back of the rising *Day* of Michelangelo, bodying forth the hope of resurrection. Both are key works: one in marble, the other on one of the most precious pieces of canvas in the world. In both I see a turning-point in history. It is remarkable that the sixteenth-century Sack of Rome and the schism within the Church, but above all the collapse of the medieval City of God and the beginning of a new, mechanistic, revolutionary age, coincided in time with these two figures in art. Baroque art embodies a subsequent attempt at reunification, the spiritual Counter-Reformation which spread from Europe to Asia and South America. The *cella* behind the altar, which housed the God who was now becoming slowly an Unknown God, was

expanded to the dimensions of the cosmos. The walls fell, and pagan antiquity and Catholicism came together in the dome frescoes of the churches
built by the new Third Estate. Until the French Revolution, the greatest
sculptors, architects and musicians created for the poorest of the poor, in the
remotest parishes, a festive sabbath atmosphere such as had existed in the
Renaissance only in the great houses of princes, or in the guildhalls of the
bourgeoisie. There is more to remember about the Counter Reformation
than its Inquisition. Through its art it began to take account of the poor, both
as masses and as individuals.

I have always found, when I visit museums on my travels, that visual art
has more to tell about social change, about the unceasing political struggle
to become truly human, than any historical or sociological or economic
theory. For instance, in the chaotic early days of the Reformation, painting
clarifies the differences in response between the Italians on one hand, who
counter the disruption of unity with mathematical logic and perspectival
space, and the Germans and Netherlanders on the other, who begin to
represent the self in a mood of isolation and alienation from the world, the
mood of 'the world without me'. To a Van Eyck, this utterly secular approach to reality would have been inconceivable; he was the last to give
artistic form to the City of God on earth, the last artist to whom man,
animals, plants, earth and heaven still appeared as the handiwork of the
Divine Creator. Yet it was also the portraits of Van Eyck which first succeeded in giving the individual his true face, his isolation and uniqueness,
without at the same time detaching him from a world of contemplation and
piety.

Charles V, though the ruler of a worldwide empire, failed as so many had
before him to unite mankind. He abdicated and withdrew to a monastery.
There he had himself painted by Titian, kneeling among the heavenly hosts
– though out of humility he has removed his crown and placed it at his
feet.

Both as a painter and an ambassador, Rubens represented the Hispano-
Habsburg aristocracy of the Counter Reformation. In the bodies of his
women, Greek sensuality is still victorious in all its unequivocal acceptance of
reality. But if he had to paint the Holy Family, he visualized them in a modern, bourgeois milieu, notwithstanding the feast of colour provided for the
eye. With the terror of the Thirty Years War, a Shakespearian carnality,
animality, coarseness, and also naivety, began to transform even the representation of mythological allegories. The aristocratic sensuality of a Rubens
was carried to market. Paintings of kitchen tables laden with food, carousers,

flirtatious harlots and ladies, and boorish peasants, adorned the residences of the bourgeoisie. Breugel had tried, with his Protestant morality pictures, to bring his co-religionists back to their senses; but when the Netherlands broke away from the unity of the Church, the isolation of the human individual became openly visible in art – and this is what I see in the paintings of Rembrandt.

Perhaps I feel less sympathy for the early Rembrandt, the burgomaster's son-in-law, who rose to fame and success, and who, in his megalomania and his Faustian impulse towards discovery, followed the alchemists and draped himself in Oriental garments. But with the course of world events – when England defeated Spain, and Holland was impoverished – he came to know the loneliness of bourgeois life and his eyes were opened to his times, as ours too may be if we but know how to look. As early as *The Night Watch* the burghers have become mere puppets; instead of real rapiers they carry ornamental dress-swords. Rembrandt's contemporaries had painted the civic guard companies in a traditional, official arrangement, in order of rank, meritorious service and income. One can almost sense the painter's cynical grin. *The Night Watch* presents an entirely new kind of composition, express-ing the hollowness of the progressive bourgeois order in a sort of carnival tableau.

Later, in the *Staalmeesters*, he regards his contemporaries still more closely. Here, each member of a group of distinguished-looking gentlemen seems familiar, as if we knew him personally, and yet each is also a solitary human being, despite his Rotarian air. Look closely into every face; unasked, it tells us its own personal experience. That tired man on the left almost succeeds in not being there at all; he remains seated with the others only out of polite-ness. Then the man on the right-hand side looks rather drunk; one can read the miseries of an unhappy marriage, a broken life, from the lines on his face. In the centre, naturally, sits the inevitable chairman who will bring the meeting to an end at the proper time. Perhaps in many ways the most attractive figure is the Jewish clerk in the background, who casts a melan-choly light over the whole scene. Rembrandt's contemporary Frans Hals only once, in two group portraits of almshouse governors painted about this same time, succeeded in capturing the total isolation of modern man in old age.

In Stockholm, after an interval of fifty years, one cold, wet November morning before the visitors were admitted to the museum I saw again Rembrandt's *Conspiracy of the Batavians under Claudius Civilis*, where finally the artist has full command of all the resources that he needed to overcome the problem of light and shade. Chiaroscuro – the word itself is a mere cliché – is quite wrongly associated with him; it would stand better as a motto for the bourgeois society whose Enlightenment had ended in darkness. The nationalist Enlightenment was a failure; the scientific analysis of optics has done nothing to resolve the alternations of dark and light in which, as in a nightmare, we spend our lives. For Rembrandt the materialist conception of light was not enough. In the *Conspiracy of the Batavians under Claudius Civilis,* an episode from the history of a Germanic people, we become aware of a menace. Figures sit or stand apart from one another, at a large table; though dimly discernible in the semi-darkness they lack clear physiognomical attributes. It might equally well be ourselves gathered round that table, which like a frozen sea holds everyone apart, as if on so many ice-floes, in nervous expectancy, from the central figure of the chieftain Claudius Civilis. Can he see us? Do we deserve to be seen? He holds his sword up for the oath, the blades of the others cross it, and it seems to hang threateningly over their heads – and over ours – like the sword of Damocles. With one blow the smooth, gleaming surface of our daily life can be shattered – if we break our oath.

The whole composition is bathed in light. We are startled by the unexpected brilliance. We have no trust in our neighbours round the table, or in the everyday surroundings to which we cling like shipwrecked men. In this painting the light has nothing to do with the colour white, or indeed with any colour at all; it is no longer the light of day – which illuminates objects, and which the human retina detects – but an awesome, inner, spiritual light. On that early morning – usually I'm not fully awake at that time of day – I was overwhelmed by the revelation that an artist of a long-past age could so forcibly dramatize the very essence of our own uneasy experience. The same is true of the light in the Rembrandt engraving of the Saviour with the two crucified robbers. It takes time – and it is right that it should – or one must grow older, in order to be vouchsafed such an experience.

At the time when Rembrandt painted the *Conspiracy of the Batavians under Claudius Civilis,* he had passed with open eyes through many rapidly shifting situations both in the life of society and in his private life. New continents, unknown races of men, had been discovered. The Habsburg hegemony was in ruins, and in the Thirty Years War a large part of Europe had been reduced to ashes. Catholic France had called Turks and Mongols into Europe as its allies. The secular authority of the new bourgeois society in the Netherlands began to crumble.

In the *Night Watch* Rembrandt grappled like a Titan, for one last time,

with the light and shade, the chiaroscuro, of his own society. Then he withdrew into obscurity and did etchings and drawings in the Amsterdam ghetto.
In the *Conspiracy of the Batavians under Claudius Civilis*, all the ideologies of
his time, including alchemy, astrology, and Christian mysticism, are opposed
by his own vision of the inner light, the only true human vision.

Here I would like to recall a self-portrait by Rembrandt which hangs in the
National Gallery in London and is dated 1669; it is his last. I saw it properly
for the first time on one of those London winter days when, without the
means to survive, I felt myself to be on the outer fringes of human existence.
The picture gave me courage to take up my life again. Rembrandt was
suffering from dropsy; his eyes ran continually, and his sight was failing.
How firmly he studies in the mirror the end of his own life! The artist's
spiritual objectivity, and his ability to draw up a balance-sheet of his own life
and give it pictorial form, convey themselves powerfully to the beholder.
To look at one's own physical decay, to see oneself as a living being in the
process of changing into a carcass, goes far beyond the revolutionary
Goya's *Plucked Turkey*, a dead bird in a still-life. For there is a difference, after
all, between being involved, oneself, and seeing it happen to another. A
human spirit is about to be extinguished, and the painter records what he sees.

Think back to the body of the Saviour in the lap of Titian's blue-clad
Madonna, or to Michelangelo's *Day*, who stretches upwards, full of hope,
but remains locked in the dead stone. The expression of true humanity is
given to art alone.

For centuries, artists tried to find a solution to the problem of the gradual
fading of the inner light; there were experiments, for example, with two-
fold lighting, candle-flames and moonlight – as in different ways with
Altdorfer and Caravaggio, or in El Greco's use of tinfoil-like colour. In the
eighteenth century this curiosity was replaced by sentimental escapism.
Rousseau preached the return to Nature, claiming that savages are better
people. The ladies of the aristocracy dressed up as shepherdesses; soon
their bleeding heads would roll into baskets of sand, under the guillotine of
Marat or Robespierre. Only our ignorance of history – of all those other
societies that have collapsed under strain – spares us a full knowledge of the
bestiality of man. For thousands of years, it seems to us, man waited in a
state of lethargy until his eyes were opened by the Greek artist, and the
Greek experience taught him the meaning of life. It is depressing to reflect
that so much depended upon one fortuitous event.

Few of the historians of the age of rationalism, and none of those who speak today in the name of Progress, have thought to say that the true main-spring of human life is the individual vision of human existence, the inevitable context in which one lives. Many books extol the Greek statesmen, who made it possible for their people to construct through law a democratic pattern of society. But the human image, which we associate with the concept of Greek democracy, was created by the artists. Of the fresco paintings of an Apelles or a Zeuxis all we know is that birds are said to have pecked at the painted grapes. This is a late and ignorant way of describing the impression these pictures must have made on the people of Athens; it is a misunderstanding limited to the rationalistic attitude to seeing. From the paintings on antique vases, one can tentatively form some idea of the greatness and the significance of the Greek paintings in which the ancient view of the world expressed itself. Athens was sacked by the Roman general Sulla. He was not the first nor the last general to plunder a city, and the booty he took home with him was far from the best that was there.

Earthquakes and invasions laid waste the Greek temples; they were not, after all, built of reinforced concrete but put together by mere masons. These masons, however, were also sculptors and painters, members of a freemasonry of true craftsmen who for hundreds of years in the course of their wanderings built everywhere in the known world. Nowadays the artist is no longer a member of a craft guild. Architects work from blueprints; painters, sculptors and writers confuse art with fashion. The Greek artists created a tradition: today fashions in art change as quickly as skirt-lengths. Yet it was thanks to the Greek tradition that freemasons were able to build the Gothic cathedrals of Europe when the temples of antiquity were in ruins and the remaining sculptures mainly copies. It was the Romans who started the habit of making do with copies – just as today we derive our education in artistic matters largely from cheap reproductions in books.

These modest Greek craftsmen migrated by way of Alexandria along the coasts of North Africa and Asia, where the Roman élite formerly sought refuge in times of political unrest at home. European art eventually took its inspiration from them and was reborn, like a phoenix from the ashes.

To my younger readers all this may sound like a melancholy wail; if so, let them reflect that life is too short, and contemporary art too senseless, to permit one the luxury of going in pursuit of Romantic illusions or utopias, of Platonic idealism. I travel in the world of antiquity because there I feel at home, far removed from the vain search for Nature, as expressed in the twentieth century by the imitation of primitive art or the attempt to avoid the human image altogether.

For some time now I have owned an impression of Dürer's copper engraving *Melencolia*, a sheet which Dürer's wife perhaps hawked from her dog-drawn barrow at a fair. My wife gave it to me once for my birthday. This engraving represents the human reaction to fear, as I have always known it in my own inner life, hand in hand with hope. It shows the seated figure of a woman, her head adorned with a wreath. She is not just gazing into space; she is staring into emptiness: *sie stiert ins Leere*, as people used to say in Vienna. 'Staring into emptiness' does not mean fatalistically surrendering to the sight of the Gorgon; it means knowing oneself to be trapped in space and time. Perhaps it is presumptuous of me to draw conclusions from this Dürer print to the *Zeitgeist* of today. It is too long ago since, in 1514, Dürer did this engraving after the death of his mother. Strangely, the only analogy I can find for it is Michelangelo's Day.

A new age had put an end to the medieval city of God, when in Florence the Renaissance began its triumphal progress. The Florentine bourgeois attempted to rival antiquity. The discovery of buried works of ancient art confirmed to them their Graeco-Roman origins. Centralized perspective – a new conception of space, a mathematical, geometrical interpretation of existence – was invented. But the Renaissance vision of a new humanity was still so closely tied up with superstition, astrology, alchemy and theology, that Faustian delusions made man forget his human origins. Only a genius could give humanity hope. Titian in his *Pietà*, Michelangelo in his *Day* and Dürer in his *Melencolia* give witness, for our seeing eyes, to the truth of the humble origin of progressive human ambitions. At the very same time as Dürer engraved the *Melencolia* – this most disturbing of all expressions of the profoundly human mood of fear and despair – the Renaissance asserted that the world had emerged from its medieval panic, its fear of the Black Death and the Millennium, and that with the arrival of a new philosophy a new future was being born. We make the same assertion today.

A lot of people worry themselves about the explanation, for instance, of the slate in Dürer's design (above the sleeping *putto*), with its figures which always give the same total, in whatever direction they are added up; or of the empty purse at the feet of the solitary female figure. At the same period other painters were using the full purse, in the hand of the confidence-inspiring financier, as the symbol of bourgeois affluence. Obviously the figures on the slate are not to be understood as a list of banknotes. The bourgeoisie had ceased to chase after profit when the Third Estate, under the emblem of the clog, the *Bundschuh*, rose in revolt and laid waste the cities and provinces of

Germany. Luther sallied forth to meet revolution with theological arguments; in his ninety-five theses he rejected the authority of the Church and asserted the individual's right of direct communication with the Creator – thus making the priest's authority, but not that of the civil Establishment, redundant. Dürer bought up all the Lutheran pamphlets he could; but he did not become a Protestant, or enlist in the service of the new *Zeitgeist*. He engraved the *Melencolia* instead.

Once more there was a fear in Germany that the end of humanity was in sight. The *Melencolia* is the expression of this fear. This sister of Michelangelo's *Day* is looking neither at the sunset, nor at the pots in which an alchemical brew is simmering, nor at the geometers' and surveyors' tools, nor, strangely, at the crystalline meteorite which lies at her feet as if it had just fallen from the moon. Nor does she see the dog, although that animal is often the solitary person's only companion in life. Almost with aversion, it seems, she thrusts aside a book of revelations, probably the product of mystical utopianism and fanaticism. All alone, she waits for the experience of becoming truly human.

At that moment in history the brilliance of the Greek sky finally faded.

Postscript

Remigius Netzer

Oskar Kokoschka has recorded the decisive experiences of his life. The painter has undertaken to retrace the path that he has followed, his encounters, his disappointments, his successes, and to recall those things that have decisively influenced him.

Everything Kokoschka creates is the product of experience: fire, which has excited him since childhood; fear and awe of Woman, whose influence has often overwhelmed him; wonder at the suddenly intensified reality of the Other – that moment, anxiously awaited in the course of painting a portrait, when the sitter will show his true face, the characteristic expression on which the artist pounces at once.

Even as a student at the Kunstgewerbeschule in Vienna, where he pioneered the use of life models in motion, Kokoschka established that the draughtsman's true objective is to capture and record the moment in all its purity. Later, he stationed himself close to the bars of the tigon's cage in order to experience the shock of its spring; what he painted was not the animal's exotic colourfulness but its wildness and fierceness.

Kokoschka is not an Impressionist, assembling the chromatic sensations of the hour into a pictorial combination; he is not one who pursues the course of a shadow in order to make a composition of it. The structure of his paintings is formed by the visions which sights and events have provoked in his mind. He cannot turn his back on reality. He paints, almost always, from nature. But he must encounter reality anew, within himself: it must touch him, fascinate him, move him.

His portraits are not photographs but encounters with the human individual; his landscapes are not meteorological bulletins but combinations of different views and diagonally ranged horizons, producing a global unity. His figure paintings are not classical structures but statements about what is seen and what is lived. *The Bride of the Wind* is the resolution of the drama of his relationship with Alma Mahler; *The Knight Errant* expresses premonitions of war and wounding; *The Woman in Blue* transposes into art the state of spleen in which he once commissioned a needlewoman to make him a likelike doll.

The 'Fortuna' of the title print of the lithograph series *O Ewigkeit – du Donnerwort (Bach Cantata)* also formed the subject of a painting, in 1915; almost three decades later he painted 'Liberty', fleeing with her chains broken after the burning of Athens by the barbarians, and holding out her hand to the spectator. Kokoschka does not fear allegory in its wider sense: it is part of a tradition to which he holds fast, and on which he lays emphasis. Allegory – felt, not reasoned – is very much a part of his artistic personality.

Kokoschka declares that he never starts out with a plan or a recipe for a picture: he waits for the moment of true feeling, the stimulus, the sensation of living reality. This is the emblem of his lasting Expressionism, in the true sense of that word. He has, of course, often and rightly rejected attempts to include his art within the ambit of the stylistic term 'Expressionism'. Expressionism as a style means the use of large surfaces tending towards decorative painting, thickness of contour and to the point of destruction of painterly quality, stylization of natural forms to the point of rigidity, emotional turmoil to the point of ecstasy. All this has absolutely nothing in common with Kokoschka's feelings or with his ideas, which are directed towards a continuation of the great expressive art of the past.

He has always made statements about other artists: Albrecht Altdorfer, whose painting *The Battle of Issus* he reinterpreted in his essay 'Das Auge des Darius'; Franz Anton Maulbertsch, whose frescoes gave him the visual experience of 'the inner fire of the colours of the painter of luminosity'; Dürer, Michelangelo and Titian; Rembrandt – whose chiaroscuro leaves him cold, while his 'inner light' fascinates him – and others, right up to Georges Seurat and Giorgio Morandi.

Kokoschka looks at art from the standpoint of the creative personality. This is why he is so sceptical about purely art-historical stylistic categories, not to speak of sociological analyses of art. He identifies himself with Expressionism only as it shares his own pursuit of the moment of greatest expressive power. In his essay 'Der Expressionismus Edvard Munchs', he praises Munch for his 'Greek eye', and defines his idea of true Expressionism thus:

'Expressionism . . . shapes life into true experience. What marks off true experience from all 'grey theory' [Goethe's phrase] is this: that something which is of this world embraces something which lies beyond it – a single moment appearing in the guise of eternity – and that the dull edge of human desires in itself sets off the divine ray of light, just as silence is broken by a cry, or as the dullness of habit is broken by the unexpected. Expressionism is the forming of experience, and as such requires a medium; it is a message from the I to the Thou. Like love, it takes two. True Expressionism does not live in an ivory tower; it addresses itself to a fellow being, whom it awakens. And so, if this power, which is capable of giving form to the human and to the inanimate, is denied in art – then those who carry Progress on their banner are denying the essence of progress. From the stereotype of man as a herd-animal, which lies within every one of us, only decisive experience can release us, can lead to humanization. With every such experience our humanity is renewed.'

Arnold Schönberg, who has also been called an Expressionist, provoked with his music the same sort of scandals in pre-1914 Vienna as did Kokoschka with his paintings and his plays. (Kokoschka painted him playing the 'cello.) From the depths of his own self-knowledge, Schönberg said: 'Kokoschka is one of those strong natures who can afford to express *themselves*, aware that they are thereby making their contribution to the expression of everyone and everything: the universe itself. This is without any doubt the task of the great artist. Even if the lesser ones, and the public, call it Expressionism.'

When Kokoschka speaks, the experience underlying his pictures are present. When he sang of the northern maiden Li, he accompanied his words with the lithograph portfolio *The Dreaming Youths*. When he compressed his own man–woman problem into the expressive power of the play *Mörder, Hoffnung der Frauen*, he did drawings of the characters, exposing, with fine strokes of the pen, the lines of their facial nerves. At the time, these drawings had the characteristic of absolute novelty. On the poster advertising his drama, he painted the man red, the colour of life, and the woman white, the colour of death, signifying both eternity and victory. And so, through the medium of art, he interprets and explains his own words.

He illustrated the poems of *Der gefesselte Kolumbus*, and the enigmatic lyric 'Allos Makar' – an anagram of 'Alma Oskar' – as well as his plays *Hiob* and *Orpheus und Eurydike*; he set forth his own love story, in sequences full of premonitions and visions, on the swan-skin fans he painted for Alma Mahler; and he later created a graphic accompaniment to his own story 'Ann Aliza Reed'.

Conversely, he has sometimes given explanations in words of what he has created on canvas or on paper, and has afforded insight into one or other of the themes he has treated: in his message to the young artists of Europe ('An die künstlerische Jugend Europas') he speaks of the ceiling paintings *The Legend of Prometheus*; and he describes his triptych *Thermopylae* as a critique. of the 'modern disease of belittling, devaluing and vilifying all that in the past was considered great and worthy of reverence'.

Much earlier, in 1912, he spoke of what he regarded as essential in his art – its spiritual content – in his Vienna lecture 'Von der Natur der Gesichte' ('On the Nature of Visions'). On the poster for the lecture he showed himself in the role of protester against the society of the 'Adults' (as he and his friends called the members of the Establishment), with shaven head and pointing to an open wound in his chest – a reminder of his revolt at the 1909 Kunstschau in Vienna and of the scandalous première of *Mörder, Hoffnung der Frauen*. In Dresden, during the revolutionary period at the end of the First World War, he wrote his individualistic anti-manifesto – matched exactly, if an illustration were required, by works such as a 1917 chalk sketch of *Soldiers Fighting with Crucifixes*. He wrote from a deep sense of personal despair and sadness, which can be detected in the nearly contemporaneous painting *The Emigrés*, in which the artist himself appears, standing in a barren landscape behind his friends Käthe Richter and Fritz Neuberger.

In an open letter from Paris, in May 1933, to the *Frankfurter Zeitung* (which that paper had the courage to publish), Kokoschka paid his tribute to Max Liebermann Two years later, at Moravská Ostrava, when Kokoschka heard the news that his art had been outlawed in Germany, he gave his answer to the bureaucrats with his self-portrait, *Portrait of a Degenerate Artist*: 'Look, this is what I am!'

During the 1940s, in the middle of the Second World War, Kokoschka spoke on the BBC and gave expression to his involvement in the events of public life; he took up a critical position on the issues of the day – condemning the British bombing of Dresden – and at the same time painted political allegories in which, for example, the decline of British maritime power is symbolized by Queen Victoria riding on a whale in stormy seas; Mussolini and Hitler are shown, together with a cat and a lion to symbolize France and England respectively, sitting down to a red egg which clangs on to the plate as the plucked roast chicken, Czechoslovakia, flies away; Hjalmar Schacht and Montague Norman (Governor of the Bank of England until 1944) are juxtaposed with French generals and a priest who blesses the war. The sardonic title is *What We Are Fighting For*.

He never falls silent. He speaks because it is important to him to be understood, and because he wants to convince. Of course he is first and foremost a

painter. Kokoschka hardly ever includes a word in a picture. He may, however, write on the back of the canvas an extended ironical comment, such
as that addressed to Karl Kraus in 1925, which speaks of the failure of the
work of those 'who were born with their foreheads boarded in' – or the
politically intended, sarcastic pseudo-dedication to the clown Cookie, in
1949: 'Fools of the world *UNITE*'.

His paintings are free of literary sentiment, of formalistic games with
letters or figures. Rather, his narrative is deeply embedded in the medium of
painting, and cannot be detached from it.

When he lays down his pencil or his brush, he sometimes writes – but
this is still not 'literature'. In words, he is as little concerned with propa-
gating artfully contrived versions of events, or descriptions, or syntheses –
let alone ideologies – as he is concerned in his pictures with the use of
colours and colour values for political agitation. Karl Kraus's words exactly
apply to him: 'An agitator seizes upon a word; the artist is seized upon
by the Word.'

Kokoschka is seized upon by the Word, caught up by his own actions, his
own will, in the necessity of self-expression. And this lends weight to what
he says. And yet reflection, surely a propensity of every truly important
artist, has always been part of his nature. The more one studies him and his
art, the more one becomes aware that his extraordinarily many-sided artistic
expression originates in his delight at making distinctions, tracing processes
of decline and resurgence, investigating the origins and the paths of art, or
working out what is exactly right for the individual (whether himself or
another). No wonder Kokoschka was fascinated by Karl Kraus's ways of
thought; he has said, in an interview, that Kraus taught people to speak
again.

The style known as Jugendstil or Art Noveau, which was taught at the
Kunstgewerbeschule when Kokoschka was a student, had reached Vienna
from many different sources at once. He learned from it the necessity of a
rediscovery of craftsmanship, a doctrine which came principally from
England, from the theories of men such as William Morris. Kokoschka
himself, for example, made a thorough study of the crafts of book production. He began his studies at the end of 1904, under Carl Otto Czeschka. He
worked in accordance with the modern ideas proclaimed by Koloman
Moser and Josef Hoffmann in their programme for the Wiener Werkstätte,
where they referred to the 'limitless damage caused in the field of the applied
arts by shoddy mass production, on the one hand, and the unthinking imitation of the styles of past ages, on the other.' Their demand was that 'the

value of artistic work and of the Idea must once more be recognized and properly assessed.'

But Kokoschka soon learnt to mistrust the decorative Art Nouveau tendency: the curlicue with its pretensions to autonomy, the wavy 'floral' line. He was confirmed and supported in the development of his personal aesthetic by his friendship with Adolf Loos, whom he met in 1908. It was Loos who 'most urgently called for an ethos of craftsmanship which had been entirely forgotten', and who, long before his 1908 essay 'Ornament und Verbrechen', had echoed the American architect Louis H. Sullivan's exhortation to renounce ornament entirely for a number of years, so that thinking could be concentrated on the construction of buildings whose effect was made purely through their bareness.

The beauty of bareness, which Loos achieved in the few buildings he built himself, was to be a decisive influence on a whole epoch of architectural history, and also on other arts influenced by architecture. In Kokoschka's own work, bareness takes the form of directness of expression without graphic or rhetorical trimmings; here are no intricate lines or phrases but the spontaneous fulfilment of the thought in words or images. Kokoschka was still – just – able to thank Klimt, that 'principal exponent of the decorative'. Jugendstil', who helped him so much at the first Kunstschau, and whom he respects to this day as 'an innovator in art, with eyes open to the spiritual tendencies of his age', by dedicating to him *The Dreaming Youths*; a little later, and the thanks would have been expressed in a work entirely antithetical to Klimt's own artistic style.

Certainly the extent to which Kokoschka learnt from Loos has never before been sufficiently emphasized; but perhaps even more important is the stimulus that Loos received from Kokoschka. Elsie Altmann-Loos writes in her memoir of Loos that his eyes used to fill with tears when he spoke of Kokoschka: 'In Kokoschka he worshipped the artist, and he loved him like his own son.'

In 1910, Herwarth Walden came to visit Karl Kraus in Vienna, and met Kokoschka, whom he invited to Berlin. The magazine *Der Sturm* was founded, and Kokoschka drew and wrote for it. Kraus, who gave financial support to this organ of cultural polemic, contributed articles of his own; topics in the first few issues included 'Pro domo et mundo', 'style' and 'aphorisms'. Loos wrote about ladies' fashions, architecture, and 'walking, standing, sitting, lying, sleeping, eating, drinking'. At the time of *Der Sturm*'s foundation, Loos also lectured in Berlin at Paul Cassirer's salon.

Walden, in the importance of his relationship with Kokoschka, ranks alongside Kraus and Loos. In his first *Der Sturm* exhibition in March 1912 – in the Tiergartenstrasse – he showed pictures by Kokoschka, some of which had been hanging in the editorial offices of his 'review of culture and the arts' ever since its launching. And when Kokoschka returned to Vienna after his year in Berlin, the paper's imprint included the by-line: 'editorial director for Austria–Hungary: Oskar Kokoschka'.

On the occasion of the 'Erster Deutscher Herbstsalon' in 1913 – at 75 Potsdamer Strasse, with about four hundred works by European artists – Walden wrote the following words, which could equally well have come from the pen of Kokoschka: 'Art is the personal forming of a personal experience. . . . Art is something given, not reproduced . . . the painter paints what he sees with his innermost senses, the expression of his being . . . every outer impression becomes, for him, an inner expression. He bears, and is borne by, apparitions, inner visions. Can he help it if mere appearances, faces, look different?'

A year before, Kokoschka had reflected, in his Vienna lecture 'On the Nature of Visions', on the artistic consciousness: 'the awareness of imagery is a part of living. It is life selecting from the forms which flow towards it, or refraining, at will. A life which derives its power from within itself will focus the perception of . . . images'.

Kokoschka owes allegiance only to his own personality. He never hides behind other artists or styles. His personal way of thought is full of expressiveness and – yes – modesty. I am thinking in this connection of Cézanne, who was able to say with perfect self-assurance, 'With an apple I will astonish Paris.' Again, when talking to Emile Bernard about Balzac's *Le Chef-d'œuvre inconnu* and its protagonist the painter Frenhofer – who could not finish his greatest masterpiece but carried it to the point of bewildering complexity – Cézanne pointed to himself with evident emotion. It remains only to add that Cézanne sought to dissociate himself from the simplified portrayal of a painter given by his friend Zola in his novel *L'Oeuvre,* and also that Balzac had learned his profound and accurate ideas on art and artists from Delacroix.

In April 1965, after Kokoschka had spent a morning in the Glyptothek in Munich looking at the figures from Aegina (which had just been freed from Thorvaldsen's nineteenth-century restorations and completions), I heard him speak in the main studio of Bavarian State Radio. Even shortly beforehand, he admitted that he had no idea what he was going to say; in a vague way, a possible theme had been agreed, which was 'art and progress'. And then, in an impromptu but utterly convincing speech, he proclaimed his allegiance to Greek art as the first spiritual manifestation of western civilization; and a large studio audience was swept along by the momentum of his thought.

These spontaneous associations of ideas produced so powerful an effect only because they sprang from the fund of ideas created by all his previous reflections on art; but they came as well from a personal knowledge of Greece and of individual works of art, studied down to the last detail and experienced anew in his crayon drawings (see the evidence of this in his Greek sketchbooks and lithographs), works he had long reflected upon in their artistic, political and cultural context.

Loos never ceased to reiterate that 'the optics of Greek buildings are human and not abstract', and taught that a Greek temple always conveyed the impression – in contradistinction to the decorative, two-dimensional façades of neoclassicism – of being built by hand and built as a space. It was he who initiated Kokoschka into the true nature of Greek art.

In 1929 on a Mediterranean journey with Albert Ehrenstein, who wanted to visit Palestine, Kokoschka climbed the Acropolis, all alone. His intention was to paint it; but he was so moved, so overwhelmed, that he gave up. He has spoken several times of what the idea of Hellas means to him: 'Light is not only a gift; it is also a human invention. I would say that before the Greek light was not known: illumination was known, but not light in the sense of movement and humanity. The gesture, mobility, the play of light on the skin, or in the facial expression – the play of expressions was invented by the Ionian Greeks.'

Pictures and writings are Kokoschka's journal of his life, testimonies to what he has seen and what he has sensed.

In the winter of 1969–70, in a series of lengthy recording sessions at Kokoschka's house at Villeneuve, his reminiscences were put on tape to provide the documentary basis for this book. I noticed his sudden emotion when he spoke of Dürer, with whom, 'probably because we both have the same basic attitude to the mystery of the origin of form', he feels an affinity. To explain a point, he held out the copper engraving of *Melencolia*, which his wife Olda had bought at an auction, years before, as a present for his birthday. Kokoschka was too moved to go on speaking.

His life has brought us many affirmations, in his art above all, but also in words. Whichever of the 'images which flood in upon him' his awareness of visions may choose – whatever he reflects upon, and however he may express it, in pictorial terms or in speech, in a drawing or in a poem – Kokoschka remains consistent in all his statements. In an interview with Wolfgang Fischer, he has summed all this up:

'I am always myself. I do only what moves me personally. I know only my own world, which expands, opens out. All these traces of Greek antiquity, or of the *Bach Cantata*, were lying ready inside me. I think I can say that I never really change, only widen my range and extend myself. The dynamics of expression may be different in old age, but the figures are all equally close to me, that is, they are all totally identified with me. I am always myself. Everything is equally close, at all times. I could just as easily have done the *Bach Cantata* now as the Greek lithographs. They are all my creations.'

The educational theories of the Moravian teacher Jan Amos Comenius have been especially important to Kokoschka since his earliest youth. As a child he was given by his father a polyglot edition of Comenius's *Orbis pictus*, a pictorial reading-book dating from the year 1654, which shows a strong emphasis on visual experience.

In his exhortatory lecture 'On the Nature of Visions', Kokoschka carries on an imaginary dialogue with a chorus of the masses: 'you who listen with your patient long ears only to words as an end in themselves, you who drone out the baneful faith all over the world, open your eyes at last and see! ... To whom are given the visions of life? Whose is the creative joy of making out of earth the images of his own imagination? ... Now I will open the book of the world for you. And there are no words in it, only pictures.'

This summons to knowledge through insight was subtitled by Kokoschka 'preface to the *Orbis pictus*'. Kokoschka has many times spoken of Comenius in speeches and in interviews. In 1935–36, when he spent several months painting a portrait of the President of the Czechoslovak Republic, Tomáš G. Masaryk, the two men discussed the ideas of Comenius at length, and a vision of Comenius appears in the portrait. It was at that time that Kokoschka embarked on a play about Comenius, to which he returned during the early years of the war in London, and which – still a fragment – was first published by his biographer Hans Maria Wingler in his 1955 edition of Kokoschka's literary works. It includes a fictitious encounter between Rembrandt and Comenius. In 1670, one year after Rembrandt, Comenius died in Amsterdam, following a precarious life full of successes and disappointments, and after many years of wandering and exile. And, of course, in the 'School of Seeing' which Kokoschka conducted with such great enthusiasm, Comenius's central educational idea – that of knowledge through learning to see – was put into practice.

When one talks about Kokoschka's own *orbis pictus* – his 'painted world' – what is usually meant are the landscapes of his years of travel, the great panorama of views of Europe, the images of the journeys which took him to the outer limits of the old Roman Empire, and of the Occidental world; and yet, in fact, the title *orbis pictus* applies equally to his whole *œuvre*, including portraits and still-lifes, political paintings, figure-compositions and allegorical representations. All this is a narration born of the artist's desire to convey the nature of the world. People reinterpret a phrase which originally stood for the world of perceptible objects, *orbis sensualium pictus*, and take it to mean the world of geography, *orbis terrarum pictus*. Indeed, there is something fascinating about the enormous upsurge of artistic power in the 1920s, the sudden intensification of artistic activity. It seems to represent a creative purging of the bad years of the war, and an end to the wound and the slow process of healing; a liberation from the terror of the post-war political upheavals and from the melancholy of the collapse of the old order; and a complete return to physical and mental health. Of the ninety paintings which Kokoschka completed in the years from 1923 – when he suddenly threw up his teaching post in Dresden and went on his travels – to 1930, nearly two-thirds are landscapes. Paintings from all over Europe: cities, famous places, historic views; and among the non-landscape paintings of these years quite a few are really travel pictures: the *Nude in Landscape near Avignon*, the *Monte Carlo Chambermaid,* the *Street Scene in Lisbon*, the *Arab Women with Cigarette Lighter*, the *Portrait of the Marabout of Temacin*, who was Kokoschka's host, out on the fringe of the desert. Other memories of his travels include the *Flowers at a Window* painted at Scheveningen – a still-life whose contrast with the translucent, billowing curtain captivated him – and the animal pictures painted at London Zoo.

To travel is to see new and different things. All at once, the world opened up before the artist's eyes. He was no longer trying to get himself a hearing in one place, in one city; no longer trying to convince or shock society. His only desire was to be on the move. He discovered his ability to put the past behind him. On his travels he discovered himself, his own secret intimations, his own ideas. More than a decade before, returning from his first, happy visit to Italy with Alma Mahler, he had captured, in a dark green landscape painted on the pass of Tre Croci in the Dolomites, a premonition of oblivion and parting. This melancholy premonition reappeared, with a similar enamel-like lustre of paint, in *The Bride of the Wind*; it took poetic form in the fragmentary poem, spoken aloud to himself in the field hospital at Wladimir-Wolhynsk, which became the drama *Orpheus und Eurydike*. This

is by no means to say that Kokoschka's landscapes always reflected sad
or painful moods. Not at all. The more places and countries he experienced
the more he fulfilled his own destiny as an artist.

He was in search of a new and dynamic form of perspective – as Paul
Stefan had realized as long ago as 1913, when he saw the landscape of the
Dents du Midi which Kokoschka had painted from the window of his attic
room in the sanatorium at Leysin. Stefan declared, in his foreword to an
edition of Kokoschka's plays and pictures (*Dramen und Bilder* 1913), that
'Kokoschka, through the deliberate adoption of a number of different
"points of intensity", is in the process of achieving a new spatial effect.' The
Boats at the Dogana of 1924 shows Kokoschka's characteristic breadth of view
across a light blue horizon, a suggestion of a *Weltkreis*, a cosmic full-circle.
This principle underlies all his 'end-to-end' pictures; it is the Baroque conception of infinite, diverging perspectives, realized, as he describes it, by
painting from two different windows of a corner room. The same effect
appears in the *View of the Paris Opera*, painted from the penthouse suite of a
hotel which overlooked it; and in the panorama of Madrid, with the Plaza
de Neptune below, which he painted from a tower room in the Hotel Ritz.
Other comparable perspectival *fuites* are his views of the waterways of the
Kloveniersburgval in Amsterdam, the Thames at Tower Bridge, and the
Bosphorus outside Istanbul.

His favourite angle of view is a high one, from a top floor, or a tower, or
from rising ground; he needs all-round vision. Kokoschka has told us how
his wartime experience of lying wounded, half-buried in the earth, aroused
in him the will to paint the world, if ever he got out of there alive, from a
high viewpoint. Breadth, bigness, height, attract him, just as in his portraits
he looks for strength of personality, whether artistic or political; he is attracted by the stronger or more sensitive individual, by the person who is larger
than life. 'I had to find myself the highest mountain there was,' he said of
his painting *Chamonix – Mont Blanc*. In a view of Santa Maria della Salute,
seen from the other side of the Grand Canal, the solemn dignity of the great
church itself hardly finds a place; by contrast, the remoteness of the desert
valley seen from the Col de Sfa, near Biskra, with its tiny figures, recalls the
fateful moment of the biblical Exodus. Even a short-range view of a landscape whose sky is not seen, such as that of the *Scottish Waterfall*, is not an
idyll but a concentrated expression of the power of nature.

The moods of his paintings are as rich in meaning as his viewpoints are
manifold. 'Just as every human being is a new case,' wrote Paul Westheim,
the author of the first monograph on Kokoschka (1918), 'every picture by

Kokoschka is a case in its own right, a daring enterprise renewed every time, a kind of Mount Everest expedition, undertaken with all possible forethought and strategic cunning from one new angle after another.' The most utterly different and contrary elements, from serenity to sorrow, from excitement to tranquillity, are built into his pictorial world. The process is not that of creating 'landscape paintings': these are narrations, stories which the painter has seen and invented – unliterary, essentially pictorial realizations of the interplay between nature and the artist's vision.

The discovery attendant on all Kokoschka's travels is a process of self-realization, an intensification of his own expressive resources. Travelling, for Kokoschka, is partly the overcoming of inner remoteness. It has come to mean much more to him than a mere sum total of the long journeys he undertook in the second half of the 1920s. He has gone on travelling ever since. Even today, 'every spring, when the light gets brighter', as he said recently, he would like to go on his travels again. And he added, 'I am a gipsy.'

His travels have left behind more than bundles of sketches. Every one of his pictorial records is a reflection of the state of mind which arose in the moment of his encounter with reality. One cannot simply read his travels into any single painting, or any group of drawings. The idea of travel is inherent in all Kokoschka's work. He gives up one place and goes to find another: a new situation, a new set of circumstances, a new problem. His feeling for permanence, for tradition, goes along with him, but he has no luggage. Time and again, he has left everything behind – often abandoning valuable, rare and beautiful things – and gone on his travels. But, every time, the idea of what he wanted to say was all the while in his mind, and became a composition while he was still on the move.

He never used to bother about what happened to his finished pictures; what was done was done. Others – friends, helpers, companions, interested outsiders – packed his paintings up in the hotels and sent them off to Loos, to Cassirer, and later to whomsoever attached value to them – usually in the most literal sense of the world.

Typical of Kokoschka, too, is his confession that he never wants to return to places he has 'experienced'. This is not to be taken absolutely literally. He has said 'Prague no longer interests me', which is partly a political statement, of course; and yet once, after painting the old city centre sixteen times while he lived there, he painted a picture from memory – the only one of his landscapes to come from his imagination. This was the painting done in London in 1938, to which he gave the title *Nostalgia*. This too was a journey.

Other journeys in his career are the voyages of discovery to Greece, into which he put all his expressive power, his feeling for the communication of emotion. The urge in Kokoschka to keep endlessly on the move is no more than a sign of his determination to pursue the truth, never to let the quarry out of his sight, and to start his journey always anew.

He has seldom had a studio. Once he had one, in Vienna: the room that he painted black after his parting with Alma Mahler, and where – with Georg Trakl looking on – *The Bride of the Wind* was painted. As an art-school professor in Dresden he had a lofty studio on the Brühlsche Terrasse, in which he endowed his paintings, above all *The Power of Music*, with a particular radiance recalling stained glass. But mostly he has painted in ordinary rooms – preferably ones with more than one view – or from hotel windows; or worked in the presence of nature. At Villeneuve, the room he paints in is called 'the library'. He paints in his sitter's house, or in the house of an acquaintance – just where it happens to suit him, where someone has kept a place for him: he is always on the move.

Is this escape, or is it pursuit? It is hard to tell. He is escaping from what he has just experienced, finished with; he is pursuing all that is still undone, still to be subdued, still to be held fast – all that, for him, is capable of permanence.

For a long time he refused to paint New York; and then, in 1966, came a view of the Manhattan skyline: not, of course, a monumental, decoratively conceived *veduta*, but a pictorial experience in terms of a spatial perspective which leads into the picture from two viewpoints, just as in *Boats at the Dogana*, forty-two years before. A new image for his *orbis pictus*. Like an acute accent, the rust-red line of the Empire State Building rises over the close-packed buildings of New York, up into the orange-tinted, hazy blue sky; it emerges from the urban space, which itself derives its breadth from light. Once again, the emphasis is on volume.

But what of the perspective of colour? In what way has the substance of Kokoschka's painting changed? If one follows the road taken by his painting, which leads through explosions of strange greens and burning reds, im-pastoed flecks of cobalt blue and umber, all these *furioso* gradations and overlappings of the colours of the spectrum, one is constantly aware of the artistic excitement aroused in the painter by experience.

The 'painterly' painters of tone-values, and their myriad virtuoso varia-tions of shimmering light, have never interested Kokoschka. The Impres-sionists' colour never appealed to him, because it serves only as a means to the exact description of lighting, of the choicest moments in the experience of nature. He rejected the colour of the Pointillists or Divisionists, because the scientific method used to reproduce them held no promise, for him, of artistic effect or of life. Kokoschka values Seurat for the strength of his compositions, and for his ability to bring a subject to life through the use of light – especially in the *Baignade* – but not for the discovery of the analysis of colour into pure tones.

Colour, for Kokoschka, has always meant intensification; its function is to give depth to the spaces within the picture, to give dynamism to the composition, and to embody the artist's vision.

Colour has always been important to him: it is a source of life. With coloured crayons he has copied ancient sculptures and reliefs in order to enhance his own visual awareness of them. Colours are the element of movement in Kokoschka's pictures.

Over the decades, Kokoschka's colours have become brighter, and – without loss of intensity – more differentiated. The incomprehension which often greets the works of Kokoschka's late period springs from a failure to see.

His capacity for sensation – metamorphosed into the psychic structure of his compositions of colours and spaces – has become more refined. A mood of euphoria, revelling in the fact of being older and wiser, gives rise to a certain summariness, a delight in the sureness of the initial stroke; and sometimes the artist takes pleasure in the game of making an image brighter by overpainting with lighter and lighter colours. The colour-combinations in Kokoschka's late works give off a sweetness which can appear in such perfection only in the works of maturity.

It is understandable that Kokoschka, who was once attracted by the powerful twisting movement of Titian's *Assumption* in the church of the Frari in Venice, now, in all humility, attributes ultimate perfection to Titian's last and probably unfinished, work, the *Pietà*, in the Accademia. In the apparent dissolution of form in that painting lie painterly strength, sublimity and wisdom. The fruits of a lifetime's journey.

In the course of Kokoschka's continuing process of self-liberation, his constant pursuit of new goals – ever since Loos, his Vergil, led him to knowledge of the ancient world – he has made the powerful narrative of the Odyssey so much his own that he has succeeded in retelling it in graphic terms, and has thereby given a new confirmation of his ability to record the world through the eyes of the spirit.

And now, once more, he has painted Berlin. In 1925 he painted the Brandenburg Gate (near which lived Max Liebermann, to whom Kokoschka dedicated a lithograph portrait of his mother); in 1965 he painted the view across into the eastern sector of the divided city. A new theme, a different image, which embodies, apart from its characteristic breadth of view, political perspectives as well: a reproach and a statement of fact – a truth. Kokoschka has never dissembled his will or his beliefs. He needs no one's propaganda to impel him to record something which belongs to his own world.

His image of the world, as reflected in his pictures and in his stories, is predestined, even though he must still bring it out, as he says, from behind the canvas or the sheet of paper, calling into play the fruit of unceasing meditation and unceasing experience.

His recourse to the past, to the great men, to the old masters, is both emotion and reflection: enthusiasm tempered by study. He learnt to understand Shakespeare in his youth, through his English master, Dr Leon Kellner. From the days when Kokoschka bought Reclam pocket classics with his daily break allowance, and studied the literature of the world, the drama always fascinated him. As early as 1918, he did a lithograph of a scene from Shakespeare's *The Tempest*. Evidence of his passion for the theatre is provided by his own plays, completed and uncompleted, and by stage designs, portraits, friendships with leading theatrical figures: actors, directors and musicians from Max Reinhardt to Donald Wolfit, the great interpeter of King Lear, and Wilhelm Furtwängler. Opera, in the guise of set and costume designs, occupies an important place in his work. He used to go to the glittering performances at the Burgtheater in Vienna – what Viennese has not been brought up on them? – and those in the Yiddish theatre in the Leopoldstadt, where he enjoyed himself hugely in the company of his friends Loos and Kraus. And the Vienna State Opera, on the Ringstrasse, where Mahler was the conductor. Kokoschka sat before stages in Berlin and Dresden, Prague and London – the last-named during the bombing, when the show went on in spite of the sirens.

The lessons of years of study, life and experience are summed up in Kokoschka's artistic statements. His saying that 'art must be communicable' means that art must match the stature of man, must be human in its reference, The artist's illustrations to *King Lear*, done at the age of seventy-seven, are the result of a journey into a past which cannot be chronologically defined; they are testimonies to the artist's comprehension of the psychology, the realism and the poetry of Shakespeare, with whose characters Kokoschka has created an utterly compelling *mise en scène* of his own. The face and expression of Lear, and the inner destruction menacing him, become plastic and alive; the human being becomes visible through the tragedy of his life. Characters, gestures and scenes attain pictorial reality. The mad Lear's upraised hand, pointing at phantoms as he sits in judgment in the hovel with the Fool; the spectral depths of the open field over which the blinded Gloucester is led by the Old Man at night: 'I have no way, and therefore want no eyes.'

Kokoschka has brought the world of antiquity to dramatic life in his drawings and etchings inspired by Heinrich von Kleist's play *Penthesilea*. The spiritualization of the artist's record of life, which Kleist achieved in words, is captured by Kokoschka in drawings such as the *Fall of Achilles*, in which there is tension in every stroke, in every curve, in every short straight line – all springing from the artist's power of visualization and his mastery of draughtsmanship and composition.

Kokoschka's output of statements in graphic form has increased in quantity in his old age. Three series of lithographs, *Journey in Apulia*, *Tribute to Hellas* and *The Odyssey*, are the result of his travels in Greece and Italy, pilgrimages of the mind into the history of man. In the wanderings and return of Odysseus, 'there is much that harmonizes with my ideas about the Greeks ... who discovered the individual. I don't mean the fighting, or the Trojan War, but Odysseus as the vagabond, almost as an eternal wanderer, so that I might almost identify myself with the character.' Escape is a characteristic element in all travel; but here it is escape from the ephemeral, the contingent. Escape into permanence – a symbolic flight from the unendurable everyday world.

In 1966 Kokoschka took up, in a painting, the idea for another graphic sequence of narrative. On New Year's Day he began to paint *Saul and David*. The garment worn by the pensive, pallid Saul ranges from tender violet to salmon pink. The colours of the painting come close to being an affirmation of a renewed will to live. In the summer of the same year, when Kokoschka exhibited the picture for the first time at the Kunsthaus in Zürich, he said on opening day: 'He – Saul – can't endure it – in all his strength – that he is eighty, and the other, David, still so young; eighteen as I once was. How annoyed he is, this Saul!' And Kokoschka pointed to himself and said: 'I think I have managed to express this at my first attempt. Sometimes it takes a very long time for me to find my picture; sometimes it comes to me right away, as it has here.' In April 1971 the painting was sent as a gift from the artist to the new museum in Tel Aviv.

In 1967, there followed the first of the sketches and drawings on the theme of *Saul and David*, which were printed as a portfolio of lithographs by Wolfensberger in Zürich and published in 1969 by Marlborough Fine Art. A journey into legend? Certainly, but only in order to confirm and reproduce, from within himself, the actualities of life, its eternally decisive emotions. In *Saul Dismembers Two Cattle*, there is a demonstration of will, the expression of one who feels himself to be righteous in his anger; in *David Dancing Before the Ark*, there is the God-favoured, God-fearing victor and his exalted joy in physical movement; in *David in his Old Age*, the sensual wrath and life given by the beautiful maiden Abishag of Shunam.

In a 1969 self-portrait, there appear, behind the painter's back, menacing and enticing, the figures of Death and Beauty, the Unattainable and the Beloved. He who has lived, has learnt.

Irony and scepticism paved Kokoschka's way to the symbolic theatre of Aristophanes, to the creation of the eleven drypoint engravings illustrating *The Frogs*. Kokoschka prefaced the series with an *Imaginary Portrait of Aristophanes*, for which there also exist sketches. Every line of these fantasy portraits reveals the artist's concern with the rightness of his knowledge and the precision of his imagination. His visual demonstration shows total commitment. Reading supplies the theme; experience makes it plain.

The sophistical image of the slave Xanthias, who complains of his burden and is forced to carry his own donkey, has been realized by Kokoschka in graphic terms. The Frogs themselves – who form the chorus which welcomes Dionysus on his way to the underworld, where he will arbitrate between Euripides and Aeschylus – also appear in a painting by Kokoschka: menacingly large, they crouch, in a dim light, in a waste land. 'I painted this picture under the impact of the Russian invasion of Czechoslovakia. One day, there might be a world in which only frogs and toads are left alive.'

Oskar Kokoschka, artist and cosmopolitan, who was born in Habsburg Austria, who chose British citizenship both freely and under compulsion, escaping from terror and seeking freedom, has now told the story of his life; he has taken his thoughts at their word. It is a life which will remain something of a mystery to philistines young and old – and not only those of Germany, from whom he has suffered so much, and of whom he has learnt to be wary. This is not an unusual state of affairs. The artist who sets his course neither by the sentimentalities of the so-called contemporary sensibility, nor by the intellectual fashions of the age – the artist who sets out in his art to give concrete expression to truth – is never readily understood.

The public has in fact been readier to acknowledge Kokoschka's standing than to understand him: the great outsider has been fittingly cheered and even very well paid. But Karl Kraus's remark about the public still sounds as if it had been written for Kokoschka: 'I and my public understand each other very well: they don't hear what I say, and I don't say what they'd like to hear.'

In Kokoschka's statements, ideas take shape.

Location of Works
Mentioned in the Text

List of Illustrations

Dresden, produced 3 June 1918. *Photo Ullstein Bilderdienst, Berlin.*

12. *OK as a dragoon*

13. *On the Isonzo Front, 1916*

14. *Daisy Spies sitting for OK*
The painting of the ballet-dancer was begun in the house of Paul Cassirer in Berlin, 1927, but was never completed. *Photo Ullstein Bilderdienst, Berlin.*

15. *Olda*
Lithograph from the portfolio *Olda*, published by Friedrich Welz, Salzburg, 1956.

16. *In London, 1942*
The artist standing in front of his painting, *Anschluss – Alice in Wonderland,* one of the political allegories in which he protested against the Third Reich.

17. *In Hyde Park, 1962*
On the occasion of the Tate Gallery exhibition. *Photo Horst Tappe, Vevey.*

18. *In the 'library' at Villeneuve*
Studio in the house built on Lake Geneva in 1953. On the easel is the painting of Herodotus. *Photo Gertrude Fehr, Territet, 1960.*

19. *At work*

20. *OK with Olda in their garden at Villeneuve.*
OK painting *Penthesilea.* Begun 1954 it was shown, still unfinished, at the exhibition in the Kunsthaus, Zürich.

Photographs from Kokoschka's archives in Vevey, except where otherwise stated.

Index

Figures in italic refer to illustrations